句型应用大全：看模板学句型，看这本就够了

史风莉●主编
易人外语教研组●编著

U0833260

江苏凤凰科学技术出版社

图书在版编目（CIP）数据

句型应用大全：看模板学句型，看这本就够了 / 史风莉主编；易人外语教研组编著 . -- 南京：江苏凤凰科学技术出版社，2019.8

（易人外语）

ISBN 978-7-5713-0351-8

Ⅰ . ①句… Ⅱ . ①史… ②易… Ⅲ . ①英语—句型—自学参考资料 Ⅳ . ① H314.3

中国版本图书馆 CIP 数据核字 (2019) 第 097456 号

句型应用大全：看模板学句型，看这本就够了

主　　编　史风莉
编　　著　易人外语教研组
责任编辑　葛　昀
责任监制　曹叶平　方　晨

出版发行　江苏凤凰科学技术出版社
出版社地址　南京市湖南路 1 号 A 楼，邮编：210009
出版社网址　http://www.pspress.cn
印　　刷　天津旭丰源印刷有限公司

开　　本　718mm × 1 000mm　1/16
印　　张　22
版　　次　2019年8月第1版
印　　次　2019年8月第1次印刷

标准书号　ISBN 978-7-5713-0351-8
定　　价　52.00元

Preface 前言

英语作为一门重要的语言工具，在我们的日常生活中一直占据着举足轻重的位置。很多读者由于受传统教学方法的影响，英语口语水平远远低于阅读能力。而提高基本的英语口语能力对很多人来说也越来越有必要。

对于很多读者来说，虽然已经学习了很多年英语，也掌握了一定的词汇量和语法知识，但是在与老外的实际交流中，往往不知道该如何利用这些知识来表达自己的想法。所谓英语口语学习，其实就是句型的学习。只要掌握一定量的句型，口语水平就能迈上一个新的台阶。因此，相信广大读者急需一本英语句型书来提高自己的口语能力。

本书分为五大板块，依次为“交际用语”“情绪用语”“思想表达”“叙述用语”以及“疑问用语”，涉及多个情景主题。每个板块均采用 4 步学习法：对话示例——句型分析——句子示例——重点单词。对话示例取材广泛，内容全面实用，几乎涵盖了日常生活中的各个场景，让你切实体会到在什么情境下使用这个句型。句型分析从读者的角度出发，力求简单清晰，让读者能全面深入地掌握句型。同时书中的句子示例贴近日常生活，帮助读者更好地掌握句型的表达方式。最后还给出了对话示例中所出现的重点单词，单词涉及全面，同时呈现了音标、词性、词义，让读者在学习句型的同时也能提升自己的词汇量。

最后，衷心希望本书能给广大读者带来实际的帮助，也希望通过本书，广大读者能提高自己的英语口语能力，轻轻松松学英语！当然，本书在编写过程中，还存在不足之处，希望各位读者能多提宝贵意见。

史风莉

Contents

目录

User's Guide

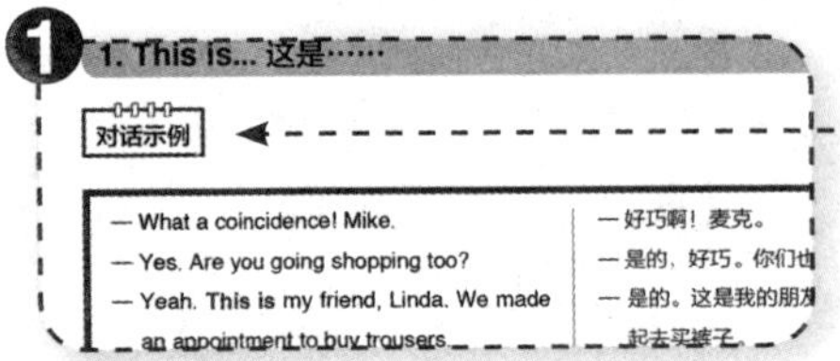

1. This is... 这是……

对话示例

— What a coincidence! Mike. — 好巧啊！麦克。
— Yes. Are you going shopping too? — 是的，好巧。你们也
— Yeah. This is my friend, Linda. We made an appointment to buy trousers. — 是的。这是我的朋友……一起去买裤子。

1. 对话示例，感知情境

本书摒弃了传统句型学习的弊端，首先给出了句型的相应情景对话，情景对话中英结合，让读者在学习句型之前先熟悉句型使用的场合。把句型学习放到不同的生活场景中，让读者再也不用为在什么场景、什么场合下使用该句型而苦恼。

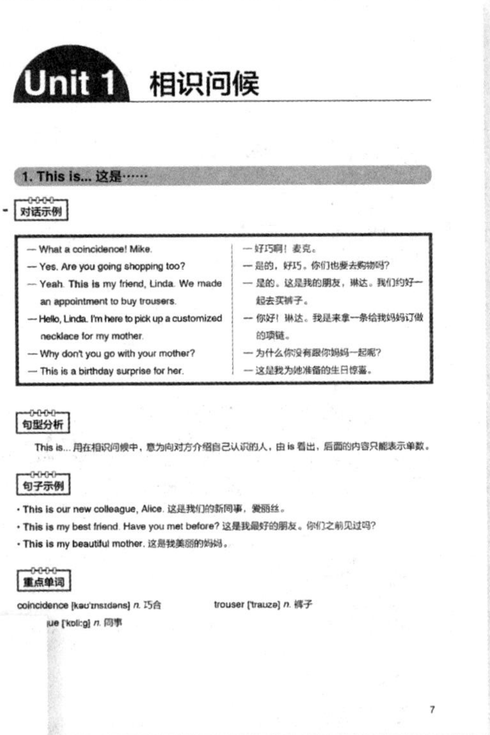

Unit 1 相识问候

1. This is... 这是……

对话示例

— What a coincidence! Mike.	— 好巧啊！麦克。
— Yes. Are you going shopping too?	— 是的，好巧。你们也要去购物吗?
— Yeah. This is my friend, Linda. We made an appointment to buy trousers.	— 是的。这是我的朋友，琳达。我们约好一起去买裤子。
— Hello, Linda. I'm here to pick up a customized necklace for my mother.	— 你好！琳达。我是来拿一条给我妈妈订做的项链。
— Why don't you go with your mother?	— 为什么你没有跟你妈妈一起呢?
— This is a birthday surprise for her.	— 这是我为她准备的生日惊喜。

句型分析

This is... 用在相识问候中，意为向对方介绍自己认识的人，由 is 看出，后面的内容只能表示单数。

句子示例

- This is our new colleague, Alice. 这是我们的新同事，爱丽丝。
- This is my best friend. Have you met before? 这是我最好的朋友。你们之前见过吗?
- This is my beautiful mother. 这是我美丽的妈妈。

重点单词

coincidence [kəu'ɪnsɪdəns] n. 巧合　　trouser ['trauzə] n. 裤子

…ue ['kɒli:g] n. 同事

7

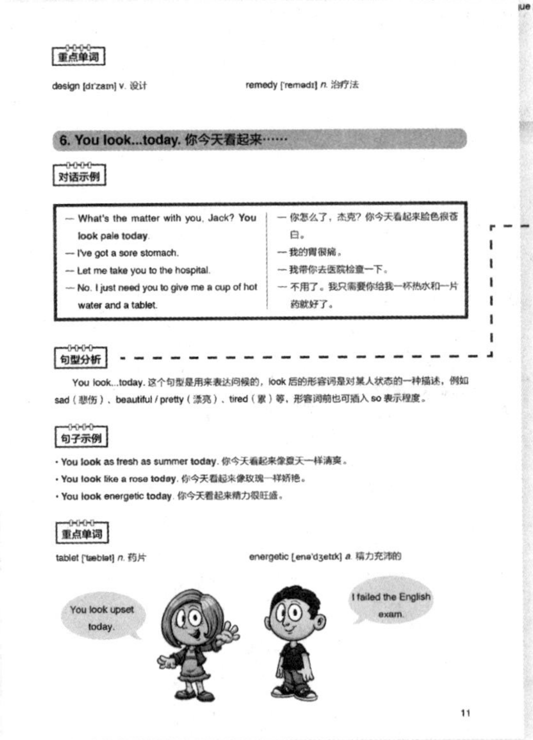

重点单词

design [dɪ'zaɪn] v. 设计　　remedy ['remədɪ] n. 治疗法

6. You look...today. 你今天看起来……

对话示例

— What's the matter with you, Jack? You look pale today.	— 你怎么了，杰克? 你今天看起来脸色很苍白。
— I've got a sore stomach.	— 我的胃很痛。
— Let me take you to the hospital.	— 我带你去医院检查一下。
— No. I just need you to give me a cup of hot water and a tablet.	— 不用了。我只需要你给我一杯热水和一片药就好了。

句型分析

You look...today. 这个句型是用来表达问候的，look 后的形容词是对某人状态的一种描述，例如 sad（悲伤）、beautiful / pretty（漂亮）、tired（累）等，形容词前也可插入 so 表示程度。

句子示例

- You look as fresh as summer today. 你今天看起来像夏天一样清爽。
- You look like a rose today. 你今天看起来像玫瑰一样娇艳。
- You look energetic today. 你今天看起来精力很旺盛。

重点单词

tablet ['tæblət] n. 药片　　energetic [ˌenə'dʒetɪk] a. 精力充沛的

11

句型分析

You look...today. 这个句型是用来表达问候的，
sad（悲伤）、beautiful / pretty（漂亮）、tired（累

2. 详细解析，一看就会

本书的句型分析，能够帮助读者在很短的时间内，掌握该句型中出现的语法点，句型使用的场合、表达意图，以及相似句型等内容，让读者一看就会，迅速掌握使用方法。

使用说明

responsibility. Please have a look first.	职责，请先看一下。
— OK. Could you tell me our working hours?	— 好的。你能告诉我我们的上班时间吗？
— From eight to five and we have an hour off at noon.	— 早上八点到下午五点，我们中午有一个小时休息时间。

句型分析

Let me introduce... 这个句型是用来作介绍的，在口语中使用频率很高，可将自己介绍给别人，或者将自己认识的人介绍给第三者。

句子示例

- Let me introduce our partners. 让我介绍一下我们的合作伙伴。
- Let me introduce John, one of the new members of our team. 让我介绍一下约翰，我们团队新来的成员之一。
- Mr. White, let me introduce you to some of our sponsors. 怀特先生，让我向你介绍几个我们的赞助商。

重点单词

responsibility [rɪˌspɒnsəˈbɪlətɪ] *n.* 职责，责任　　partner [ˈpɑːtnə] *n.* 合伙人

sponsor [ˈspɒnsə] *n.* 赞助商，倡议者

4. Allow me to introduce... 请允许我来介绍……

对话示例

— Allow me to introduce our new partner, Mr. Jones.	— 请允许我来介绍一下，这是我们新的合伙人，琼斯先生。
— Hello, Mr. Jones. I am Andy. I'm in charge of the project.	— 你好，琼斯先生。我是安迪，这个项目的负责人。
— Hello, Andy. I hope we can cooperate happily.	— 你好，安迪。希望我们合作愉快。
— Sure.	— 当然。

3

句子示例

- Let me introduce our partners. 让我介绍一下我们的合作伙伴。
- Let me introduce John, one of the new members of our team. 让……来的成员之一。
- Mr. White, let me introduce you to some of our sponsors. 怀特先生……助商。

3. 经典例句，把握用法

给出多个例句，使读者能在句型的实际运用中掌握知识点。这些例句内容涉及生活中的方方面面，在一定程度上帮助读者把握句型的具体使用方法。

句型分析

I live in... 表示我在哪里居住，in 后跟表示地点的名词，且后面的内容通常是相对较大的地点，如国家、城镇等。

句子示例

- I live in a very small village. 我住在一个很小的村庄里。
- I live in an apartment surrounded by beautiful gardens. 我住在一个公寓里，周围环绕着美丽的花园。
- I live in the dormitory near an amusement park. 我住在一个离游乐园很近的宿舍里。

重点单词

apartment [əˈpɑːtmənt] *n.* 公寓　　dormitory [ˈdɔːmətrɪ] *n.* 宿舍

amusement [əˈmjuːzmənt] *n.* 娱乐

9. I come from... 我来自……

对话示例

— Hello! I am from Beijing. Where do you come from?	— 你好，我来自北京。你来自哪里？
— Hello! I come from Pasadena.	— 你好！我来自帕萨迪纳市。
— Is it in California? Can you speak Chinese?	— 是在加利福尼亚州吗？你会说中文吗？
— Yes, it's in southern California and I can speak a little Chinese.	— 是的，它在南加利福尼亚。我会说一点点中文。

句型分析

I come from... 这个句型是在表达我来自的地方，come from 是一个动词词组，充当谓语，因为 come 是一个不及物动词，需要跟 from 来引导后面的地点。

句子示例

- I come from Malaysia, but I live in London. 我来自马来西亚，但现在住在伦敦。
- My name is Will and I come from a small town in Mexico. 我叫威尔，来自墨西哥的一个小村庄。
- I come from the country and this is the local specialty of my hometown. 我来自农村，这是我家乡的土特产。

13

4

重点单词

apartment [əˈpɑːtmənt] *n.* 公寓　　dormito

amusement [əˈmjuːzmənt] *n.* 娱乐

4. 单词呈现，拓展词汇

设置重点单词，配有国际音标，能够让读者迅速掌握单词的正确发音并记忆单词，不仅能增加读者的词汇量，还可以帮助读者在阅读中扫除障碍。

Chapter 1
交际用语句型

Unit 1 相识问候

Unit 2 保持联络

Unit 3 拜访聚会

Unit 1 相识问候

1. This is... 这是……

对话示例

— What a coincidence! Mike.	— 好巧啊！麦克。
— Yes. Are you going shopping too?	— 是的，好巧。你们也要去购物吗?
— Yeah. **This is** my friend, Linda. We made an appointment to buy trousers.	— 是的。这是我的朋友，琳达。我们约好一起去买裤子。
— Hello, Linda. I'm here to pick up a customized necklace for my mother.	— 你好！琳达。我是来拿一条给我妈妈订做的项链。
— Why don't you go with your mother?	— 为什么你没有跟你妈妈一起呢?
— This is a birthday surprise for her.	— 这是我为她准备的生日惊喜。

句型分析

This is... 用在相识问候中，意为向对方介绍自己认识的人，由 is 看出，后面的内容只能表示单数。

句子示例

- **This is** our new colleague, Alice. 这是我们的新同事，爱丽丝。
- **This is** my best friend. Have you met before? 这是我最好的朋友。你们之前见过吗?
- **This is** my beautiful mother. 这是我美丽的妈妈。

重点单词

coincidence [kəʊ'ɪnsɪdəns] *n.* 巧合

trouser ['traʊzə] *n.* 裤子

colleague ['kɒli:g] *n.* 同事

2. My name is... 我叫……

对话示例

— Good morning, sir. **My name is** Daniel. I'm here for a job interview.	— 早上好，先生。我叫丹尼尔。我今天是来面试的。
— Good morning. What job do you want?	— 早上好！你想面试什么工作?
— Manager assistant.	— 经理助理。
— Do you have experience of a smilar job?	— 你之前有过类似的工作经历吗?
— Yes. I was a secretary.	— 是的，我曾经是一名秘书。

句型分析

My name is... 通常用于正式场合中，也是自我介绍中的必备句。有时也可用 I am... 来替换。

句子示例

- **My name is** Mike. I come from England. 我叫麦克，来自英国。
- By the way, **my name is** Dean. 对了，我的名字叫迪恩。
- Hello, **my name is** Feynman and I have a reservation for dinner at six tonight. 你好！我叫费曼。我预订了今晚 6 点在这里用餐。

重点单词

reservation [ˌrezəˈveɪʃn] *n.* 预约　　　　assistant [əˈsɪstənt] *n.* 助理

3. Let me introduce... 让我来介绍一下……

对话示例

— **Let me introduce** myself. My name is Andy. This is my first day at work. Please give me your advice.	— 自我介绍一下。我叫安迪。这是我第一天来这里上班。请多多指教。
— Hello, Andy. I am Finn. This is our job	— 你好，安迪。我叫费恩。这是我们的工作

responsibility. Please have a look first.	职责，请先看一下。
— OK. Could you tell me our working hours?	— 好的。你能告诉我我们的上班时间吗?
— From eight to five and we have an hour off at noon.	— 早上八点到下午五点。我们中午有一个小时休息时间。

句型分析

Let me introduce... 这个句型是用来作介绍的，在口语中使用频率很高，可将自己介绍给别人，或者将自己认识的人介绍给第三者。

句子示例

- **Let me introduce** our partners. 让我介绍一下我们的合作伙伴。
- **Let me introduce** John, one of the new members of our team. 让我介绍一下约翰，我们团队新来的成员之一。
- Mr. White, **let me introduce** you to some of our sponsors. 怀特先生，让我向你介绍几个我们的赞助商。

重点单词

responsibility [rɪˌspɒnsə'bɪlətɪ] *n.* 职责，责任

partner ['pɑ:tnə] *n.* 合伙人

sponsor ['spɒnsə] *n.* 赞助商，倡议者

4. Allow me to introduce... 请允许我来介绍……

对话示例

— **Allow me to introduce** our new partner, Mr. Jones.	— 请允许我来介绍一下，这是我们新的合伙人，琼斯先生。
— Hello, Mr. Jones. I am Andy. I'm in charge of the project.	— 你好，琼斯先生。我是安迪。这个项目的负责人。
— Hello, Andy. I hope we can cooperate happily.	— 你好，安迪。希望我们合作愉快。
— Sure.	— 当然。

句型分析

Allow me to introduce...introduce 后面的人物是我要介绍的对象，是为了让某人了解某人。根据 introduce 的用法，其后的句式为 introduce sb to sb。

句子示例

- **Allow me to introduce** Mr. Black to you. 请允许我向你介绍一下布莱克先生。
- **Allow me to introduce** my college roommate to you. 请允许我向你介绍一下我的大学室友。
- **Allow me to introduce** you to my classmates. 请允许我把你介绍给我的同学。

重点单词

project ['prɒdʒekt] *n.* 项目

roommate ['rʊmmeɪt] *n.* 室友

5. Please give my wishes to... 请代我向……问好。

对话示例

— Long time no see. What have you been doing lately?	— 好久不见。你最近在忙些什么？
— I've been designing remedies at home.	— 我最近一直在家设计治疗方案。
— And how are your parents doing? **Please give my wishes to** them.	— 你父母好吗？请代我向他们问好。
— Thank you. They are fine.	— 谢谢。他们都很好。

句型分析

Please give my wishes to... 这个句型常用来表示我请求某人向某人转达问候或祝福，to 后面跟的对象通常是请求对象所认识或熟知的人。

句子示例

- **Please give my wishes to** your family. 请代我向你的家人问好。
- **Please give my wishes to** Mike. 请代我向麦克问好。
- **Please give my wishes to** your brother. 请代我向你的兄弟问好。

重点单词

design [dɪ'zaɪn] v. 设计　　remedy ['remədɪ] *n.* 治疗法

6. You look...today. 你今天看起来……

对话示例

— What's the matter with you, Jack? **You look** pale **today**.	— 你怎么了，杰克？你今天看起来脸色很苍白。
— I've got a sore stomach.	— 我的胃很痛。
— Let me take you to the hospital.	— 我带你去医院检查一下。
— No. I just need you to give me a cup of hot water and a tablet.	— 不用了。我只需要你给我一杯热水和一片药就好了。

句型分析

You look...today. 这个句型是用来表达问候的，look 后的形容词是对某人状态的一种描述，例如 sad（悲伤）、beautiful / pretty（漂亮）、tired（累）等，形容词前也可插入 so 表示程度。

句子示例

- **You look** as fresh as summer **today**. 你今天看起来像夏天一样清爽。
- **You look** like a rose **today**. 你今天看起来像玫瑰一样娇艳。
- **You look** energetic **today**. 你今天看起来精力很旺盛。

重点单词

tablet ['tæblət] *n.* 药片　　energetic [ˌenə'dʒetɪk] *a.* 精力充沛的

7. Have you met...? 你见过……吗？

对话示例

— Selena, this is my friend, Angel. **Have you met** each other before?	— 赛琳娜，这是我的朋友，安琪儿。你们之前见过面吗？
— No, we're strangers. But I am willing to make friends with her. Can you give me her phone number?	— 没有，我们不认识。但是我很愿意跟她做朋友。你能把她的电话号码给我吗？
— Of course. But I should ask for her permission first.	— 当然可以。但是我应该先征求她的同意。
— All right.	— 好的。

句型分析

Have you met...? 这个句型中用的是 Have...met（现在完成时态），表明对现在的对话有一定的影响，met 后面直接跟“你有没有见过面”的对象。

句子示例

- **Have you met** Mr. Mason, our manager? 你见过我们的经理梅森先生吗？
- **Have you met** all of your roommates? 你和所有的室友都见过面了吗？
- Mr. Hill, **have you met** our executive manager? 希尔先生，你见过我们的执行经理吗？

重点单词

permission [pə'mɪʃn] *n.* 允许，批准

executive [ɪg'zekjətɪv] *a.* 执行的，管理的

8. I live in... 我住在……

对话示例

— Where do you live? Is it near our school?	— 你住在哪里？离我们学校近吗？
— Not very far. **I live in** the apartment on the north side of the park next to the school.	— 不是很远，我住在学校旁边的那个公园北面的公寓里。
— How long will it take you to get to school?	— 你到学校需要多长时间？
— It's about 15 minutes' walk.	— 步行大约 15 分钟。

句型分析

I live in... 表示我在哪里居住，in 后跟表示地点的名词，且后面的内容通常是相对较大的地点，如国家、城镇等。

句子示例

- **I live in** a very small village. 我住在一个很小的村庄里。
- **I live in** an apartment surrounded by beautiful gardens. 我住在一个公寓里，周围环绕着美丽的花园。
- **I live in** the dormitory near an amusement park. 我住在一个离游乐园很近的宿舍里。

重点单词

apartment [ə'pɑ:tmənt] *n.* 公寓

dormitory ['dɔ:mətrɪ] *n.* 宿舍

amusement [ə'mju:zmənt] *n.* 娱乐

9. I come from... 我来自……

对话示例

— Hello! I am from Beijing. Where do you come from?	— 你好，我来自北京。你来自哪里?
— Hello! **I come from** Pasadena.	— 你好！我来自帕萨迪纳市。
— Is it in California? Can you speak Chinese?	— 是在加利福尼亚州吗? 你会说中文吗?
— Yes, it's in southern California and I can speak a little Chinese.	— 是的，它在南加利福尼亚。我会说一点点中文。

句型分析

I come from... 这个句型是在表达我来自的地方，come from 是一个动词词组，充当谓语，因为 come 是一个不及物动词，需要跟 from 来引导后面的地点。

句子示例

- **I come from** Malaysia, but I live in London. 我来自马来西亚，但现在住在伦敦。
- My name is Will and **I come from** a small town in Mexico. 我叫威尔，来自墨西哥的一个小村庄。
- **I come from** the country and this is the local specialty of my hometown. 我来自农村，这是我家乡的土特产。

重点单词

southern ['sʌðən] *a.* 南方的

country ['kʌntrɪ] *n.* 乡下，地区

specialty ['speʃəltɪ] *n.* 专长，特点，特产

10. My job is... 我的工作是……

对话示例

— Hello, may I ask what you do for a living? Are you a salesman?	— 你好！请问你是做什么工作的？你是推销员吗？
— No, **my job is** to provide sales proposals to customers actually.	— 不是，事实上我的工作是给客户提供销售方案。
— Great. Our manager is looking for a company to provide us with sales programs. Can you tell me the price of it?	— 太好了。我们经理正在找一家公司为我们提供销售方案。你能告诉我价格吗？
— I can send it to you by mail. It contains different packages.	— 我可以通过邮件的方式发送给你。它包含着不同的套餐。

句型分析

My job is... 虽然指的是“我的工作是什么”，但是 is 后面通常不是跟职业名称，而是用来描述一种职业的性质或内容，所以 is 后面常跟 to，构成 My job is to，to 是不定式，后面要跟动词原形。

句子示例

- **My job is** to write a brief report for the manager. 我的工作是为经理写简短的报告。
- **My job is** to sort out the documents for the manager and arrange the meeting agenda for him. 我的工作是为经理整理文件以及为他安排会议流程。
- **My job is** to provide graphic design for clients occasionally. 我的工作是偶尔为客户提供平面设计。

重点单词

package ['pækɪdʒ] *n.* 套餐，包裹

agenda [ə'dʒendə] *n.* 议程

proposal [prə'pəʊzl] *n.* 建议，提议

graphic ['græfɪk] *a.* 形象的，图解的

11. I have heard a lot about... 我对……久仰大名了。

对话示例

— Hello, **I have heard a lot about** you. But I didn't expect to meet you today.	— 你好，久仰大名。没想到今天能见到你。
— Hello, are you a friend of Bob's? He often mentions you to me.	— 你好，你是鲍勃的朋友吗？他经常跟我提起你。
— So, why don't we have a cup of coffee to get to know each other better?	— 既然这样，我们何不喝杯咖啡增进我们之间的了解呢？
— It sounds great.	— 好主意。

句型分析

I have heard a lot about...这个句型中的"久仰"指的是听说过某个人好的方面，表示对某人的敬仰，这里的 about 后面跟久仰大名的某人，have heard 用的是现在完成时态，也就是以前就对某人有了解，对现在的情况还有影响。

句子示例

- **I have heard a lot about** your father. 我对你的父亲久仰大名。
- **I have heard a lot about** your friend, John. 我对你的朋友约翰久仰大名。
- **I have heard a lot about** you. I finally have the chance to meet you. 久仰大名。今天我终于见到你了。

重点单词

expect [ɪk'spekt] *v.* 期望，预期

mention ['menʃn] *v.* 提及

12. Best wishes for... 给……最好的祝愿

对话示例

— Linda, I heard that you've been preparing for the exam recently.	— 琳达，我听说你最近一直在为考试做准备。
— Yes, it is very important to me.	— 是的，这次的考试对我来说很重要。
— **Best wishes for** passing the examination.	— 那我在此预祝你考试通过。
— Thank you.	— 谢谢。

句型分析

Best wishes for... 这个句型的主干是 best wishes，一般来说，for 后面通常接 sth，表示祝福的具体内容，有时 for 后面也接 sb。

句子示例

- **Best wishes for** a happy marriage. 祝你们的婚姻幸福美满。
- **Best wishes for** a speedy recovery. 衷心祝你早日康复。
- **Best wishes for** you. 献上最美好的祝愿。

重点单词

examination [ɪɡˌzæmɪ'neɪʃn] *n.* 检查，考试

recovery [rɪ'kʌvərɪ] *n.* 恢复

13. ...be interested in... ……对……感兴趣。

对话示例

— John, I found you **are interested in** wildlife conservation.	— 约翰，我发现你对野生动物保护很感兴趣。
— Yes, because there are many rare animals that are nearly extinct.	— 是的。因为有很多珍稀动物几乎要濒临灭绝了。
— That's right. Do you have any plans?	— 没错，那你有什么计划吗?
— Yes, I'm going to publish articles on rare animals and their situations on the web.	— 有，我准备在网站上发表关于珍稀动物和它们的现状的文章。

句型分析

... be interested in... 这个句型的主语是某人或者其他有生命的东西。in 后面指的是某人或者有生命的东西所感兴趣的某方面，in 后跟的是名词或者动名词。

句子示例

- I'm **interested in** the customs of every country. 我对各个国家的风俗习惯都很感兴趣。
- Ants **are interested in** sugary foods. 蚂蚁对含糖类的食物都很感兴趣。
- I used to **be interested in** horse racing. 我过去对赛马很感兴趣。

重点单词

wildlife ['waɪldlaɪf] *n.* 野生生物

extinct [ɪk'stɪŋkt] *a.* 灭绝的

sugary ['ʃʊgərɪ] *n.* 含糖的

conservation [ˌkɒnsə'veɪʃn] *n.* 保护

14. How old ...? ……几岁了?

对话示例

— Is there someone's birthday today?	— 今天有人过生日吗?
— Yes, it's Daniel's birthday. I plan to have a birthday surprise for him.	— 是的，是丹尼尔的生日。我计划为他准备一个生日惊喜。
— **How old** is he? I can try to get him a birthday cake.	— 他多大了? 我可以设法为他弄一个蛋糕。
— Thank you. That's really nice of you.	— 谢谢。你真是太好了。

句型分析

How old ...? 这个句型是对年龄的提问，询问某人现在多大岁数。How 作特殊疑问词，old 作形容词，其后跟的是要询问的对象，即 be 动词 + 主语。

句子示例

- **How old** are you? 你多大了?
- **How old** is your friend? 你的朋友多大了?
- **How old** are those lambs? 那些羊羔有多大?

重点单词

surprise [sə'praɪz] *n.* 惊喜，惊奇

lamb [læm] *n.* 羊羔

15. I haven't seen you for... 我……没见你了。

对话示例

— Guiney? Where've you been? **I haven't seen you for** three months.	— 吉尼？你去哪儿了？我已经三个月没有看到你了。
— I've been on a business trip to Australia lately. The scenery in Australia is really beautiful.	— 我最近一直在澳大利亚出差。澳大利亚的风景真是美丽。
— Yes. So I always want to go there again.	— 确实。所以我一直很想再去一次那里。
— Maybe we can go together next time.	— 或许下次我们可以一起去。

句型分析

I haven't seen you for... 这个句型用的是现在完成时态，“没有见到”这个事实是从过去就开始，对现在还有影响，for 后面跟表示时间的词。

句子示例

- **I haven't seen you for** a long time. 我已经很长时间没有见过你了。
- **I haven't seen you for** a year. 我已经有一年没有见过你了。
- What a pleasant surprise! I **haven't seen you for** ten years. 真叫人惊喜！我已经十年没有见到你了。

重点单词

scenery ['si:nərɪ] *n.* 风景　　business ['bɪznəs] *n.* 生意，商业

16. I'm going to... 我将要……

对话示例

— Do you have any plans for the weekend?	— 你这周末有什么打算吗？
— **I am going to** pay a visit to one of my old friends.	— 我打算去看我的一位老朋友。
— Where does he live?	— 他住在哪里？
— He lives in a small town in Australia.	— 他现在住在澳大利亚的一个小村庄里。
— What a coincidence! My uncle lives there, too.	— 好巧。我的叔叔也住在那里。

句型分析

I'm going to... 这个句型表示的是一般将来时态，to 后面跟的事情通常指的是计划、打算、将要做的事情，表示一种主观的态度，也许是马上做的事情，to 后跟动词原形。

句子示例

- **I'm going to** dinner at Mr. White's tonight. 今晚我要去怀特先生家赴宴。
- **I am going to** go skiing this week. 我计划这周去滑雪。
- **I'm going to** go to the aquarium with my parents at the beginning of next month. 我打算下个月初带着我的父母去海洋馆。

重点单词

ski [skiː] *v.* 滑雪

aquarium [əˈkweərɪəm] *n.* 海洋馆

17. I will come back... 我……时候会回来。

对话示例

— John, I heard you're going to London tomorrow.	— 约翰，我听说你明天要去伦敦了。
— Yes, there are some financial problems that need me to solve in our branch.	— 是的，我们的分公司里出现了一些财务上的问题需要我去解决。
— Oh, when will you be back? I'd like to invite you to have a barbecue.	— 哦，那你什么时候回来？我想邀请你去吃烧烤。
— Okay. **I'll be back** in a week.	— 好的。一个星期后我就会回来。

句型分析

I will come back... 从这个句型中的 will 可看出是表示一般将来时，通常 come back 后面跟表示时间的短语，也就是我回来的时间。

句子示例

- **I will come back** three months later. 我会在三个月后回来。
- Wait for me, please. **I will come back** after a while. 请等我一下，我一会儿就回来。
- Don't worry. **I will come back** next month. 不要担心，我下个月就回来了。

重点单词

financial [faɪˈnænʃl] *a.* 财务的

branch [brɑːntʃ] *n.* 分公司，分支

barbecue [ˈbɑːbɪkjuː] *n.* 烤肉

18. We should have a farewell party for... 我们应该为……开一个欢送会。

对话示例

— Do you know that Mike quit? He'll be living in Australia in the future.	— 你知道麦克辞职了吗？他以后就在澳大利亚生活了。
— No. He is an old employee of our company and has taught us a lot of things. **We should have a farewell party for** him.	— 不知道。他是我们公司的老员工了，并且教会了我们很多东西，我们应该给他举办一个欢送会。
— That sounds good. Do I need to have a reservation now?	— 好主意，需要我现在去订位吗？
— Okay. But you should make sure of the time for dinner.	— 好的，不过你应该先确定一下聚餐的时间。

句型分析

We should have a farewell party for... farewell party（欢送会）决定了这个句子的主题，for 后面要跟的是 sb，也就是我们举办欢送会欢送的对象，从 we should 可以看出这是对我们的一种建议，主语是 we。

句子示例

- **We should have a farewell party for** our manager. 我们应该为我们的经理举办一个欢送会。
- **We should have a farewell party for** Linda who is leaving tomorrow. 我们应该为琳达举办一个欢送会，她明天就要离开了。
- **We should have a farewell party for** our roommate Daniel tonight. 今晚我们应该为我们的室友丹尼尔开一个欢送会。

重点单词

farewell [ˌfeəˈwel] *n.* 欢送，告别

quit [kwɪt] *v.* 辞职，离开

19. ...left without saying goodbye. ……一声招呼没打就走了。

对话示例

— Jack called me yesterday and asked me where you were. He also said he hadn't seen you for a long time. Didn't you tell him you went to Singapore?	— 昨天杰克打电话问我你去哪里了，还说他已经很久没有见到你了。你没有跟他说你去新加坡了吗?
— Yes, I **left without saying goodbye**.	— 是的，我没有跟他打招呼就走了。
— Well. You should have said goodbye to him, after all he was so good to you.	— 好吧。其实你本应该跟他说一声再见的，毕竟他以前对你那么好。
— I just don't want to see him.	— 我只是不想见到他。

句型分析

... left without saying goodbye. 这个句型后面的意思为“不辞而别”，而 left 前面则是主语，指的是不辞而别的人。

句子示例

- I was going to have a farewell party for him, but he **left without saying goodbye.** 我本来打算为他举办一场欢送会的，但是他一声招呼没打就走了。
- I don't know he had gone to Singapore, he **left without saying goodbye.** 我不知道他已经去新加坡了，他一声招呼没打就走了。
- My good friend **left without saying goodbye**, so I am angry with her. 我的好朋友一声招呼没打就走了，所以我对她很生气。

重点单词

without [wɪ'ðaʊt] *prep.* 没有

Singapore [ˌsɪŋgə'pɔː] *n.* 新加坡

20. I have to go now because... 我现在必须得走了，因为……

对话示例

— Jack, **I have to go now because** I have to prepare the information of the interviewees for the manager in the afternoon.	— 杰克，我现在必须得走了，因为我下午还要为经理准备面试者的资料。
— But it's time for lunch now. You can leave after the meal.	— 但是现在到了吃午饭的时间，你可以吃完饭再走。
— Fine, but I need to arrive at office before 2:00 p.m.	— 可以，但是我需要在两点之前到办公室。
— I can drive you there.	— 我可以开车送你过去。
— Okay. Thank you.	— 好的。谢谢。

句型分析

I have to go now because... 这个句型表明了我现在要走的动作，表达说话者急切的情绪，because 后面只能跟句子。

句子示例

- **I have to go now because** I must attend the training seminar on time. 我现在必须得走了，因为我得准时参加培训研讨会。
- **I have to go now because** I have to prepare some materials for the negotiation this afternoon. 我现在必须得走了，因为我要为今天下午的谈判准备一些资料。
- **I have to go now because** I need to get to the railway station before six p.m. 我现在必须得走了，因为我需要下午六点前赶到火车站。

重点单词

seminar ['semɪnɑː] *n.* 研讨会

negotiation [nɪˌgəʊʃɪ'eɪʃn] *n.* 谈判

Unit 2 保持联络

1. This is...speaking. 我是……

对话示例

— Hello! **This is** Mr. Green **speaking**. May I speak to Mr. White?	— 你好！我是格林先生，我能和怀特先生讲话吗?
— I'm sorry. Mr. White is out. Can I take a message for him ?	— 不好意思，怀特先生现在不在。需要我转告吗?
— No thank you. I'm so sorry to disturb you so early.	— 不用了，谢谢。实在不好意思，这么早打扰你。
— No problem.	— 没关系。
— May I know when he will be back?	— 我能知道他什么时候回来吗?
— About three hours later.	— 大约三个小时后。

句型分析

This is...speaking. 这个句型是电话用语，用来表明自己的身份。This is 后面跟说话者的名字，is speaking 表明了正在说话的动作。

句子示例

- Is that Mr. Black? **This is** Mario **speaking**. 是布莱克先生吗? 我是马里奥。
- Good morning. **This is** Mrs. Carter **speaking**. 上午好，我是卡特太太。
- **This is** his wife **speaking**. 我是他的太太。

重点单词

message ['mesɪdʒ] *n.* 信息

disturb [dɪ'stɜ:b] *v.* 打扰

2. Is this...speaking? 你是……吗?

对话示例

— Hello, who do you wish to talk to ?	— 你好。请问你找谁?
— Hello! **Is this** Mrs. Green **speaking**?	— 你好。你是格林太太吗?
— Yes, speaking.	— 是的，请讲。
— My son fought with your son at school. The school says that they will solve this problem, but I think we can solve it privately. What do you think?	— 我的儿子在学校和你儿子打架了。学校说他们会解决这件事情，但是我认为我们可以私底下解决，您觉得呢?
— I think so. Maybe we should talk to them first.	— 我也这样认为。或许我们应该先跟他们沟通一下。

句型分析

Is this...speaking? 这个句型是对 This is...speaking. 句型的转换，用来询问对方的身份，Is this 后面跟的是我所猜测的人物。

句子示例

- **Is this** Susan **speaking**? 是苏珊吗?
- Hello, **is this** Mary **speaking**? 你好，是玛丽吗?
- Good afternoon. **Is this** Helen **speaking**? 下午好，是海伦吗?

重点单词

privately ['praɪvətlɪ] *ad.* 私下地，不公开地

problem ['prɒbləm] *n.* 问题

3. May I speak to...? 可以让……接电话吗?

对话示例

— Hello. This is Melissa speaking. **May I speak to** Mary?	— 你好，我是梅莉莎，可以让玛丽接电话吗?
— I'll just find out for you ...Uh, I am sorry,	— 我给你看看她在不在。不好意思，她不在。

she is not available. Can I take a message for her?	要我帮你留言吗?
— Yes, please tell her that the manager asked us to come to the company at 3 p.m. to discuss the material benefits and regulations of the company.	— 是的，请告诉，她经理要求我们下午三点到公司讨论公司的福利待遇和一些规章制度。
— No problem.	— 没问题。

句型分析

May I speak to...? 这个句型是一种电话用语，用于请求和某人讲话，to 后面的某人与说话者不是一个人，而是是我想要找的人，May 用于此表明我说话时委婉的语气。

句子示例

- **May I speak to** your boss? 我能和你的老板讲话吗?
- Hello, this is Max. **May I speak to** Frank, please? 你好，我是麦克斯，我能和弗兰克说话吗?
- Hello! I am from Green Company. **May I speak to** Mr. Cook? 你好！我来自格林公司，我能和库克先生讲话吗?

重点单词

benefit ['benɪfɪt] *n.* 福利，利益

regulation [ˌregjʊ'leɪʃn] *n.* 规章制度

4. There is a call for ... 这儿有……的电话。

对话示例

— Mr. White, **there is a call for** you.	— 怀特先生，这里有一个电话找你。
— Thank you. I'll take it here.	— 谢谢。接下来就交给我吧。
— Yes, sir. You'd better hurry, because I heard someone crying.	— 好的，先生。不过您最好快一点，我听到有人在哭泣。
— Do you have any idea?	— 你知道原因吗?
— Maybe it's because of damage and compensation of the car.	— 可能是因为车的损坏和赔偿。
— I know, thank you.	— 我知道了。谢谢。

句型分析

There is a call for ... 这是一个电话用语，for 后面跟的是电话需要转交的某人。这里的 call 作名词使用。

句子示例

Sorry to bother you, but **there is a call for** you. 对不起打扰了，有您的电话。

Dad, **there is a call for** you. 爸爸，有您的电话。

Black, **there's a call for** your student. 布莱克，有个电话找你的学生。

重点单词

damage ['dæmɪdʒ] *n.* 损坏，赔偿金　　　　compensation [ˌkɒmpen'seɪʃn] *n.* 赔偿

5. Please ask...to ring me back. 请让……给我回电话。

对话示例

— Hello! Is Frank there?	— 你好。是弗兰克吗?
— No, this is Jenney. May I have your name, please?	— 不，我是珍妮。请问您是?
— I'm Frank's colleague, Mike. May I speak to him?	— 我是弗兰克的同事，麦克。我能和他通电话吗?
— Sorry, he went to the countryside to spend his holiday with his grandmother.	— 不好意思，他去乡下陪他的姥姥度假了。
— All right. **Please ask** him **to ring me back**.	— 好吧，那请让他给我回个电话。
— Okay.	— 好的。

句型分析

Please ask...to ring me back. 这个句型中的 ring me back 意思是“给我回电话”，ask 后要跟 sb，也就是我通过电话要找的某人。

句子示例

- **Please ask** your manager **to ring me back.** 请让你的经理给我回个电话。
- **Please ask** John **to ring me back** when he gets back. 约翰回来时请让他给我回个电话。

• **Please ask** Mr. Parson **to ring me back** if he comes back. 如果帕森先生回来请让他给我回个电话。

重点单词

countryside ['kʌntrɪsaɪd] *n.* 乡村　　holiday ['hɒlədeɪ] *n.* 节日，休息日

6. I'm writing to inform you... 我写信是要告诉你……

对话示例

— Peter, is this the letter you wrote to me?	— 皮特，这是你给我写的信吗?
— Yes, **I'm writing to inform you** that I've decided to quit my present job. Thank you for helping me all the time.	— 是的，我写信是要告诉你我已经决定辞掉我现在的工作了。谢谢你一直以来对我的照顾。
— You're welcome. But I've explained to you the downside of quitting now.	— 不客气。但是我已经给你解释了现在辞职的不利之处了。
— I'm sorry, but I really don't want to work here.	— 不好意思，但是我真的不想在这里工作了。

句型分析

I'm writing to inform you... 这个句型较常用于书面表达中，指出写信的目的。inform you 后面可跟 that 从句或介词短语。

句子示例

• **I'm writing to inform you** of my new address. 我写信是要告诉你我的新住址。

• **I'm writing to inform you** about my decision to join your team. 我写信是要告诉你我决定加入你的团队。

• **I'm writing to inform you** that I met your ex-husband in Australia. 我写信是要告诉你我在澳大利亚见到了你的前夫。

重点单词

downside ['daʊnsaɪd] *n.* 不利方面　　explain [ɪk'spleɪn] *v.* 解释

present ['preznt] *n.* 礼物，现在 *a.* 现在的，出席的

7. I'm looking forward to... 我期待……

对话示例

— I heard you appreciate Mr. Finn, don't you?	— 我听说你很欣赏芬恩先生，不是吗?
— Yes, **I'm looking forward to** working with him. He is one of the most competent people I know.	— 是的，我期待着能和他一起工作。他是我认识的人中工作能力最强的一个。
— Really? Maybe you can introduce him to me.	— 是真的吗? 或许你可以把他介绍给我认识一下。
— Of course. We're going to have dinner together this week. Do you want to go with me?	— 当然可以。这周我们要一起吃饭，你要和我一起去吗?
— Sure.	— 好的。

句型分析

I'm looking forward to... 这个句型用 be looking forward 强调正在进行的事情，to 在这里是介词，后接名词或动名词。

句子示例

- **I'm looking forward to** paying a visit to you this week. 我期待着这周去拜访你。
- **I'm looking forward to** attending your speech contest next month. 我期待着参加你下个月的演讲比赛。
- **I'm looking forward to** your visit tomorrow evening. 我期待着你明天晚上的光临。

重点单词

competent ['kɒmpɪtənt] *a.* 有能力的　　appreciate [ə'priːʃɪeɪt] *v.* 欣赏，感激

8. Can you help me...? 你可以帮我……吗?

对话示例

— Anna, I can't move my leg for a while. **Can you help me** contact the doctor?	— 安娜，我的腿暂时不能移动，你能帮我联系一下医生吗?

— No problem. What is the doctor's telephone number?	— 没问题，医生的电话号码是什么？
— It's in the notebook on the table.	— 号码在桌子上的那个笔记本里。
— Is that the blue notebook?	— 是蓝色的那个笔记本吗？
— Yes.	— 是的。

句型分析

Can you help me...? 由这个句型中的 help 可知，me 后面要跟的内容需要符合 help 的固定搭配，即 ① Can you help me + to do sth? ② Can you help me + do sth? ③ Can you help me with sth?

句子示例

- **Can you help me** with my chemistry? 你可以帮我学化学吗？
- **Can you help me** put my computer into the locker? 你可以帮我把我的电脑放进储物柜里吗？
- **Can you help me** give this letter to Paul? 你可以帮我把这封信交给保罗吗？

重点单词

medicine ['medsn] *n.* 药物

backpack ['bækpæk] *n.* 背包

chemistry ['kemɪstrɪ] *n.* 化学

9. You can ask...for help. 你可以向……求助。

对话示例

— What's wrong with you?	— 你怎么了？
— I can't contact with my father.	— 我找不到我爸爸了。
— Don't worry. **You can ask** the police **for help**. I think they could help you find your father.	— 不要担心，你可以向警察求助。我想他们可能帮你找到你的爸爸。
— Where should I go to find them?	— 我应该去哪里找他们？

句型分析

You can ask...for help. 这个句型中的 ask sb for help 是固定搭配，help 在这里作名词使用，help 也可以当作动词，表示“帮助”。

句子示例

- This question is somewhat abstract. **You can ask** your teacher **for help**. 这个问题有些抽象，你可以向你的老师求助。
- **You can ask** Information Center **for help**. 你可以向信息中心求助。
- I don't know the duration of the activity. **You can ask** the volunteers **for help**. 我不知道这个活动的持续时间，你可以向志愿者求助。

重点单词

attendant [əˈtendənt] *n.* 服务人员

abstract [ˈæbstrækt] *a.* 抽象的

duration [djʊˈreɪʃn] *n.* 持续时间

10. Are you free for...? 你有空……吗?

对话示例

— Mary, **are you free for** lunch next Monday? Can I invite you to a banquet?	— 玛丽，你下个星期一午餐的时候有空吗?我能否邀请你参加一个宴会?
— I'd like to, but I am having a meeting then.	— 我很愿意去，但是我那时正在开会。
— What a pity! My colleagues would like me to introduce you to them.	— 真遗憾！我的同事都很想让我把你介绍给他们。
— Maybe we can make an appointment next time.	— 或许我们可以约下一次。

句型分析

Are you free for...? 这个句型是用来询问对方是否有空，for 后不能直接跟表时间的短语，而应跟我询问的目的，然后可以加上时间短语。

句子示例

- **Are you free for** my birthday party this Monday evening? 你这周一晚上有空参加我的生日聚会吗?

- **Are you free for** lunch on Friday, Sept.4, 2017? 您能否在 2017 年 9 月 4 日，周五中午与我们共进午餐?
- **Are you free for** my visit at 8:30 tomorrow evening? 我明天晚上八点半去拜访你，方便吗?

重点单词

banquet ['bæŋkwɪt] *n.* 宴会

appointment [ə'pɔɪntmənt] *n.* 约会，约定

11. We can meet at... 我们可以在……见面。

对话示例

— Are you free tomorrow night? I want to play poker with you.	— 你明天晚上有空吗? 我想和你打扑克牌。
— Sure. Where would you like to meet?	— 可以。你想在哪里见面?
— **We can meet at** your house or mine, as you wish.	— 我们可以在你家或者我家见面，随便你。
— Well, then, we can meet at my home. My family is out.	— 那样的话，我们可以在我家见面，我的家人都不在家。
— Okay.	— 好的。

句型分析

We can meet at... 这个句型 at 后面跟的应是表示时间和地点的词汇。

句子示例

- **We can meet at** seven this evening. 我们可以今天晚上七点见面。
- **We can meet at** the movies and I have bought two movie tickets. 我们可以在电影院见面，我已经买了两张电影票。
- **We can meet at** 3:30 tomorrow afternoon in your office. 我们可以明天下午三点半在你的办公室见面。

重点单词

poker ['pəʊkə] *n.* 扑克

ticket ['tɪkɪt] *n.* 票

12. Could you tell me...? 你可以告诉我……吗?

对话示例

— **Could you tell me** something about your experience in Mexico?	— 你能告诉我一些你在墨西哥的经历吗?
— Of course. What impressed me most is its topography and monuments. I believe you will love the city.	— 当然可以。最令我印象深刻的就是它的地貌和古迹。我相信你也会喜欢那个城市的。
— Yes, how long are you staying there?	— 是的，你在那里住了多长的时间?
— About three years.	— 大约三年。

句型分析

Could you tell me...? 这个句型中的 Could 使句子的语气更委婉，tell 在这里接双宾语，因此 me 后面要跟的是 sth；me 后面也可以接宾语从句。

句子示例

- **Could you tell me** where the telephone booth is? 你可以告诉我电话亭在哪里吗?
- **Could you tell me** how to take the shortcut? 你可以告诉我如何抄近道吗?
- **Could you tell me** the time? 你可以告诉我现在几点了吗?

重点单词

monument ['mɒnjʊmənt] *n.* 纪念碑，遗迹　　topography [tə'pɒgrəfɪ] *n.* 地貌

shortcut ['ʃɔːtkʌt] *n.* 捷径，近道

13. Would you like to...? 你愿意……吗?

对话示例

— Amy, **would you like to** go for a walk with me tomorrow evening? I have so many words to tell you.	— 艾米，你愿意明天晚上陪我散步吗? 我有很多话想对你说。
— Sure. But I won't be free until after eight because I have to send snapshots to my	— 可以。但是我八点以后才有空，因为我还要给我叔叔送快照照片。你介意吗?

uncle. Do you mind?	
— No, I can write my report first.	— 不介意，我可以先去写我的报告。
— OK, see you at eight.	— 好的，那八点见。

句型分析

Would you like to... 这个句型中 would like 是固定搭配，意为“想要”，这种询问方式相对委婉，用于礼貌地提出请求、建议或者征求对方的意见。由 like 后的 to 可知，后面要跟动词原形。

句子示例

- **Would you like to** change U.S. dollars into Japanese yen? 你想要把美元兑换成日币吗?
- **Would you like to** arrange for me to meet Mr. Mike? 你愿意安排我和麦克先生会面吗?
- **Would you like to** go to the library to read magazines with me? 你愿意跟我一起去图书馆看杂志吗?

重点单词

snapshot ['snæpʃɒt] *n.*（快照）照片

magazine [ˌmægə'zi:n] *n.* 杂志

yen [jen] *n.* 日元

14. Please confirm that... 请确认……

对话示例

— Hello, what can I do for you?	— 你好，有什么需要帮助的吗?
— Hello, this is Jack from Green Company. Your order has arrived. **Please confirm that** the production date and expiry date of the products are not wrong.	— 你好。我是格林公司的杰克。你们预订的产品已经到了。请确认一下这些产品的生产日期和有效期没有问题。
— OK. Give me a minute. I will arrange someone to take charge of this.	— 好的，等我一下。我会安排一个人去负责这件事情。
— OK.	— 好的。

句型分析

Please confirm that... 这里的 that 引导宾语从句，这里省略了主语 you，用 please 增强这个句子的委婉语气。

句子示例

- **Please confirm that** this phone number is not wrong. 请确认一下这个电话号码没有错误。
- **Please confirm that** the date and price on the invoice are correct. 请确认一下发票上的日期和价格是正确的。
- **Please confirm that** this is the way you choose to receive goods. 请确认一下这是您选择的收货方式。

重点单词

expiry [ɪk'spaɪərɪ] *n.* 满期，终止　　confirm [kən'fɜ:m] *n.* 确认

15. You need to... 你需要……

对话示例

— Jones, I'm going to open a fried chicken restaurant here next year. What do you say?	— 琼斯，我打算明年在这里开一家炸鸡店。你认为呢？
— That sounds good, but **you need to** make some preparations before you open the fried chicken restaurant.	— 听起来不错，但是你在开炸鸡店之前需要先做一些准备。
— What should I do?	— 我要做什么？
— My suggestion is that you get the information of all the businesses in this area, and the number of households in the neighborhood. This can help you determine if you can successfully open a fried chicken restaurant in this area.	— 我的建议是你需要收集这个地区所有商家的信息，以及附近小区的住户数量。这能帮你判断你能否在这个地区成功开一家炸鸡店。
— That's right. How can I get information about the businesses and households?	— 没错。那么我如何获得商家和住户的信息呢？
— Maybe you can get it from the government office.	— 或许你可以从政府的办事处获得。

句型分析

You need to... 这里的 need 是作实义动词使用，构成 need to + do sth，表示我对你需要做的事情的建议，接近于命令的语气。

句子示例

- **You need to** put these crabs into the steamer as soon as possible. 你需要尽快把这些螃蟹放进蒸锅里。
- **You need to** fry the potato chips until they're crisp. 你需要把土豆片炸到脆为止。
- **You need to** be familiar with the company's rules and regulations. 你需要对公司的规章制度了如指掌。

重点单词

household ['haʊshəʊld] *n.* 住户

steamer ['sti:mə] *n.* 蒸锅

crisp [krɪsp] *a.* 脆的，易碎的

16. Do you know...? 你知道……吗?

对话示例

— **Do you know** who the man we saw today is?	— 你知道我们今天见到的那位男士是谁吗?
— No, I just know he is an important client of our company.	— 不知道，我只知道他是我们公司的一个重要客户。
— That's right. He is a big client of our company. It is because of him that the profits of our company doubled. That's why we always welcome him so ceremoniously.	— 没错，他是我们公司的大客户。正是因为他我们公司的利润增大了一倍。这就是我们每次都这么隆重地欢迎他的原因。
— He's really a very capable person, and he's also very kind.	— 他真的是一个很有能力的人，而且还很和蔼。

句型分析

Do you know...? 这个句型中 Do you know 本身就是完整的句子，后面若跟句子就构成宾语从句，从句必须用陈述语序；know 后面也可以跟名词。

句子示例

- **Do you know** how to deactivate the car bomb? 你知道如何拆除这个汽车炸弹吗?
- **Do you know** why he has always hung up? 你知道为什么他最近总是心神不宁吗?
- **Do you know** the time of the next subway? 你知道下一趟地铁的时间吗?

重点单词

deactivate [ˌdiːˈæktɪveɪt] *v.* 使无效，使不活动

ceremoniously [ˌserəˈməʊnɪəslɪ] *ad.* 隆重地

17. Do you want to...? 你想……吗?

对话示例

— **Do you want to** buy a down jacket?	— 你想买羽绒服吗?
— Yes, can you recommend one for me? I'll send you some pictures later, and their details.	— 是的，你能帮我推荐一款吗? 稍后我给你发几张图片，以及它们的详细信息。
— Of course. Hum, I think the style of first one is very suitable for you; its cashmere rate also reached 99.9%. And it looks very fashionable. Do you like it?	— 可以。嗯，我感觉第一款的风格很适合你，其含绒量也达到了 99.9%。而且它看起来很时尚。你喜欢吗?
— Ah, I don't like this color. You know, I like light-colored clothes.	— 啊，我不喜欢这个颜色。你知道的，我喜欢浅色的衣服。

句型分析

Do you want to...? 这个句型的问法比较直接，常用在熟人之间，这里的 to 是不定式，后面跟动词原形，也就是 want to + do sth。

句子示例

- We are going to play football, **do you want to** join in? 我们要去踢足球，你来不来?
- **Do you want to** eliminate the generation gap between you and your dad? 你想消除你和你爸爸之间的代沟吗?
- **Do you want to** improve your Chinese? 你想提高你的汉语水平吗?

重点单词

eliminate [ɪˈlɪmɪneɪt] *v.* 消除

generation [ˌdʒenəˈreɪʃn] *n.* 一代人，一代

18. I'd like to make an appointment... 我想预约……

对话示例

— Good afternoon. This is Dr. Hammer's office. What can I do for you?	— 下午好。这里是哈默医生的诊所，有什么事吗？
— Good afternoon. **I'd like to make an appointment** with Dr. Hammer. Could you arrange it for me?	— 下午好。我想预约哈默医生。你能为我安排吗？
— Of course. Just a minute, please. Let me check his schedule. How about Friday morning at 10:00?	— 可以。请稍等，我看一下他的日程表。星期五上午十点可以吗？
— That's fine. Thank you.	— 可以。谢谢。
— You're welcome. May I have your name and phone number, please?	— 不客气。能告诉我你的名字和电话吗？
— Certainly. My name is John Wilson. My phone number is 216-254-426.	— 当然可以。我是约翰·威尔逊。我的电话是 216-254-426。

句型分析

I'd like to make an appointment... 这个句型的用法相对正式，通常用于谈公事。make an appointment 是固定搭配，would like to 表明我的意愿。如果表示“我想与某人预约”用 with；若想表示预约的目的，这个句型后可跟 to + 动词原形；若想表示预约的时间，则可跟介词 for 连用。

句子示例

- **I'd like to make an appointment** for next Monday at 5 p.m. 我想要预约下个星期一下午五点。
- **I'd like to make an appointment** to see Mr. Daniel. 我想约个时间去看丹尼尔先生。
- **I'd like to make an appointment** with the accountant. 我想预约会计谈一下。

重点单词

appointment [ə'pɔɪntmənt] *n.* 约会，任命

accountant [ə'kaʊntənt] *n.* 会计师，会计人员

schedule ['ʃedju:l] *n.* 日程

19. I couldn't keep the appointment because... 我不能赴约，因为……

对话示例

— What's up, Harry?	— 怎么了，哈利?
— I am so sorry, Henry. **I couldn't keep the appointment because** I've caught a bad cold today and have a fever. I went to see the doctor, and he said I'd better have a good rest.	— 真的不好意思，亨利。我不能赴约了，因为我得了重感冒并且发烧了。我已经去看过医生了，医生说我最好在家好好休息。
— That's all right. You have a good rest at home. We can make an appointment next time.	— 没关系。你在家里好好休息。我们可以下次再约。
— Okay. I'll contact you when I'm well.	— 好的。等我病好后，我会立刻联系你。

句型分析

I couldn't keep the appointment because... 这个句型中的 keep the appointment 是“赴约”的意思，这里是要讲述不能赴约的原因，其后跟句子。

句子示例

- **I couldn't keep the appointment because** my shower facility is dribbled all the time. 我不能赴约了，因为我家的淋浴设备一直漏水。
- **I couldn't keep the appointment because** my parents came to see me. 我不能赴约了，因为我的父母来看我了。
- **I couldn't keep the appointment because** my manager asked me to work overtime tonight. 我不能赴约了，因为我的经理要求我今天晚上加班。

重点单词

facility [fə'sɪlətɪ] *n.* 设备　　dribble ['drɪbl] *v.* （液体）滴下；细流

20. He has to cancel his appointment because... 他不得不取消他的约会，因为……

对话示例

— I am calling about your appointment with Mr. Clinton. **He has to cancel his appointment because** he must fly to New York now to deal with the problems about the contract for the company.	— 我打电话来是想说你和克林顿先生预约的事。他不得不取消他的预约，因为他必须现在就飞往纽约，为公司解决有关合同的问题。
— When will he come back?	— 他什么时候能回来?
— About five days later. You can make an appointment on Friday.	— 大约五天后。你们可以约在星期五。
— Well. Please arrange it for me.	— 那好吧。请帮我安排一下。

句型分析

He has to cancel his appointment because... 这个句型中的 has to 表明了这个约会的取消是因为客观存在的问题，because 引导取消约会的原因。

句子示例

- **He has to cancel his appointment because** he has something urgent to deal with. 他不得不取消他的预约，因为他有紧急的事情要处理。
- **He has to cancel his appointment because** he needs to execute the chairman's temporary request. 他不得不取消他的预约，因为他需要执行董事长的临时要求。
- **He has to cancel his appointment because** all the flights are booked today. 他不得不取消他的预约，因为今天所有的航班都预订完了。

重点单词

contract ['kɒntrækt] *n.* 合同

urgent ['ɜ:dʒənt] *a.* 紧急的

execute ['eksɪkju:t] *v.* 执行

Unit 3 拜访聚会

1. I want to eat... 我想吃……

对话示例

— **I want to eat** out with my friends tonight. Will you join me?	— 今晚我想出去和我朋友一起吃，你要跟我一起吗?
— No, I have a lot of documents to check. Could you bring me a combination salad when you come back?	— 不了，我还有很多的文件要检查。你回来的时候能帮我带一份什锦色拉吗?
— Sure. Anything else?	— 当然可以了。还要其他的吗?
— No, thank you. There's bread and milk in the fridge.	— 不用了，谢谢。冰箱里还有面包和牛奶。

句型分析

I want to eat... 这个句型明确了我想要做的动作。因动词是 eat（吃），故后面常跟各类食物。这个句型可单独使用，但其后的省略号表明需要在 eat 后面加上宾语才能使句子完整。

句子示例

- **I want to eat** a sandwich, as well as the apple and radish. 我想吃一个三明治，还有苹果和萝卜。
- I don't want sandwiches; **I want to eat** dumplings. 我不想吃三明治，我想吃饺子。
- **I want to eat** omelettes; can you cook it? 我想吃蛋饼，你会做吗?

重点单词

combination [ˌkɒmbɪ'neɪʃn] *n.* 结合

sandwich ['sænwɪtʃ] *n.* 三明治

omelette ['ɒmlət] *n.* 煎蛋饼

2. I'd like... 我想要……

对话示例

— Do you have any plans for the weekend?	— 你这周末有什么计划吗?
— **I'd like** to pay a visit to my grandpa.	— 我想去拜访我的爷爷。
— Do you know how to get there? Maybe I can drive you there.	— 你知道怎么去那里吗? 或许我可以载你去那里。
— No, thank you. My uncle will pick me up.	— 不用了，谢谢。我叔叔会来接我。

句型分析

I'd like... 这个句型中的 I'd like 是 I would like 的缩写，在表示“请求”和“愿望”时 would like 相当于 want，所以其常用的结构为：I'd like + to do（动词） sth / I'd like + sth（名词）。

句子示例

- **I'd like** a large coke and a hamburger. 我想要一个大杯可乐和一个汉堡。
- **I'd like** to drink a glass of milk. 我想喝一杯牛奶。
- **I'd like** to go to summer camp to master more skills. 我想要去参加夏令营来掌握更多的技能。

重点单词

master ['mɑ:stə] *v.* 掌握

hamburger ['hæmbɜ:gə] *n.* 汉堡

3. I just stop by to... 我来拜访只是为了……

对话示例

— How are you, Mr. Cook? I'm glad you've come.	— 你好吗，库克先生? 欢迎光临。
— I am fine. Thank you. **I just stop by to** borrow some charcoal.	— 我很好，谢谢。我来拜访只是为了借一些木炭。
— OK. Wait me for a minute. I'll take it at once.	— 好的，稍等一下。我马上给你拿来。
— Thanks a lot.	— 多谢。

句型分析

I just stop by to... 这个句型中的 stop by 是固定搭配，意为“顺便拜访”，to 在这里是不定式，需跟动词原形。

句子示例

- **I just stop by to** say hello. 我来拜访只是为了问个好。
- **I just stop by to** tell you the truth. 我来拜访只是为了告诉你事实的真相。
- **I just stop by to** give you some special products. 我来拜访只是为了给你一些特产。

重点单词

charcoal ['tʃɑ:kəʊl] *n.* 木炭，竹炭

special ['speʃl] *a.* 特殊的，专门的

4. I forgot... 我忘记……了

对话示例

— Sorry, Jenney. **I forgot** to come to your birthday party.	— 不好意思，珍妮。我忘记去参加你的生日聚会了。
— That's all right. My birthday party has been adjusted to tomorrow evening.	— 不要紧。我的生日聚会调整至明天晚上了。
— Great. I'll be on time this time. What time does the party start?	— 太好了。这次我一定准时参加。聚会几点开始?
— At 8:00.	— 八点。

句型分析

I forgot... 这个句型中的 forgot 是 forget 的过去式，表示我忘记的内容。可表达两种意思：一种是 forget to do sth，指的是忘记去做某事，意味着“这件事未做”，另一种是 forget doing sth，指的是忘记做过某事，意味着 “这件事已做” 。此外，I forgot 后面还可跟 that 引导的宾语从句。

句子示例

- **I forgot** to give him the crystal ball. 我忘记把这个水晶球给他了。
- **I forgot** that I had given the keys to the secretary. 我忘了我已经把钥匙交给秘书了。
- **I forgot** turning off the air conditioner. 我忘记我已经关掉空调了。

重点单词

conditioner [kən'dɪʃənə] *n.* 调节器

adjust [ə'dʒʌst] *v.* 调整

crystal ['krɪstl] *n.* 水晶

5. Do you still remember...? 你还记得……吗?

对话示例

— Daniel, **do you still remember** our monitor in high school?	— 丹尼尔，你还记得我们高中时期的班长吗?
— Yes. What's up?	— 记得，他怎么了?
— I met him at the party two days ago. He is now a manager of a company. It is said that he is well known in the sales field.	— 我前两天在宴会上碰见他了。他现在已经是一家公司的主管。据说他在销售行业里很有名。
— Wow, he's always been excellent. Did you say hello to him?	— 哇。他一直很优秀。你有和他打招呼吗?
— Yes, we talked for nearly two hours.	— 是的，我们聊了将近两个小时。

句型分析

Do you still remember...? 这个句型后可跟三种形式：引导宾语从句，从句需是陈述语序；句型后跟 sth，构成 remember sth；最后一种就是 remember doing sth（表示记得做过某事，表示说话的时候动作已完成）和 remember to do sth（表示记住去做某事，表示这件事还没有做）。

句子示例

- **Do you still remember** how to open the safe? 你还记得如何打开这个保险柜吗?
- **Do you still remember** what we talked about last month? 你还记得我们上个月的谈话吗?
- **Do you still remember** that roommate from Turkey? 你还记得来自土耳其的那个室友吗?

重点单词

safe [seɪf] *n.* 保险柜

supervisor ['su:pəvaɪzə] *n.* 主管

6. ... is coming. ……节日就要到了。

对话示例

— Thanksgiving Day **is coming**, I brought you a white wine. Have you figured out what you're ready to eat?	— 感恩节就要到了，我给你带了白葡萄酒。你已经想好准备什么食物了吗?
— Sure. I have booked two turkeys, and I'm going to cook some English cheese pies, pumpkin pies, and mashed sweet potato etc. Do you want to join us?	— 当然了，我已经预订了两只火鸡，我还准备制作一些英国奶酪派、南瓜派、红薯泥等。你要加入我们吗?
— No, thank you. I also prepared a lot of food. I wish you have a good time that day.	— 不了，谢谢。我也准备了很多的食物。祝愿你在那天过得愉快。
— Thank you.	— 谢谢。

句型分析

... is coming. 这个句型是正在进行时表将来，意为“就要来了”，而在这里限定的是“节日”，因此 is 前面需要加上节日名称。对外国人而言比较重要的节日有：圣诞节（Christmas Day）、万圣节前夕（Halloween）、感恩节（Thanksgiving Day）、情人节（Valentine's Day）等。

句子示例

- Christmas Day **is coming**; how are you going to spend the time with your husband? 圣诞节就要来了，你打算怎么和你的丈夫度过这段时间?
- Thanksgiving Day **is coming**; I am looking forward to eating pumpkin pie made by my mom. 感恩节就要来了，我很期待吃到妈妈制作的南瓜饼。
- Valentine's Day **is coming**; what kind of present are you going to give your girlfriend? 情人节就要来了，你打算送你女朋友什么礼物?

重点单词

pumpkin ['pʌmpkɪn] *n.* 南瓜

Valentine ['væləntaɪn] *n.* 情人

7. Thanksgiving Day is a / (an)...day. 感恩节是一个……的节日。

对话示例

— **Thanksgiving Day is an** important **day**, do you have any plans for that day?	— 感恩节是一个很重要的节日，你那天有什么计划吗？
— Yes, I intend to participate in volunteer activities after lunch with my family.	— 是的，我打算吃完午饭和家人去参加志愿者活动。
— Wow, you must have a meaningful day. I've been involved in it several times.	— 哇，那你肯定会度过有意义的一天。我也参加过好几次了。
— By the way, what do I need to pay attention to?	— 顺便问一下，我需要注意什么？

句型分析

Thanksgiving Day is a...day. 这个句子是要对 Thanksgiving Day（感恩节）作一个介绍，缺少了形容 day 的各类形容词。day 有时会与 family 连用，构成 family day，意为“家庭日”。

句子示例

- **Thanksgiving Day is a** special and important **day**. 感恩节是一个特别而又重要的节日。
- **Thanksgiving Day is a** meaningful **day**. 感恩节是一个非常有意义的节日。
- **Thanksgiving Day is a** family **day**; my family usually celebrate with a big dinner and a reunion. 感恩节是一个家庭日，我的家人通常以盛大的晚餐和团聚庆祝。

重点单词

celebrate ['selɪbreɪt] *v.* 庆祝

reunion [riː'juːnɪən] *n.* 聚会

8. It's fun to...on Christmas Day. 在圣诞节……是一件有趣的事。

对话示例

— Do you know? **It's fun to** dress up as Santa Claus to give candy to kids **on Christmas Day**.	— 你知道吗？在圣诞节扮圣诞老人给小朋友发糖果真的是一件有趣的事。
— Really? I haven't tried. But I can experience	— 真的吗？我还没有尝试过。不过我可以在

it this time.	这次的圣诞节体验一下。
— Yes, I'm sure you'll have a good time.	— 是的，我相信你一定会玩得很开心。
— Would you come with me?	— 你会跟我一起吗?

句型分析

It's fun to... on Christmas Day. 这个句型中的 fun 在这里作名词，表示“有趣的一件事”，It's fun 后面接的是 to，因此 to 后面要跟动词原形；如果 fun 前有 no、much、great 或 a lot of 等修饰时，It's fun 后通常跟 V-ing 形式。而要表达“在圣诞节”可用 at Christmas 或者 on Christmas Day。

句子示例

- **It's fun to** visit New York **on Christmas Day**. 在圣诞节去纽约游玩是一件有趣的事。
- **It's fun to** go shopping with friends **on Christmas Day**. 在圣诞节和朋友们去购物是一件有趣的事。
- **It's fun to** distribute sweets in the street to children **on Christmas Day**. 在圣诞节到大街上为小朋友分发糖果是一件有趣的事。

重点单词

Santa ['sæntə] *n.* 圣诞老人

distribute [dɪ'strɪbjuːt] *v.* 分发

sweet [swiːt] *n.* 糖果

9. Would you like to join...party? 你愿意来参加……派对吗?

对话示例

— Mike, **would you like to join** us in the dancing **party**?	— 麦克，你愿意来参加我们的舞会吗?
— When and where is it held?	— 它什么时候在哪儿举办?
— It's held in our apartment tonight. You can also invite more friends to come here.	— 今天晚上在我们的公寓里举办。你可以邀请更多的朋友来。
— Great. I'm only available tonight. See you soon.	— 太棒了，我就今晚有空。稍后见。

句型分析

Would you like to join...party? 这个句型用 Would you like to 作询问，主要是为了更加委婉、客气地提出邀请，join 后面通常引导“什么样的”聚会。

句子示例

- **Would you like to join** a cocktail **party**? 你愿意参加鸡尾酒会吗?
- **Would you like to join** the birthday **party**? 你愿意来参加生日聚会吗?
- **Would you like to join** a costume **party**? 你愿意来参加化妆舞会吗?

重点单词

cocktail ['kɒkteɪl] *n.* 鸡尾酒

costume ['kɒstju:m] *n.* 戏服

10. My favorite festival is... 我最喜欢的节日是……

对话示例

— **My favorite festival is** Valentine's Day. I can receive my favorite rose and chocolate on that day. What about you, Alice?	— 我最喜欢的节日是情人节。在那天我可以收到我最喜爱的玫瑰花和巧克力。你呢，爱丽丝?
— My favorite festival is Halloween because I can go to the parade in ghoulish clothes.	— 我最喜欢的节日是万圣节，因为我可以穿令人毛骨悚然的服装去巡游。
— Well, I still remember that the child was frightened into crying by your terrible mask last year.	— 好吧，我仍然记得你去年戴了一个可怕的面具，把一个小孩吓哭了。
— Ha-ha.	— 哈哈。

句型分析

My favorite festival is... 这个句型中的 My favorite festival 确定了这个句子的主题，因此 is 后面需要引导的是各类节日名称，且只能跟一个节日名称。

句子示例

- **My favorite festival is** Christmas, because I can see lots of Santa Clauses and mascots. 我最喜欢的节日是圣诞节，因为我可以看到很多圣诞老人和吉祥物。

- **My favorite festival is** Thanksgiving Day, because I can be with my parents. 我最喜欢的节日是感恩节，因为我可以和我的父母团聚。
- **My favorite festival is** Carnival, because I can see beautiful women dancing the Samba. 我最喜欢的节日是狂欢节，因为我能看到美丽的女士跳桑巴舞。

重点单词

parade [pə'reɪd] *n.* 游行

mascot ['mæskət] *n.* 吉祥物

11. It's the custom to... at ... 在……做……是一种习俗。

对话示例

— You know the customs of many countries, don't you?	— 你知道很多国家的习俗，不是吗?
— Yes, I've been to many places before. And I have a general understanding of their customs before I go.	— 是的，我以前去过很多地方。在去之前我对它们的风俗习惯都有个大致的了解。
— Can you tell me some? Like the place we live in.	— 你能告诉我一些吗? 比如我们生活的这个地方。
— Certainly. **It's the custom to** eat all the food on your plate **at** table.	— 当然。用餐时吃光你盘子里的食物就是这里的一种习俗。

句型分析

It's the custom to... at ... 这个句型中的 to 是作不定式使用，后面接动词原形，指的是做什么事情是一种习俗。

句子示例

- **It's the custom to** decorate a Christmas tree **at** Christmas. 在圣诞节装扮圣诞树是一种习俗。
- **It's the custom to** make lanterns with pumpkins **at** Halloween. 在万圣节前夕用南瓜制作灯笼是一种习俗。
- **It's the custom to** dress up as Santa Claus to give children gifts **at** Christmas. 在圣诞节装扮成圣诞老人给小孩送礼物是一种习俗。

重点单词

decorate ['dekəreɪt] *v.* 装饰　　lantern ['læntən] *n.* 灯笼

12. When is...? ……是什么时候?

对话示例

— Daniel, **when is** John's celebratory dinner?	— 丹尼尔，约翰的庆功晚宴什么时候举行?
— He said to me that he put the time in tomorrow afternoon temporarily. What's up?	— 他说暂时安排在明天下午，怎么了?
— I have to go to London for a week because I have some urgent things to solve. I'm afraid I can't attend it.	— 我要去伦敦一周，因为我有一些急事需要处理，我恐怕没有办法参加了。
— It's a pity. But maybe he could adjust the time to next Friday.	— 真遗憾。不过或许他会把时间调整至下个星期五。

句型分析

When is...? 这个句型用的特殊疑问词是 when，表明了要询问时间，is 是 be 动词，后可接名词或者动词，但要注意 is 和动词之间的关系。

句子示例

- **When is** the movie coming out? 这部电影什么时候上映?
- **When is** the next flight to Australia? 去澳大利亚的下一趟航班是什么时候?
- **When is** the best time to tell Jane about this? 什么时候是告诉简这个消息的最好时机?

重点单词

celebratory [ˌseləˈbreɪtərɪ] *a.* 为了庆祝的，表示庆祝的

temporarily [tempəˈrerɪlɪ] *ad.* 暂时地

13. We can ... at ... 我们可以在……做……

对话示例

— Halloween is coming. What do you want to do?	— 万圣节要来了，你有什么想做的事情吗？
— I have no idea. I might hitch a ride to an outing.	— 我不知道。我可能搭个顺风车去郊游。
— Come on. **We can** wear clothes like a ghost to find our friends **at** Halloween.	— 不要了吧。我们可以在万圣节穿上像鬼的衣服去找我们的朋友。
— That sounds great. But I don't have that kind of clothes.	— 听起来不错。但是我没有那样的衣服。

句型分析

We can ... at... 这里的 can 表示现在的能力，也就是我们能做的事情，at 后面跟节日的名称，can 后面引导可以做的事情。

句子示例

- **We can** hang a sock on the head of the bed **at** Christmas. 我们可以在圣诞节的时候在床头挂上一只袜子。
- **We can** make all kinds of strange clothes to sell **at** Halloween. 我们可以在万圣节的时候制作各种奇怪的衣服去卖。
- **We can** put a lot of pink balloons in the house **at** Valentine's Day night. 我们可以在情人节的晚上在房子里放很多的粉色气球。

重点单词

hitch [hɪtʃ] *v.* 搭乘

ghost [gəʊst] *n.* 鬼，（电视屏幕上的）重影

14. How do you plan to celebrate...? 你打算怎么庆祝……？

对话示例

— Valentine's Day is coming. **How do you plan to celebrate** it?	— 情人节要来了。你打算怎么庆祝它？

— I plan to propose to my girlfriend. Can you help me to decorate the room?	— 我打算向我的女朋友求婚。你能帮我布置房间吗?
— Of course, but I suggest that you'd better arrange the place in the park because the park is more suitable for hydrogen balloons and roses.	— 当然可以了，不过我建议你最好把地点安排在公园。因为公园更适合放置氢气球和玫瑰花。
— That's a wonderful idea.	— 好主意。

句型分析

How do you plan to celebrate...? 这个句型中的特殊疑问词 how 是用来询问庆祝的方式，plan to 表示“计划做”。

句子示例

- **How do you plan to celebrate** the promotion? 你打算怎么庆祝这次升职?
- **How do you plan to celebrate** the birthday of Kelley? 你打算怎么庆祝凯利的生日?
- **How do you plan to celebrate** this successful negotiation? 你打算怎么庆祝这次谈判的胜利?

重点单词

propose [prə'pəʊz] *v.* 求婚

hydrogen ['haɪdrədʒən] *n.* 氢

promotion [prə'məʊʃn] *n.* 升职

15. I wish you... 我祝你……

对话示例

— Valentine's Day is coming, **I wish you** to find your other half.	— 情人节要到了，祝你早日找到你的另一半。
— Thank you. By the way, can you introduce your college classmate to me?	— 谢谢。对了，顺便问一下，你能把你的那个大学同学介绍给我吗?
— Sure. But do you mind that she's five years older than you?	— 可以。但是你介意她比你大五岁吗?
— No, I just hope we can enjoy each other. Can you arrange for us to meet tonight?	— 不介意，我只希望我们能互相喜欢。你能安排我们今晚见面吗?

句型分析

I wish you... 这个句型中的 wish 后是 you，根据这个结构可知 wish 后可接复合宾语和双宾语，既可表示“祝愿”，也可表示“希望”。

句子示例

- **I wish you** a pleasant journey. 祝你旅途愉快。
- **I wish you** would turn the television down. 我希望你能把电视的声音调低一些。
- **I wish you** to know that I have been accustomed to the life here. 我希望你知道我已经习惯了这里的生活。

重点单词

journey ['dʒɜːnɪ] *n.* 旅行　　accustom [ə'kʌstəm] *v.* 使习惯

16. What's your wish on...? 你……节日的愿望是什么？

对话示例

— Amy, **what's your wish on** your birthday?	— 艾米，你生日时的愿望是什么？
— I wish my family a happy and prosperous life.	— 我希望我的家人生活幸福、万事如意。
— You don't want gifts?	— 你不想要礼物吗？
— No, but I would prefer my family to be happy.	— 想，但是我更希望我的家人过得快乐。
— Since you are so sensible, I give you this as a gift.	— 既然你这么懂事，我就把这个作为礼物送给你。

句型分析

What's your wish on...? 这个句子里on的意思是“关于，有关”，也就是询问你的愿望是关于什么的。

句子示例

- **What's your wish on** Christmas Day? 在圣诞节的时候你的愿望是什么？
- **What's your wish on** Valentine's Day? 在情人节的时候你的愿望是什么？
- **What's your wish on** Thanksgiving Day? 在感恩节的时候你的愿望是什么？

重点单词

prosperous ['prɒspərəs] *a.* 运气好的

sensible ['sensəbl] *a.* 明智的，通情达理的

17. Have a...day! 祝你玩得……

对话示例

— Tom, the party is not over, where are you going?	— 汤姆，聚会还没有结束，你要去哪里?
— I have to go back to the company to learn about the changes in financial indicators. Maybe I have to work overtime tonight again.	— 我必须要回公司了解财务指标的变化。可能今晚我又要加班了。
— Do you want to take some midnight snacks?	— 那你要不要带一些夜宵回去?
— No, I don't have that habit. Bye, **have a** nice **day**!	— 不用了，我没有那个习惯。我走了，玩得愉快!

句型分析

Have a...day! 这个句型缺少形容词来形容 day，通常可用 fine、nice 或 good 来表示。这句话主要用于道别时，表示良好的祝愿。

句子示例

- **Have a** nice **day**! 祝你玩得愉快!
- My pleasure, madam. **Have a** good **day**! 我的荣幸，女士。玩得愉快!
- Thank you in advance. **Have a** fine **day**! 先行致谢，祝您愉快!

重点单词

indicator ['ɪndɪkeɪtə] *n.* 指示

midnight ['mɪdnaɪt] *n.* 午夜

18. I met...in the party. 我在聚会上遇见了……

对话示例

— Jones, **I met** our former classmate in high school **in the party**, Marie. She turned and ignored me deliberately when I walked towards her. Maybe she doesn't forgive me.	— 琼斯，我在聚会上碰见了我们以前的高中同学，玛丽。我向她走去时她转身故意不搭理我。可能她还是没有原谅我。
— Maybe she just did not see you. It has been five years since it happened. I believe that no one can remember that thing.	— 可能她只是没有看见你。那件事已经过去五年了，我相信没有人会记得那件事。
— Maybe. Should I give her a ring to say hello?	— 或许。我是不是应该给她打个电话打声招呼呢?
— You'd better say it when you meet.	— 你最好在你们见面的时候说。

句型分析

I met...in the party. 这里用过去式 met 表明在聚会上已经见过了，met 后通常跟的是所见的人物。

句子示例

- **I met** my ex-husband **in the party**. 我在聚会上见到了我的前夫。
- **I met** a famous singer and got his autograph **in the party**. 我在聚会上见到了一个著名的歌手并得到了他的亲笔签名。
- **I met** most of her family **in the party**. 我在聚会上见到了她的大部分家人。

重点单词

deliberately [dɪˈlɪbərətlɪ] *ad.* 故意地　　autograph [ˈɔːtəgrɑːf] *n.* 亲笔签名

19. It is a ... party. 这是一个……的聚会。

对话示例

— John, **it's a** pity that Daniel didn't come to the **party**.	— 约翰，很遗憾丹尼尔没有来参加这个聚会。
— Indeed. After all, we do not know when we can meet again. Do you have his phone number? I want to ask about his illness.	— 确实，毕竟我们再见面也不知道是何时了。你有他的电话号码吗？我想要问一下他的病情。
— I have asked. His father said that he has been through a dangerous period.	— 我已经问过了。他爸爸说他已经度过了危险期。
— Great, it's worth celebrating.	— 太棒了，这值得我们庆祝一番。

句型分析

It is a ... party. 这个句型中的 a 表示后面应跟一个名词，常用的有 pity 和 honor，而 party 前可跟一系列的形容词，来形容这是一个什么样的聚会。

句子示例

- **It is a** great honor for me to be present at this evening **party**. 对我来说能参加这个晚会是一种荣幸。
- **It is a** pity that you didn't come to our **party**. 很遗憾你没有参加这个聚会。
- **It is a** pity that you forgot to attend the unforgettable **party**. 很遗憾你忘记参加这个难忘的聚会。

重点单词

unforgettable [ˌʌnfəˈgetəbl] *a.* 难忘的　　dangerous [ˈdeɪndʒərəs] *a.* 危险的

20. The dish is... 这道菜……

对话示例

— Mike, **the dish is** not bad. Would you like to taste a piece of it?	— 麦克，这道菜的味道真的不错。你要尝一块吗?
— Yes, I also like sweet food. It seems our tastes are very similar.	— 好的。我也喜欢吃甜的食物。看来我们俩的口味很相似。
— Yes, can I invite you to my home for dinner tomorrow night? You can have a taste of my cuisine.	— 是的。我能邀请你明晚去我家吃晚饭吗?你可以尝一尝我的手艺。
— No problem.	— 好的，没问题。

句型分析

The dish is... 这个句子 is 后引导的内容是用来修饰 dish 的，通常用形容词，也可以用固定搭配，例如 be made from，意为“这道菜由……制成”。此外，dish 也可作“盘子”使用。

句子示例

- **The dish is** made from potatoes. 这道菜的原料是土豆。
- **The dish is** too salty to swallow. 这道菜太咸了以至于难以下咽。
- **The dish is** a local snack in London. 这道菜是伦敦的地道小吃。

重点单词

cuisine [kwɪ'zi:n] *n.* 烹饪，菜肴

swallow ['swɒləʊ] *v.* 咽，忍受

21. Welcome to... 欢迎来到……

对话示例

— **Welcome to** my home. I have prepared a sumptuous meal for you. I believe you will love it.	— 欢迎来到我家，我已经为你准备了很丰盛的食物，相信你一定会喜欢的。
— Thank you. This is your gift.	— 谢谢。这是我送你的礼物。
— Thank you. Please sit down. What would you like, coffee or orange juice?	— 谢谢，请坐。你想喝点什么，咖啡还是橙汁?
— Orange juice, please.	— 橙汁，谢谢。

句型分析

Welcome to... 这个句型是用来表达我对某人的热情欢迎，to 后通常跟欢迎来到的“地点”，也就是 Welcome to + n 形式。

句子示例

Welcome to Mexico. 欢迎来到墨西哥。

Welcome to our hotel; what can I do for you? 欢迎来到我们的旅馆，有什么需要帮助的吗？

Welcome to my school; let me show you around. 欢迎来到我的学校，让我带你参观一下吧。

重点单词

sumptuous ['sʌmptʃʊəs] *a.* 豪华的，奢侈的

Mexico ['meksɪkəʊ] *n.* 墨西哥

Chapter 2
情绪用语句型

Unit 1 高兴

1. I'm glad to... 我很高兴……

对话示例

— **I'm glad to** know the news that my brother will return from abroad.	—我很高兴得知我哥哥要从国外回来的消息。
— How many years has your brother stayed in Canada?	—你哥哥在加拿大待了多少年?
— About 4 years. Now he will graduate from the university.	—大约 4 年。现在他要从大学毕业了。
— Your parents must be very happy now.	—你父母现在肯定很开心。
— Yes, they clean my brother's room every day.	—是的，他们每天打扫我哥哥的房间。

句型分析

I'm glad to... 句型中的主干是主系表结构，to 在该句型中是动词不定式的标志，不定式结构作主语的补足语。I'm glad to... 也可用 I'm happy to... 来替换。

句子示例

- **I'm glad to** receive your flowers. 我很高兴收到你的花。
- **I'm glad to** be dressed up by my mother. 我很高兴被妈妈梳妆打扮。
- **I'm glad to** meet Jack who often played with me at the childhood. 我很高兴和杰克见面，小的时候他经常和我一起玩耍。

重点单词

graduate ['grædʒʊeɪt] *v.* 毕业，渐渐

receive [rɪ'si:v] *v.* 收到，接收

childhood ['tʃaɪldhʊd] *n.* 童年，儿童时期

2. I find great pleasure in... 我很喜欢……

对话示例

— Carrie, what would you like to do when you are free?	— 卡丽，你在空闲时间喜欢做什么？
— **I find great pleasure in** the violin, so I have been practicing playing the violin all the time.	— 我很喜欢小提琴，所以我一直在练习拉小提琴。
— When did you start to learn?	— 你从什么时候开始学的？
— At the age of eight when my mother took me to the mall and a violin caught my sight.	— 在我 8 岁时候，妈妈带我去商场，我立即就被小提琴吸引了视线。

句型分析

I find great pleasure in... 句型的主干是主谓宾结构，介词 in 后接名词或动名词构成介词短语作状语。该句型也可被 I like ... very much 替换。

句子示例

- **I find great pleasure in** making handicrafts. 我很喜欢制作手工艺品。
- **I find great pleasure in** fashion design. 我很喜欢服装设计。
- **I find great pleasure in** traveling in places with mountains and rivers. 我很喜欢在有山有水的地方旅游。

重点单词

violin [ˌvaɪə'lɪn] *n.* 小提琴

handicraft ['hændɪkrɑ:ft] *n.* 手工艺品

fashion ['fæʃn] *n.* 时装，时尚

3. ...make me so happy. ……让我很高兴。

对话示例

— Carl, shall we go to have a coffee after work?	— 卡尔，下班后我们去喝咖啡，好吗？

— For what?

— Finishing the sales on time **makes me so happy** that I want to treat you a coffee.

— That's good. But I have to work overtime today.

— Well, work is the most important.

— 为了什么呢?

— 按时完成销售量让我很高兴，我决定请你喝咖啡。

— 那是好事，但是我今天要加班。

— 好吧，工作最重要。

句型分析

... make me so happy. 句型缺少了主语，主语可以是名词、动名词或名词性从句，谓语动词 make 的单复数形式取决于主语的单复数形式。

句子示例

- His words **make me so happy**. 他的话让我很高兴。
- What they said just now **makes me so happy**. 他们刚才说的话让我很高兴。
- Being the only one to know the truth **makes me so happy**. 我是唯一一个知道真相的人，这让我很高兴。

重点单词

treat [tri:t] *v.* 对待，治疗

overtime ['əʊvətaɪm] *ad.* 加班地 *n.* 加班

truth [tru:θ] *n.* 真相，事实

4. I will feel happy if... 如果……我会感到很高兴

对话示例

— Why are you not happy?

— **I will feel happy if** you can help me with these data.

— These are your company's financial data. I know nothing about accounting.

— Only if you sort them out can I make them out easily.

— I will try it.

— 你为什么不高兴?

— 如果你能帮我解决这些数据我将会感到很高兴。

— 这些是你们公司的财务数据，我不懂会计。

— 只要你把它们分类，我就会计算得容易点。

— 我试试。

句型分析

I will feel happy if... 句型包含一个 if 引导的条件状语从句，这类从句的时态规则是：主句用一般将来时，从句用一般现在时。在该句型中主句是主系表结构。

句子示例

- **I will feel happy if** you can repair the bike for me. 如果你能帮我修理自行车，我会感到很高兴。
- **I will feel happy if** you buy me a lot of flowers. 如果你给我买很多花，我会感到很高兴。
- **I will feel happy if** I can win the first prize. 如果我能获得第一名，我会感到很高兴。

重点单词

financial [faɪˈnænʃl] *a.* 财务的，金融的

accounting [əˈkaʊntɪŋ] *n.* 会计

prize [praɪz] *n.* 奖励

5. It's nice to... 很高兴……

对话示例

— Do you know what David is busy with?	— 你知道大卫在忙什么吗？
— He is busy collecting a biography of a writer. You know, **it's nice to** interview a literary figure for him.	— 他在忙着收集一位作家的生平资料。你知道的，他很高兴采访一位文学人物。
— Yeah, but whom will he interview?	— 是的，但是他要采访谁呢？
— David's favorite contemporary French novelist. It is said David has contacted the writer's assistant.	— 大卫最喜欢的法国当代小说家。据说大卫已经和那位作家的助理联系上了。

句型分析

It's nice to... 句型中的 it 是形式主语，真正的主语是不定式结构表示的内容，nice 在该句型中是形容词作表语。nice 也可被 glad, happy 替换。

句子示例

- **It's nice to** attend my best friend's birthday party. 参加我最好朋友的生日宴会，我很高兴。
- **It's nice to** help my mother take care of my younger sister. 帮助妈妈照顾妹妹我很高兴。

• **It's nice to** eat an ice cream on such a hot day. 在如此热的天气吃一个冰淇淋很高兴。

重点单词

biography [baɪ'ɒgrəfɪ] *n.* 个人简介，传记

figure ['fɪgə] *n.* 人物，数字

contemporary [kən'temprərɪ] *a.* 当代的，同时代的

6. I was so pleased to...that... ……我是如此高兴，以至于……

对话示例

— **I was so pleased to** finish the paper **that** I didn't sleep well last night.	— 完成了论文我很高兴，以至于我昨晚没有睡好。
— No wonder you seem to be tired today.	— 难怪你今天看起来很累。
— I would go to bed early tonight. By the way, have you finished your paper?	— 我今晚要早点睡。顺便问一下，你的论文完成了吗?
— I finished it as early as last week.	— 早在上个星期我就完成了。
— I really envy you.	— 我真羡慕你。

句型分析

I was so pleased to ... that... 句型中的 so 是副词，与后文的 that 构成 so ... that... 结构，that 引导的是结果状语从句。句型中的 to 是不定式，不定式结构作主语补足语。该句型的主句是一般过去时态，所以从句也要用过去时态。

句子示例

• **I was so pleased to** know the result **that** I jumped. 知道结果我很高兴，我跳了起来。

• **I was so pleased to** get an award from the teacher **that** I told my best friends. 从老师那里得到了奖品我很高兴，我告诉了我最好的朋友。

• **I was so pleased to** see my grandparents **that** I bought a lot for them. 见到我的祖父母我很高兴，我为他们买了很多东西。

重点单词

wonder ['wʌndə] *a.* 好奇的 *n.* 奇观

envy ['envɪ] *v.* 羡慕，嫉妒

award [ə'wɔːd] *n.* 奖品 *v.* 奖励

7. That's great to... ……真是太好了

对话示例

— Lisa, your promotion application has been approved. Congratulations.	— 丽萨，你的升职申请已经被批准了。恭喜。
— **That's great to** hear the news. When will the company issue the announcement?	— 听到这个消息真高兴。公司什么时候发公告呢?
— Don't worry. According to the regulation, the announcement will be made a week later.	— 别着急。按照规定，公告将在一周后发布。
— I feel I can't wait any more.	— 我感觉我已经等不及了。

句型分析

That's great to... 句型可被 It's great to... 替换，真正的主语是不定式结构所表示的内容。

句子示例

- **That's great to** listen to good music. 听美妙的音乐很高兴。
- **That's great to** have the meals cooked by mom. 吃妈妈做的饭很高兴。
- **That's great to** live in such a big house. 在这么大的房子里居住真是太好了。

重点单词

promotion [prə'məʊʃn] *n.* 升职，提升

application [ˌæplɪ'keɪʃn] *n.* 申请，应用

issue ['ɪʃu:] *v.* 发布 *n.* 问题

regulation [ˌregjʊ'leɪʃn] *n.* 规定，规则

8. This is a happy moment that... ……，这是一个高兴的时刻。

对话示例

— **This is a happy moment that** we succeed in signing the contract.	— 我们成功签署了合约，这是一个高兴的时刻。
— Indeed. I advise we hold a party to celebrate it.	— 的确。我建议举办一场宴会庆祝一下。
— I agree, but we need to ask the manager	— 我同意，但是我们需要请示经理。

for agreement.	
— You are right. I will do this when I go to submit the report.	— 你说得对。我去提交报告的时候会提及这件事的。
— Look forward to your good news.	— 期待你的好消息。

句型分析

- This is a happy moment that... 句型中的主句是完整的，that 在这里引导的是定语从句而不是同位语从句。

句子示例

- **This is a happy moment that** everyone is here. 大家都在这里，这是一个高兴的时刻。
- **This is a happy moment that** the mother gave birth to a baby. 妈妈生了一个婴儿，这是一个高兴的时刻。
- **This is a happy moment that** they set a new record just now. 他们刚刚创造了新的记录，这是一个高兴的时刻。

重点单词

submit [səbˈmɪt] *v.* 提交，顺从

record [ˈrekɔːd] *n. & v.* 记录

9. ... couldn't be happier. ……非常高兴。

对话示例

— I have the greatest chance to win the game, and I **couldn't be happier**.	— 我有最大的机会赢得比赛，我非常高兴。
— Don't be happy so early. Although your opponent is older than you, he has rich experience.	— 不要高兴得太早。虽然你的对手比你年长，但是他有丰富的经验。
— You are right, but I've noticed that there seems to be an injury on his right leg.	— 你说得对，但是我观察到他的右腿好像有伤。
— So what? Don't underestimate anyone.	— 那又怎样？不要轻视任何人。
— I've got it.	— 我知道了。

句型分析

... couldn't be happier. 此句型缺少了主语，couldn't 在此处一般不用 can't 或其他词汇来替换，happier 是形容词的比较级作表语，在此处是用否定的形式来表示“高兴的”程度。

句子示例

- His father was promoted to manager, and he **couldn't be happier**. 他父亲升职为经理了，他非常高兴。
- My pet is trained with regularity, and I **couldn't be happier**. 我的宠物训练有素，我非常高兴。
- The mother bought him some candy, and the little boy **couldn't be happier**. 妈妈给他买了糖果，小男孩非常高兴。

重点单词

opponent [əˈpəʊnənt] *n.* 对手，敌手

underestimate [ˌʌndərˈestɪmeɪt] *v.* 低估，轻视

injury [ˈɪndʒərɪ] *n.* 受伤，损伤

regularity [ˌregjʊˈlærətɪ] *n.* 规矩，规定

10. ... jumped for joy. ……高兴地跳了起来。

对话示例

— My father said he would send me a car if I will be admitted by the university, and I **jumped for joy**.	— 我爸爸说如果我被这所大学录取，他会送我一辆车，我高兴地跳了起来。
— Are you sure you will be accepted?	— 你确定自己会被录取吗?
— I have estimated my score, which is higher than their admitted score.	— 我估算了自己的分数，比他们的录取分数高。
— I wish you a success.	— 希望你成功。

句型分析

... jumped for joy. 此句型缺少的是主语，为一般过去时态。主句前可用状语从句，也可用非谓语结构和独立主格结构。

句子示例

- After being employed by the famous company, I **jumped for joy**. 被那家知名企业录用后，我高兴

地跳了起来。

- When the young man got his first wage in his life, he **jumped for joy**. 当这个年轻人得到了人生中第一笔工资，他高兴地跳了起来。
- Though being praised by the mayor, but they didn't **jump for joy**. 虽然被市长表扬了，他们也没有高兴地跳起来。

重点单词

admit [əd'mɪt] *v.* 承认，允许

wage [weɪdʒ] *n.* 工资，薪水

estimate ['estɪmət] *v.* 估计，评价

praise [preɪz] *v.* 表扬，称赞

11. ... feel like a million dollars. ……感觉好极了。

对话示例

— How about your trip to Hawaii?	— 你在夏威夷的旅行怎么样?
— I swam in the sea every day and I **felt like a million dollars**. What's more, I learned to surf.	— 每天在海里游泳，我感到非常愉快。还有，我学会了冲浪。
— My mother has promised me to take me there next summer vacation. I can't wait to go there.	— 我妈妈答应我明年暑假带我去那里。我已经等不及要去了。
— Hawaii deserves indeed a trip, but you'd better go in the winter holiday.	— 夏威夷的确值得游玩，但是你最好寒假的时候去。

句型分析

... feel like a million dollars. 此句型是比喻句型，用来比喻高兴、愉悦的心情。like 在此处是介词而不是动词和副词，其引导的介词短语在该句型中作表语。

句子示例

- Being informed of the promotion, he **felt like a million dollars**. 被通知升职了，他非常高兴。
- Having a steady job, she feels **like a million dollars**. 拥有一份稳定的工作，她感觉好极了。
- I found the book I had always wanted, and I **felt like a million dollars**. 我找到了一直想要的书，感觉好极了。

重点单词

vacation [və'keɪʃn] *n.* 假期

deserve [dɪ'zɜːv] *v.* 值得，应得

steady ['stedɪ] *a.* 稳定的，安稳的

12. I'm delighted with... ……让我很高兴。

对话示例

— You seem to be in good mood. What happened?	— 你看起来心情很好，发生了什么事？
— **I'm delighted with** the result of the experiment we are doing. It's successful.	— 我们在做的实验结果成功了，这让我很高兴。
— That's really good news. Would you like to celebrate it?	— 那可真是好消息。你们打算庆祝吗？
— Of course. We have booked a closed room in the biggest restaurant.	— 当然。我们已经在最大的餐厅订了一个包间。

句型分析

I'm delighted with... 句型中的 delighted 是动词 delight 的过去分词，在此处用作形容词作表语。介词 with 后要接名词或动词，该句型也可写作 I'm delighted to...，但是 to 不是介词，而是不定式标志。

句子示例

- **I'm delighted with** the pet's action. 这只宠物的动作让我很高兴。
- **I'm delighted with** his obedience. 他听话的样子让我很高兴。
- **I'm delighted with** possessing a house by myself. 拥有一套自己的房子让我很高兴。

重点单词

mood [muːd] *n.* 心情，情绪

obedience [ə'biːdɪəns] *n.* 顺从，听话

possess [pə'zes] *v.* 拥有

13. ... be filled with joy. ……高兴极了。

对话示例

— When the doctor said I had recovered, I **was filled with joy**.	— 当医生说我康复了，我高兴极了。
— Did the doctor say anything you can do and can't do?	— 医生有说你能做和不能做的事情吗?
— Yes, I can't stay up late or eat spicy food. I think it's too cruel. Spicy food is my favorite.	— 是的，我不能熬夜，不能吃辛辣的食物。我觉得那太残酷了。辛辣食物是我的最爱。
— You should follow the doctor's words, or you will be in trouble again.	— 你应该听医生的话，否则你又会有麻烦了。

句型分析

... be filled with joy. 此句型是被动语态句型，with joy 是宾语补足语，be 动词的形态取决于主语，be 的时态取决于前面的句子或结构的时态。

句子示例

- The girl was elected monitor, and she **was filled with joy**. 这个女孩被选为班长，她高兴极了。
- Being hired as translators, they **were filled with joy**. 他们很高兴被雇用为翻译。
- When the baby saw her mother, she **was filled with joy**. 当婴儿看到了妈妈，她很高兴。

重点单词

recover [rɪ'kʌvə] *v.* 恢复

cruel [kru:əl] *a.* 残忍的，残酷的

14. ... luck out today. ……今天运气真好。

对话示例

— You bought the lottery and won the second prize; you **lucked out today**.	— 你买彩票中了二等奖，你今天运气真好。
— This is my first time to win a lottery.	— 这是我第一次彩票中奖。
— By the way, do you need to pay the tax?	— 顺便问一下，你需要交税吗?
— Yes, I have to pay 20% of all the money.	— 是的，我要缴纳所有金额的 20%。

句型分析

... luck out today. 此句型中的 luck out 是动词词组，其后一般只接副词或介词短语作状语。

句子示例

- He found a high-paid job, and he **lucked out today**. 他今天运气真好，找到了一份高薪工作。
- This is the last pasta and you **luck out today**. 你今天运气真好，这是最后一份意大利面。
- As soon as you went out, the rain stopped, and you **lucked out today**. 你今天运气真好，一出门雨就停了。

重点单词

lottery ['lɒtərɪ] *n.* 彩票

tax [tæks] *n.* 税 *v.* 收税

pasta ['pæstə] *n.* 意大利面

15. I'm in the mood for... 我有心情……

对话示例

— What is your hobby?	— 你的爱好是什么?
— I like playing the guitar. What is your favorite thing?	— 我喜欢弹吉他。你呢?
— I like the drum set.	— 我喜欢架子鼓。
— You must like rock music. Can you play for me?	— 那你一定喜欢摇滚音乐。你能给我表演一下吗?
— You are lucky. **I'm in the mood for** playing the drums.	— 你很幸运。我有心情给你演奏架子鼓。

句型分析

I'm in the mood for... 是一个简单的主系表结构，其中介词短语 in the mood 在句中作表语。

句子示例

- **I'm in the mood for** shrimp and crab. 我想吃虾和螃蟹。
- **I'm in the mood for** something heavier than stir-fried meat and vegetables. 我想吃一些比肉炒蔬菜更丰盛的东西。

• **I'm in the mood for** playing a joke on him. 我有心情和他开玩笑。

重点单词

drum [drʌm] *n.* 鼓

shrimp [ʃrɪmp] *n.* 虾

crab [kræb] *n.* 螃蟹

stir-fried [stə: fraɪd] *a.* 用旺火炒的

16. I can't wait to... 我迫不及待……

对话示例

— There is lots of delicious food to eat.	— 那儿有很多美味的食物。
— Who has prepared for dinner?	— 谁准备的晚饭?
— Our mother has prepared the whole evening.	— 我们的妈妈忙了一整晚。
— **I can't wait to** taste this dish.	— 我迫不及待想尝一尝这道菜。
— No, we must wait for our father.	— 不可以，我们必须等爸爸回来。

句型分析

I can't wait to... 该句型中含有一个固定用法 can't wait to do sth，表示“迫不及待想要做某事”。

句子示例

• **I can't wait to** operate this machine. 我迫不及待地想要操作这台机器。

• **I can't wait to** fish in the sea and bring in the catch. 我迫不及待地想要出海捕鱼，带回捕到的鱼。

• **I can't wait to** update the equipment. 我迫不及待地想要更新设备。

重点单词

dish [dɪʃ] *n.* 盘，一盘食物

machine [mə'ʃi:n] *n.* 机器，机械

update [ˌʌp'deɪt] *v.* 更新，校正

17. It's nice of you to... 你……真好

对话示例

— It's time to pick up my son from school.	— 该接我儿子放学了。
— When does the school finish?	— 学校什么时候放学?
— At 5:30. Would you mind looking after my daughter?	— 五点半。你介意帮我照看一下我女儿吗?
— Of course.	— 当然可以。
— **It's nice of you to** take care of my daughter.	— 你能帮我照看女儿真好。

句型分析

It's nice of you to... 该句型中，it 作形式主语，真正的主语是 to...，It's nice of you to do sth 是固定的用法，表示“你做……真好”。

句子示例

- **It's nice of you to** make an appointment to discuss the question. 你约时间讨论这个问题真好。
- **It's nice of you to** teach me about the local cuisine. 你给我介绍当地的美食真好。
- **It's nice of you to** get in touch with me. 你能跟我联系真好。

重点单词

mind [maɪnd] *v.* 介意，注意

touch [tʌtʃ] *v.* & *n.* 触摸

Unit 2 难过

1. I'm very sad to... 我很难过……

对话示例

— I heard that David was fired. Is that true?	— 我听说大卫被开除了，那是真的吗?
— Yes, **I'm very sad to** know the matter. David helped me a lot with my job.	— 是的，知道这件事我很难过。大卫对我的工作帮助颇多。
— Don't worry. David will certainly find a better job soon.	— 别担心。大卫肯定会很快找到一份更好的工作。
— I hope so.	— 希望如此。

句型分析

I'm very sad to... 句型中的主句是主系表结构，to 是不定式标志，其后接动词原形，不定式结构作主语的补足语。

句子示例

- **I'm very sad to** hear the old man's death. 听到这个老人死了，我很难过。
- **I'm very sad to** know that he gets cancer. 知道他得了癌症，我很难过。
- **I'm very sad to** see his distress. 看到他的狼狈，我很难过。

重点单词

certainly ['sɜːtnlɪ] *a.* 肯定地，确定

cancer ['kænsə] *n.* 癌症

distress [dɪ'stres] *n.* 痛苦，狼狈

2. I feel really sad about... 我真的很难过……

对话示例

— **I feel really sad about** the professor's death. He is so kind a man.	— 教授死了，我真的很难过。他是那么善良的一个人。
— I'm sad, too. The professor has taught a lot of excellent talents for the university.	— 我也很难过。教授为学校培养了许多优秀的人才。
— Let's visit the professor's wife tonight. We should give her some comfort.	— 我们今晚去拜访一下教授的夫人吧。我们应该安慰她一下。
— I agree.	— 我同意。

句型分析

I feel really sad about... 句型中的 about 是介词，其后接名词、动名词或名词性从句。about 结构在该句型中作主语的补足语。

句子示例

- **I feel really sad about** what they did to the man. 他们对这个人做的事让我很难过。
- **I feel really sad about** the failure of the negotiation. 关于谈判失败，我很难过。
- **I feel really sad about** being apart from my parents. 与父母分开，我感到很难过。

重点单词

excellent ['eksələnt] *a.* 优秀的，杰出的

talent ['tælənt] *n.* 天赋，人才

comfort ['kʌmfət] *n.* 安慰，舒服

failure ['feɪljə] *n.* 失败

3. I feel a little bit sad... ……我有点儿伤心。

对话示例

— Did you know the information that the company will lay off?	— 你听说公司要裁员了吗?
— **I feel a little bit sad** for myself. I make no outstanding contributions to the company, and I will be certainly laid off.	— 我有点为自己感到伤心。我对公司没有杰出贡献，一定会被裁掉的。

— Don't say like this, the news is not necessarily true.	— 不要这样说，这个消息不一定是真的。
— The personnel manager told me privately.	— 人事部经理已经私下告诉我了。

句型分析

I feel a little bit sad... 句型中的a little bit是副词词组，修饰形容词sad，该句型的主干是主系表结构，sad 后可接介词短语、从句或动词不定式。

句子示例

- **I feel a little bit sad** about the words he said. 对于他说的话，我感到有点儿伤心。
- **I felt a little bit sad** when he brought me the bad news. 当他给我带回这个坏消息，我感到有点伤心。
- **I feel a little bit sad** to get the worst score. 得了最差的成绩，我感到有点伤心。

重点单词

outstanding [aʊt'stændɪŋ] *a.* 杰出的，突出的

contribution [ˌkɒntrɪ'bjuːʃn] *n.* 贡献，投稿

personnel [ˌpɜːsə'nel] *n.* 人事部门，员工

4. I cried bitterly when... 当……时，我哭得很伤心。

对话示例

— **I cried bitterly when** the news came that my husband was injured.	— 当传来我丈夫受伤的消息时，我哭得很伤心。
— Did you tell the news to your children?	— 你告诉你的孩子们这个消息了吗?
— No, they were all in school and I didn't want them to worry.	— 没有，他们都在上学，我不想让他们担心。
— Did you take care of your husband by yourself only?	— 是你一个人照顾你丈夫的吗?
— No, my husband's sister sometimes would give me a hand.	— 不是，我丈夫的妹妹有时会帮助我。

句型分析

I cried bitterly when... 这是主句和时间状语从句构成的复合句型，主句的时态是一般过去时，所以从句也要用过去时。

句子示例

- **I cried bitterly when** I knew he drowned. 当我得知他溺死的时候，我哭得很伤心。
- **I cried bitterly when** I was getting an injection. 当我被打针的时候，我哭得很伤心。
- **I cried bitterly when** my wound hurt heavily. 当我的伤口很疼时，我哭得很伤心。

重点单词

bitterly ['bɪtəlɪ] *ad.* 痛苦地，伤心地

drown [draʊn] *v.* 溺水，淹死

injection [ɪn'dʒekʃn] *n.* 注射

5. It makes me grieve very much because... 我很难受因为……

对话示例

— How are you feeling now?	— 你现在感觉怎么样?
— **It makes me grieve very much because** I can't imagine I am suffering from the disease.	— 我感觉很难受，因为我无法想象我竟然患病了。
— Don't worry, the doctor has not made the final diagnosis.	— 别担心，医生还没有最终确诊。
— Maybe I should do a thorough examination.	— 也许我应该做一个全身检查。

句型分析

It makes me grieve very much because... 句型中的 grieve 是宾语 me 的补足语，very much 修饰 grieve。主句是主谓 + 复合宾语结构，because 引导一个原因状语从句。

句子示例

- **It makes me grieve very much because** my father beat me. 我很难受，因为我父亲打了我。
- **It makes me grieve very much because** I have insomnia. 我很难受，因为我得了失眠症。
- **It makes me grieve very much because** my pet is missing. 我很难受，因为我的宠物丢了。

重点单词

grieve [griːv] *v.* 难受，伤心

insomnia [ɪnˈsɒmnɪə] *n.* 失眠症

diagnosis [ˌdaɪəgˈnəʊsɪs] *n.* 诊断

6. I'm depressed about... 我对……感到沮丧

对话示例

— **I'm depressed about** failing to finish the work.	— 我对自己没有完成工作感到很沮丧。
— Never mind. You are a new man after all.	— 没关系，毕竟你是一个新人。
— But I want to quickly pass the assessment to become a regular staff member as soon as possible.	— 但是我想尽快通过考核，尽早成为一名正式员工。
— Your supervisor will have a bad impression on you if you are impatient.	— 如果你表现得急躁，你的主管对你的印象会变差。

句型分析

I'm depressed about... 句型的主句是主系表结构，介词 about 引导的内容是作主语的补足语。depressed 是动词 depress 的过去分词用作形容词，在该句型中充当表语。

句子示例

- **I'm depressed about** everything I saw last night. 我对昨天晚上看到的一切感到沮丧。
- **I'm depressed about** what my parents told me. 父母告诉我的话让我感到沮丧。
- **I'm depressed about** not being able to reach the final game. 我对没能进决赛感到沮丧。

重点单词

assessment [əˈsesmənt] *n.* 评价，评估

impression [ɪmˈpreʃn] *n.* 印象

supervisor [ˈsuːpəvaɪzə] *n.* 监管者

impatient [ɪmˈpeɪʃnt] *a.* 不耐烦的

7. ... make me sad. ……让我很难过。

对话示例

— Which book do you read recently?	— 你最近看了哪本书?
— *Pride and Prejudice*. The hero's performance at the beginning **makes me sad**.	—《傲慢与偏见》。男主人公刚开始的表现让我很难过。
— I have also read the book. I think we can learn much strength from the heroine.	— 我也看了这本书。我认为女主人公身上有很多我们可以学习的长处。
— Yes, especially she never humbles herself and is so kind.	— 是的，尤其是她从不自卑，而且很善良。
— You are right.	— 你说得对。

句型分析

... make me sad. 句型中需要填补一个主语，充当主语的可以是名词、动名词或名词性从句，谓语动词 make 需要根据主语的单复数情况来变化。

句子示例

- The reason why he didn't accept the donation **made me sad**. 他没有接受捐赠的原因让我很难过。
- What the doctor said in the ward **made me sad**. 医生在病房里说的话让我很难过。
- Not being able to pass the exam **makes me sad**. 不能通过考试让我很难过。

重点单词

heroine ['herəʊɪn] *n.* 女主人公

humble ['hʌmbl] *v.* 使谦卑 *a.* 谦虚的

ward [wɔːd] *n.* 病房

8. My heart is full of grief because... 我的内心充满了悲伤，因为……

对话示例

— **My heart is full of grief because** my pet died of disease.	— 我的宠物死于疾病，我的内心充满了悲伤。
— I'm sorry to hear it, but would you like to continue to keep a pet?	— 听到这件事我很难过，但是你想继续养一只宠物吗?

— No. I don't want to have this sad experience anymore.	— 不，我再也不想有这种难过的经历了。
— I guess so.	— 我想也是。

句型分析

My heart is full of grief because... 句型中的主句是主系表结构，介词短语 of grief 是主语的补足语，because 引导的是原因状语从句。is full of 也可被 is filled with 代替。

句子示例

- **My heart is full of grief because** the doctor diagnosed me as having a terminal disease. 我的内心充满了悲伤，因为医生诊断我得了绝症。
- **My heart is full of grief because** the novel has a sad ending. 我的内心充满了悲伤，因为这本小说有一个悲伤的结局。
- **My heart is full of grief because** my two friends had an accident. 我的内心充满了悲伤，因为我的两位朋友出了车祸。

重点单词

grief [gri:f] *n.* 悲伤，难过

continue [kən'tɪnju:] *v.* 继续，持续

terminal ['tɜ:mɪnl] *a.* 晚期的，末期的

9. ... burst into tears. ……突然哭了起来。

对话示例

— When we were seeing a film yesterday, I **burst into tears**.	— 我们昨天在看电影的时候，我突然哭了。
— For what?	— 为什么?
— The hero in the film died in a car accident, and his wife was very sad.	— 电影里的男主角在车祸中死了，他的妻子非常伤心。
— It's just a movie. They were just performing a plot.	— 那只是一部电影，他们只是在表演一个情节。
— I knew, but I couldn't control my tears. I was deeply moved by the film.	— 我知道，但是我控制不住自己的眼泪。我被这部电影深深地感动了。

句型分析

... burst into tears. 句型中的 burst 多用作不及物动词，其过去式和过去分词都是 burst。该句型中 tears 不能改变其形态，只能是复数形式。

句子示例

- Knowing he was abandoned, he **burst into tears**. 知道自己被抛弃了，他大哭起来。
- When they broke into the bedroom, the baby **burst into tears**. 当他们闯进卧室的时候，小婴儿突然哭了起来。
- Before the song ended, one of them **burst into tears**. 这首歌结束之前，他们中的一个人突然哭了起来。

重点单词

plot [plɒt] *n.* 情节，片段

control [kən'trəʊl] *v.* 控制，支配

abandon [ə'bændən] *v.* 抛弃，丢弃

10. ... be in a bad mood because... ……心情不太好，因为……

对话示例

— Be careful. The boss **is in bad mood because** there was a bad performance last month.	— 小心点，老板心情不太好，因为上个月的业绩不好。
— The sales department should be responsible for it. How does that have to do with the personnel department?	— 那应该是销售部的责任，这与人事部有什么关系?
— In short, pay more attention when you report to the boss.	— 总之，你在向老板汇报工作的时候注意点。
— I will. Thank you.	— 我会的，谢谢。

句型分析

... be in a bad mood because... 句型需填补的是主语和原因状语从句。be in bad mood 也可用 be in a bad temper, be in a bad skin 等替换。

句子示例

- My mother **is in a bad mood because** my brother was criticized by the teacher. 我妈妈心情不太好，因为我哥哥被老师批评了。
- He **is in a bad mood because** the flight is delayed. 他心情不太好，因为航班延误了。
- His wife **is in a bad mood because** he forgot their wedding anniversary. 他的妻子心情不太好，因为他忘记了他们的结婚纪念日。

重点单词

department [dɪ'pɑ:tmənt] *n.* 系，部门

criticize ['krɪtɪsaɪz] *v.* 批评

11. I have a feeling of deep sorrow to... ……让我很难过。

对话示例

— Why do you look sad?	— 你为什么看起来很伤心?
— **I have a feeling of deep sorrow to** be beat by my mother because I didn't pass the exam.	— 我母亲因为我考试不及格打了我一顿，我很难过。
— I think you always play games and seldom study, which leads to your failure in the exam.	— 我觉得你总是玩游戏而很少学习，这才导致你考试不及格。
— My mother has warned me not to play games anymore.	— 我母亲已经警告我不准再玩游戏了。
— I agree with your mother's doing.	— 我赞成你母亲的做法。

句型分析

I have a feeling of deep sorrow to... 句型的主句是主谓宾结构，of deep sorrow 是介词短语作定语，to 是不定式标志，引导的是非谓语结构。

句子示例

- **I have a feeling of deep sorrow to** see the cruel picture. 看到这幅残忍的画面，我很难过。
- **I have a feeling of deep sorrow to** be cheated by my best friend. 被我最好的朋友欺骗，我很难过。
- **I have a feeling of deep sorrow to** know his disease. 知道了他的病情，我很难过。

重点单词

sorrow ['sɒrəʊ] *n.* 伤心，悲伤　　　　warn [wɔːn] *v.* 警告

12. ... feel down today. ……今天心情不好

对话示例

— Do you know what happened to John?	— 你知道约翰发生了什么事吗?
— He **felt down today**. His design didn't get approved by the university.	— 他今天心情不好。他的设计图没有通过学校的审批。
— His design style maybe not consistent with the university's requirement.	— 可能他的设计风格和学校的要求不一致。
— I told him early, but he insisted his own thought.	— 我早就告诉他了，但是他还是坚持自己的想法。
— You know he is very stubborn and would not change his idea easily.	— 你知道的，他是一个非常固执的人，不轻易改变自己的想法。

句型分析

... feel down today. 此句型是主系表结构，feel 是系动词，down 在该句型中是形容词，意为“沮丧的”。该句型也可用 ... feel upset today. 替换。

句子示例

- Being criticized for a small error, the secretary **felt down today**. 因为一个小错误受了批评，秘书今天心情不好。
- The professor's words made him **feel down today**. 教授的话让他今天心情不好。
- The failure in the experiment is the reason why she **feels down today**. 实验失败是她今天心情不好的原因。

重点单词

consistent [kən'sɪstənt] *a.* 连续的，一致的　　　　stubborn ['stʌbən] *a.* 固执的，顽固的

error ['erə] *n.* 错误

13. ... be frantic with grief. ……悲痛得发狂。

对话示例

— Did you hear that Paul is seriously ill?	— 你听说保罗得重病的事了吗?
— Yes. He can't bear the fact that he would soon die, and he **is frantic with grief**.	— 听说了。他不能忍受自己快死的事实，悲痛得发了狂。
— It's really a pity. Paul is very talented and he has been hired by a famous company.	— 真是太可惜了。保罗非常有才华，他已经被一家知名企业录用了。
— How I wish it was false.	— 我多希望这事不是真的。

句型分析

... be frantic with grief. 句型是主系表结构，with grief 是介词短语作主语的补足语。该句型也可用 ...go mad with grief 来代替。

句子示例

- Not being able to collect enough money to help the child, she **was frantic with grief**. 没有筹集到足够的钱来帮助这个孩子，她很悲痛。
- After being thrown out from the yard, he **was frantic with grief**. 他从院子里被赶出来后，悲痛得发了狂。
- Knowing only a soldier of a thousand left, the general was **frantic with grief**. 得知一千个士兵只剩了一个，将军悲痛至极。

重点单词

frantic ['fræntɪk] *a.* 发狂的，疯狂的

pity ['pɪtɪ] *n.* 遗憾，怜悯

general ['dʒenrəl] *a.* 一般的 *n.* 将军

14. I'm sick of... 对……厌倦

对话示例

— What is your job?	— 你是做什么的?
— I am an edit. What do you do?	— 我是一个编辑。你呢?
— I am doing sales.	— 我是做销售的。

— That must be challenging.	— 那一定很具有挑战性。
— **I'm sick of** selling products. I decide to go freelance.	— 我对销售产品很厌倦。我决定去做一个自由职业者。

句型分析

I'm sick of... 该句型中，含有主系表结构，其中主语是 I，系动词是 am，表语是 sick，通常用在表达对某事的不喜欢。

句子示例

- **I'm sick of** comparing with others. 我对和别人作对比感到厌倦。
- **I'm sick of** recommending the new sample. 我对推荐新样品感到厌倦。
- **I'm sick of** the complaints. 我对投诉感到厌倦。

重点单词

freelance ['fri:lɑ:ns] *v.* 当自由职业者

recommend [ˌrekə'mend] *v.* 推荐，建议

complaint [kəm'pleɪnt] *n.* 抱怨，控诉

15. I can't stand... 我不能忍受……

对话示例

— What are you doing?	— 你正在做什么?
— I am conducting a market survey.	— 我正在进行一个市场调查。
— But you just made the market survey.	— 但是你上个月刚做过。
— Yeah, but the manager said that was an unqualified survey.	— 是的，但是经理说那个不合格。
— So, you must do it again.	— 因此，你必须再做一遍。
— **I can't stand** doing the same work.	— 我不能忍受做同样的工作。

句型分析

I can't stand... 该句型中 can't stand 有两个用法，can't stand to do sth 表示“不能忍受将要做某事”， can't stand doing sth 表示“不能忍受做某事”。

句子示例

- **I can't stand** the smell of cheap perfume. 我不能忍受廉价香水的气味。
- **I can't stand** to write the feedback. 我不能忍受去写反馈。
- **I can't stand** giving further suggestions. 我不能忍受给出进一步的建议。

重点单词

perfume ['pɜ:fju:m] *n.* 香水

feedback ['fi:dbæk] *n.* 反馈

further ['fɜ:ðə] *a.* 更远的 *ad*. 进一步地

Unit 3 担心

1. I'm afraid that... 我很担心……

对话示例

— **I'm afraid that** I can't pass the interview.	— 我很担心自己不能通过面试。
— Don't worry, you have the best qualification among us. You will be certainly hired.	— 别担心，你的资历是我们中最好的，一定会被录取的。
— This company focuses more on the working experience of the applicant than on the qualifications.	— 这家公司更看重应聘者的工作经验而不是资历。
— Didn't you do the part-time job like this while you were in college?	— 你在大学期间不是一直在从事这类兼职吗?

句型分析

I'm afraid that... 句型的主句是主系表结构，该句型在口语中可用于多个场合，常用来表示担心或提出异议，语气比较委婉。

句子示例

- **I'm afraid that** we can't get to the destination without enough gas. 我担心没有足够的汽油，我们无法到达目的地。
- **I'm afraid that** I don't have enough money to pay for the coat. 我担心我没有足够的钱来买这件大衣。
- **I'm afraid that** they have guessed our thoughts. 我担心他们已经猜出了我们的想法。

重点单词

qualification [ˌkwɒlɪfɪ'keɪʃn] *n.* 资历，资格

applicant ['æplɪkənt] *n.* 应聘者，申请者

destination [ˌdestɪ'neɪʃn] *n.* 目的地

2. What worries ... most is that... 最令……担心的是……

对话示例

— I guess your parents have got to Paris now.	— 我猜你父母现在肯定到巴黎了。
— They should according to the flight time. **What worries** me **most is that** they can't speak French or English.	— 按照航班时间，他们是该到了。最让我担心的是他们不会说法语或英语。
— Didn't you hire a translator for them?	— 难道你没有为他们请一个翻译吗?
— I would have done, but they refused. They may ask for the local travel agency.	— 我本来打算这么做，但是他们拒绝了。他们可能会找当地的旅行社。
— I hope so.	— 希望如此。

句型分析

What worries ... most is that... 句型的主语是关系代词 what 引导的主语从句，that 引导的是表语从句。该句型在口语中并不常用。

句子示例

- **What worries** the man **most is that** he will be fined. 最让这个人担心的是他会被罚款。
- **What worries** the old woman **most is that** her son doesn't have a steady job. 最让这位老妇人担心的是她儿子没有一份稳定的工作。
- **What worries** the doctor **most is that** the patient doesn't follow his advice. 最让医生担心的是病人不听从他的建议。

重点单词

agency ['eɪdʒənsɪ] *n.* 代理，代理机构

fine [faɪn] *a.* 精致的 *v.* 罚款

patient ['peɪʃnt] *n.* 病人 *a.* 耐心的

3. You needn't worry about... 你不必担心……

对话示例

— My wife is going to have a baby soon. I'm worried about her.	— 我妻子很快要生孩子了，我很担心她。
— **You needn't worry about** her so much. The medicine is so developed now.	— 你没必要这么担心，现在的医学很发达。
— You are right. The doctor told me that my wife is in good condition.	— 你说得对，医生告诉我我妻子状况很好。
— You should take it easy.	— 你应该放轻松。

句型分析

You needn't worry about... 常用来安慰对方，也可以用 You don't have to worry about... 来代替。about 后接名词、动名词或名词性从句。

句子示例

- **You needn't worry about** your children's study. 你不必担心孩子们的学业。
- **You needn't worry about** how to solve the difficult problem. 你不必担心如何解决这个棘手的问题。
- **You needn't worry about** being tested by the professor. 你不必担心被教授测试。

重点单词

condition [kən'dɪʃn] *n.* 情况，条件　　　　solve [sɒlv] *v.* 解决

4. It's a worry to... ……担心……

对话示例

— **It's a worry to** me whether I can be admitted by a music college.	— 我担心自己能否被音乐学院录取。
— Why do you want to get into a music college?	— 你为什么想进音乐学院？
— I am interested in music and I want to become a music teacher in the future.	— 我对音乐感兴趣，而且我想在将来成为一名音乐老师。
— It depends on your score in the college entrance examination.	— 这取决于你的高考成绩。

句型分析

It's a worry to... 句型中的 worry 是名词，to 是介词，后多接表示人的名词或代词，其后可接从句。

句子示例

- **It's a worry to** David what damage the accident will bring to him. 大卫担心这场事故会给他带来什么伤害。
- **It's a worry to** us whether it will stop raining tomorrow. 我们在担心明天雨是否会停。
- **It's a worry to** them that the general will give up them. 他们在担心将军会放弃他们。

重点单词

entrance ['entrəns] *n.* 入口，进入

damage ['dæmɪdʒ] *n. & v.* 损害

5. ...be very concerned that... ……担心……

对话示例

— I **am very concerned that** our product is not saleable abroad.	— 我很担心我们的产品在国外不畅销。
— Although the sales are not as good currently, considering that this is the first time we have sold them in Italy, this performance is normal.	— 虽然目前销售量不太乐观，但是考虑到这是我们第一次在意大利销售，这种业绩是正常的。
— I think we should increase the advertising.	— 我觉得我们应该加大宣传力度。
— The manager of the financial department won't agree.	— 财务部经理不会同意的。

句型分析

... be very concerned that... 句型中的主句是主系表结构，concerned 是动词 concern 的过去分词作形容词，该句型也可用 concern 的名词形式来表示，即：express concern that...

句子示例

- The Greens **are very concerned that** they will lose the property. 格林一家非常担心他们会失去财产。

• Grace **is very concerned that** her daughter will keep a bad habit. 格蕾丝非常担心她的女儿会养成不好的习惯。

• We **are very concerned that** the storm will affect the crops. 我们非常担心暴风雨会影响庄稼。

重点单词

saleable ['seɪləbl] *a.* 畅销的

property ['prɒpətɪ] *n.* 财产

normal ['nɔːml] *a.* 正常的 *n.* 正常

habit ['hæbɪt] *n.* 习惯

6. I'm worried about... 我担心……

对话示例

— The production has been half done. Why would you like to stop?	— 生产已经进行了一半，你为什么要停下来呢?
— **I'm worried about** the quality not up to the standard, and we need to check again.	— 我担心质量不合格，我们需要再检查一遍。
— It's impossible. The products we sampled are all qualified.	— 不可能。我们抽检的产品都是合格的。
— You'd better follow my words.	— 你最好听我的。

句型分析

I'm worried about... 句型在日常口语中非常常见，适用于各类场合，表示对某种不好情况的担心。about 是介词，其后接名词或者动名词。

句子示例

• **I'm worried about** the player who may be not able to attend the game. 我担心这个运动员可能不能参赛。

• **I'm worried about** being eliminated from the candidates. 我担心自己会从选手中淘汰。

• **I'm worried about** these trees which will be cut by people privately. 我担心这些树会被人们偷偷砍掉。

重点单词

production [prə'dʌkʃn] *n.* 生产

quality ['kwɒlətɪ] *n.* 品质，质量

eliminate [ɪ'lɪmɪneɪt] *v.* 淘汰，排除

7. ... feel great concern for... ……很担心……

对话示例

— I **feel great concern for** the air pollution. More and more get diseases related to the air pollution.	— 我很担心空气污染的问题，越来越多的人患有与空气污染相关的疾病。
— Indeed. But the government has taken measures, such as limiting the private cars.	— 的确。但是政府已经采取措施了，比如限制私家车。
— In fact, I would prefer everyone to go to work by bike.	— 其实，我更希望人们骑自行车去上班。
— That's not practical.	— 那不现实。

句型分析

... feel great concern for... 句型中的谓语动词虽然是 feel，但在这里并不是系动词，而是及物动词，主句是主谓宾结构。

句子示例

- I **feel great concern for** my sister who is going to study abroad. 我很担心我妹妹，她将要去国外留学了。
- I **feel great concern for** the man who has a disabled leg. 我很担心这个人，他的一条腿残疾了。
- I **feel great concern for** the quarrel between my parents. 我很担心父母之间的争吵。

重点单词

pollution [pə'lu:ʃn] *n.* 污染

prefer [prɪ'fɜ:] *v.* 宁愿，偏爱

quarrel ['kwɒrəl] *n. & v.* 吵架

8. Don't be afraid of... 不要害怕……

对话示例

— **Don't be afraid of** the dog, it never bites.	— 不要害怕这条狗，它从不咬人。
— But it looks so fierce and bigger than the	— 但是它看起来很凶，而且比一般的狗大。

normal dogs.	
— It is a well-trained dog and won't harm people without permission.	— 这是一条训练有素的狗，不经允许是不会伤害人的。
— Wow, I want to keep one, too.	— 哇，我也想养一条。

句型分析

Don't be afraid of... 句型是祈使句型，be afraid of 是固定搭配，其后接名词或动名词。该句型也可用 Don't be afraid that... 来代替。

句子示例

- **Don't be afraid of** the failure as a result of trying. 不要害怕尝试，哪怕会失败。
- **Don't be afraid of** facing others' laughter. 不要害怕面对别人的嘲笑。
- **Don't be afraid of** people with AIDS. 不要害怕患有艾滋病的人。

重点单词

bite [baɪt] *v.* & *n.* 咬

fierce [fɪəs] *a.* 凶恶的，凶猛的

permission [pəˈmɪʃn] *n.* 允许，许可

9. ... be frightened by... ……被……吓到了

对话示例

— Why is the baby crying?	— 为什么宝宝在哭?
— It seems she **was frightened by** the dog's bark.	— 她好像被狗的叫声吓到了。
— I warned you early not to let the dog be close to the baby.	— 我早就警告过你不要让狗狗离婴儿太近。
— It is my fault. I didn't notice there was a dog in the yard.	— 这是我的错。我没有注意到院子里有条狗。

句型分析

... be frightened by ... 句型是被动句型，是主谓宾结构，该句型可转化为主动句型，即：...frighten...

句子示例

- It's obvious that he **was frightened by** the explosion. 很明显，他被这次爆炸吓到了。
- I dare say you **are frightened by** the kids' practical jokes. 我敢说你被孩子们的恶作剧吓到了。
- If someone **is frightened by** your behavior, you will be responsible. 如果有人被你的行为吓到了，你应该负责。

重点单词

bark [bɑ:k] *n. & v.* 犬吠

explosion [ɪk'spləʊʒn] *n.* 爆炸

10. ... be quite anxious about... ……为……很担心

对话示例

— I heard you will be the major role in a movie.	— 我听说你要担任一部电影的主角。
— Yes, but I **am quite anxious about** my acting. I never played a main role.	— 是的，但是我很担心我的演技。我从来没有演过主角。
— Don't worry, the director must think you are the right one to play the main role. You should be confident.	— 别担心，导演肯定认为你合适才让你演主角的。你应该自信一点。
— But I haven't got the script yet, and I'm afraid the director will change the actor at the near time.	— 但是我还没有拿到剧本，我担心导演会临时换人。

句型分析

... be quite anxious about... 句型中的 quite 是副词，修饰形容词 anxious，表示担心的程度。该句型也可用 show anxiety to 来代替。

句子示例

- She **is quite anxious about** the result of the promotion application. 她很担心这次升职申请的结果。
- He **is quite anxious about** speaking loud in public. 他很担心在公共场合大声讲话。
- Everyone in the family **is quite anxious about** her competition results. 家里的每一个人都很担心她的比赛结果。

重点单词

script [skrɪpt] *n.* 剧本，脚本

competition [ˌkɒmpəˈtɪʃn] *n.* 比赛，竞赛

11. My chief worry now is that... 我现在最大的担心是……

对话示例

— Is your book going to be published?	— 你的新书是不是要出版了?
— The press hasn't sent me any news. Maybe it will be next month.	— 出版社还没有给我任何消息，可能要到下个月了。
— I can't wait to read your new book.	— 我已经等不及要看你的新书了。
— **My chief worry now is that** readers don't like the writing style of this book.	— 我现在最大的担心是读者不喜欢这本书的写作风格。

句型分析

My chief worry now is that... 句型中 that 引导的是一个表语从句，worry 在句型里是名词的用法。该句型也可用 What I concern most now is that... 来替换。

句子示例

- **My chief worry now is that** we have no enough funds to invest. 我最大的担心是我们没有足够的资金来投入。
- **My chief worry now is that** we have only ten minutes left to finish the whole design. 我最大的担心是我们只剩下十分钟来完成整个设计。
- **My chief worry now is that** they can't get one film ticket. 我最大的担心是他们买不到一张电影票。

重点单词

chief [tʃiːf] *a.* 主要的，总的

style [staɪl] *n.* 风格，格式

Unit 4 感叹

1. What a / an...! 真是……!

对话示例

— **What a** beautiful dress it is! How much is it?	— 多么漂亮的一条裙子！多少钱?
— 3,000 dollars. It is made of silk. You can try it on.	— 3000 美元。它是由丝绸制成的，你可以试穿。
— I think I needn't try. The price is beyond my imagination.	— 我想我没必要试穿了。这个价格超出了我的想象。
— The dress's material, quality and brand decide its price.	— 这条裙子的材质、质量和品牌决定了它的价格。

句型分析

What a/an 引导的感叹句，其结构是：What a/an + 形容词 + 可数名词单数 + 主语 + 谓语! What 也可引导接可数名词复数的感叹句，其结构是：What + 形容词 + 可数名词复数 + 主语 + 谓语!

句子示例

- **What an** interesting cartoon**!** 多么有趣的一部动画片!
- **What a** delicious dish**!** 多么好吃的一道菜!
- **What a** tall apple tree**!** 多么高的一棵苹果树!

重点单词

imagination [ɪˌmædʒɪ'neɪʃn] *n.* 想象，想象力

material [mə'tɪərɪəl] *n.* 原料，材料

brand [brænd] *n.* 品牌，商标

cartoon [kɑː'tuːn] *n.* 卡通，漫画

2. How...! 多么……!

对话示例

— **How** lovely the doll is! Where did you buy it?	— 这个玩偶多可爱！你在哪里买的?
— A online shop my friend recommended. There are all kinds of dolls. I believe you will certainly like them.	— 我朋友推荐的一家网店。那里有各种各样的玩偶，我相信你肯定会喜欢的。
— Can you send me the link of the shop?	— 你能把网店的链接发给我吗?
— Of course, but it's inconvenient for me now. I will do it when I get back home.	— 当然了，但是我现在不方便。我回到家之后就给你发。

句型分析

How 引导的感叹句型，其结构是：How + 形容词 + 主语 + 谓语！与 what 引导的感叹句不同，how 引导的感叹句型强调的是修饰词。

句子示例

- **How** dangerous the situation is! 情况多么危险!
- **How** cold it was yesterday! 昨天那么冷!
- **How** well he did! 他做得非常好!

重点单词

link [lɪŋk] *n.* 链接 *v.* 连接

inconvenient [ˌɪnkən'viːnɪənt] *a.* 不方便的

3. Aren't you...! 你真……!

对话示例

— George said we will have a sports meeting next week.	— 乔治说我们下周要开运动会。
— **Aren't you** stupid! Why do you believe in him? He is always telling lies.	— 你真蠢！你为什么相信他的话？他一直在说谎。
— I don't think he is telling a lie. Maybe you	— 我认为他没说谎，也许你对他有误解。

have misunderstood him.	
— I don't want to talk with you about George. I want you yourself to find the fact.	— 我不想和你讨论乔治，我希望你自己发现真相。
— I will.	— 我会的。

句型分析

Aren't you ...! 句型是用否定的修辞问句来表示感叹，可转化为一般主谓宾结构的句型，即 You are... 该句型的相似句型有：Isn't he / she ...! 和 Wasn't it...!

句子示例

- **Aren't you** a respected professor! 你真是一位备受尊敬的教授！
- **Aren't you** proud! 你真骄傲！
- **Aren't you** a considerate person! 你真是一个体贴的人！

重点单词

stupid ['stju:pɪd] *a.* 愚蠢的　　respected [rɪ'spektɪd] *a.* 备受尊敬的

considerate [kən'sɪdərət] *a.* 体贴的，考虑周到的

4. Fancy...! 想想……！

对话示例

— **Fancy** having to cook for my husband and my kids as soon as I get off work!	— 想想我一下班就要为丈夫和孩子们做饭！
— You can take turns with your husband to cook.	— 你可以和你丈夫轮流做饭。
— No way! He has no talent for cooking. My elder daughter sometimes helps me cook.	— 不行，他没有做饭的天赋，我大女儿有时会帮我做饭。
— In this case, he should be responsible for dishing.	— 这样的话，他应该负责洗碗。
— That's for sure.	— 那是当然了。

句型分析

Fancy 引导的感叹句型，表示难以想象或惊奇，其后一般接 doing sth，动名词前可接副词作修饰语，也可接逻辑主语。

句子示例

- **Fancy** getting up to study at five in the morning! 想想在早上五点就起床学习！
- **Fancy** never eating any snacks! 想想从来没吃过零食！
- **Fancy** her getting married and not telling anyone! 没想到她偷偷结了婚，没有告诉任何人！

重点单词

case [keɪs] *n.* 案例，情况，箱子　　　　snack [snæk] *n.* 零食，快餐

5. I only regret that...! 我唯一遗憾的是……！

对话示例

— Mr. Rowland, what in your life makes you regret?	— 罗兰先生，您的一生中有什么令您感到遗憾的吗？
— **I only regret that** I didn't take good care of my wife! She passed away for cancer at the age of 55. I know it was fatigue that caused her illness.	— 我唯一遗憾的是我没有好好照顾我的妻子！她在 55 岁时因为癌症去世了。我知道是劳累导致她患病。
— What kind of person was your wife?	— 您的妻子是一个怎样的人？
— She was a gentle woman, but she sometimes was very strong. She always supported me as I was down and out.	— 她是一位温柔的女性，但有时她很坚强，在我穷困潦倒的时候，她始终支持我。

句型分析

I only regret that...! 句型是主谓宾结构，that 引导的是宾语从句，该句型也可转化为 What I only regret is that... 的形式。

句子示例

- **I only regret that** I didn't see her for the last time! 我唯一遗憾的是我没有见到她最后一面！

- **I only regret that** I chose English as my major! 我唯一遗憾的是我选择英语作为我的专业!
- **I only regret that** I didn't catch the chance of this trip! 我唯一遗憾的是我没有抓住这次旅行的机会!

重点单词

regret [rɪ'gret] *v.* 遗憾，后悔

fatigue [fə'ti:g] *n.* 劳累，疲劳

support [sə'pɔ:t] *v.* 支持

6. I was floored...! ……令我感到震惊不已!

对话示例

— **I was floored** by the latest survey data! It shows more and more young people suffer from obesity.	— 最新的调查数据令我震惊不已! 数据显示越来越多的年轻人患有肥胖症。
— Yes, the ratio has doubled in five years. I think the social health department should pay more attention.	— 是的，这个比率在五年间已经增长了一倍。我想社会健康部门应该给予重视。
— Right. They should take measures to control the sales of sugary food and drinks.	— 对。他们应该采取措施控制含糖食品和饮料的销售。
— But it can't solve the problem fundamentally.	— 但是那不能从根本上解决问题。

句型分析

I was floored ...! 句型是主系表结构，其后可接介词 by 引导的介词短语或接 when 引导的从句。该句型也可用 I was shocked ...! 替换。

句子示例

- **I was floored** when I knew that they all died! 当我得知他们都死了，我感到震惊不已!
- **I was floored** by seeing the spectacle scene! 看到这壮观的景象，我感到震惊不已!
- **I was floored** by the hard work of farmers! 农民们的辛苦令我震惊不已!

重点单词

obesity [əʊ'bi:sətɪ] *n.* 肥胖

ratio ['reɪʃɪəʊ] *n.* 比率

fundamentally [ˌfʌndə'mentəlɪ] *ad.* 根本上

7. Here comes...! ……来了!

对话示例

— Hurry up! **Here comes** the bus!	— 快点！公交车来了!
— It is crowded with people. Let's wait for the next one.	— 上面挤满了人。我们等下一辆吧。
— The next one will come after twenty minutes. We will be late.	— 下一辆是在二十分钟后，我们会迟到的。
— Well, but I'm afraid we can't get on this one. The driver is stopping more people from getting on.	— 好吧，但是我担心我们上不去了。司机已经在阻止更多的人上车了。
— We should come to the bus station earlier.	— 我们应该早点来公交站的。

句型分析

Here comes...! 句型是副词 here 引导的倒装句，在该句型中主语一般是物，采用完全倒装的形式，如果主语是人称代词，那么要采用部分倒装。

句子示例

- **Here comes** the pesky fly! 讨厌的苍蝇又来了!
- **Here comes** the headmaster! 校长来了!
- **Here comes** a batch of steel! 新来了一批钢材!

重点单词

crowd [kraʊd] *v.* 拥挤 *n.* 人群

pesky ['peskɪ] *a.* 讨厌的

batch [bætʃ] *n.* 一批

steel [sti:l] *n.* 钢铁

8. Long live...! ……万岁!

对话示例

— **Long live** the vacation! I can finally go to visit my grandparents in the countryside.	— 假期万岁！我终于可以去乡下看望我爷爷奶奶了。
— Why don't they live with you in the town?	—你爷爷奶奶为什么不来城里和你们一起住呢?

— They said they can't adapt to life in the town and they are freer to live in the countryside.	— 他们说他们不适应城里的生活，在乡下生活更自由。
— How long will you stay there?	— 你要在那里待多长时间?
— A month at least. There are quite a lot of things we can't see in the town.	— 至少一个月。那里有很多我们在城里见不到的事物。

句型分析

Long live ...! 句型含有祈祷的意味，实际上是一个缩略的倒装句型。long 在该句型中是副词，修饰动词 live，也可置于动词后。

句子示例

- **Long live** the world peace! 世界和平万岁!
- **Long live** our friendship! 我们的友谊万岁!
- **Long live** the Olympic Games spirit! 奥林匹克精神万岁!

重点单词

countryside ['kʌntrɪsaɪd] *n.* 农村，乡野

adapt [ə'dæpt] *v.* 适应，改编

peace [pi:s] *n.* 和平，宁静

9. ... is simply terrible! ……简直太可怕了!

对话示例

— That the couple's house was robbed last night **is simply terrible!**	— 昨天晚上那对夫妇的房子被盗了，这简直太可怕了!
— It is said that the couple went out for a trip and weren't at home. It was their neighbor that called the police.	— 据说那对夫妇昨天出去旅行了，并不在家。是他们的邻居报的警。
— I hope the police could catch the burglar quickly, otherwise we will be worried.	— 希望警察快点抓住窃贼，要不然我们都会很担心。
— You are right. By the way, your jewelry should not be placed on the table in the bedroom in order to avoid the accident.	— 你说得对。对了，你的珠宝首饰不要放在卧室里的桌子上，以免发生意外。
— I will lock them up later.	— 我一会儿就把它们锁起来。

句型分析

... is simply terrible! 句型是主系表结构，前面可接名词性从句和独立主格结构。该句型也可转化为用 it 作形式主语的句型，即：It is simply terrible to...

句子示例

- Two parrots being shot to death, it **is simply terrible!** 两只鹦鹉被射死了，简直太可怕了！
- That the man died because of drunk driving **is simply terrible!** 那个人因为酒驾死了，简直太可怕了！
- His German pronunciation **is simply terrible!** 他的德语发音简直太可怕了！

重点单词

rob [rɒb] *v.* 抢劫

burglar ['bɜ:glə] *n.* 盗窃者

pronunciation [prəˌnʌnsɪ'eɪʃn] *n.* 发音

10. If only...! 要是……该多好啊！

对话示例

— Do you know Vivian will hold a concert?	— 薇薇安要开演唱会了，你知道吗？
— I know it will be held in New York, but the tickets have been sold out. It's a pity!	— 我知道演唱会是在纽约举行，但是门票已经全部卖完了。真遗憾！
— **If only** I knew someone who works in Vivian's company!	— 要是我认识在薇薇安的公司工作的人该多好啊！
— Don't think about it. We shall see the live telecast on the Internet.	— 别想了。我们在网上看直播吧。
— It's the only thing we can do.	— 只能这样了。

句型分析

If only 引导的感叹句型要包含虚拟语气，一般表示与现在事实或过去事实相反的情况，谓语动词要用过去时或过去完成时。

句子示例

- **If only** you were a doctor! 如果你是一个医生就好了！

- **If only** we could move away the stone in the middle of the road! 要是我们能把路中间的石头移开就好了！
- **If only** they had arrived here the day before yesterday! 如果他们前天就到这里就好了！

重点单词

telecast ['telɪkɑ:st] *n. & v.* 电视广播　　stone [stəʊn] *n.* 石头

11. It is too late to...! ……太晚了！

对话示例

— I will visit the local textile factory in Melbourne tomorrow.	— 我明天要参观墨尔本当地的纺织工厂。
— But **it is too late to** book the air ticket now! I can't make it at any websites.	— 但是现在订机票太晚了！在任何网站上都买不到票了。
— How many hours will it take from here to Melbourne to take a train?	— 乘火车从这里到墨尔本要多长时间?
— About 13 hours. I'm afraid you can't get there in time.	— 大约要 13 个小时。恐怕你不能及时到达那里。
— You can make a call to ask whether there is a refund.	— 你打电话问问有没有退票。

句型分析

It is too late to... 句型中的 too...to 是“太……而不能……”的意思，too 后接形容词或副词，to 后接动词原形。It 是形式主语，真正的主语是不定式结构的内容。

句子示例

- **It is too late to** compensate for your child! 现在补偿你的孩子太晚了！
- **It is too late to** apply for a qualification assessment! 现在申请资格评定太晚了！
- **It is too late to** save your marriage! 现在挽救你们的婚姻太晚了！

重点单词

textile ['tekstaɪl] *n.* 纺织　　refund ['ri:fʌnd] *n. & v.* 退还

marriage ['mærɪdʒ] *n.* 婚姻

Chapter 3
思想表达句型

Unit 1 相信认为

1. I mean that... 我的意思是……

对话示例

— What a fine day today! We can go for a picnic.	— 今天的天气真好！我们可以去野餐。
— I don't think this is a good idea.	— 我认为这不是一个好主意。
— Why do you say that?	— 为什么会这样说?
— **I mean that** we still have a lot of work to do. Some of the work must be finished today.	— 我的意思是我们仍然有很多工作要做。有的今天必须完成。
— What a pity!	— 多遗憾!

句型分析

I mean that... 其中 I 是主语，mean 表示“意思是”，是整个句子的谓语动词，that 引导的句子是宾语从句。

句子示例

- **I mean that** we can go on a journey. 我的意思是我们可以去旅行。
- **I mean that** the manager has gone to Paris. 我的意思是经理去巴黎了。
- **I mean that** you can work together. 我的意思是你们可以一起工作。

重点单词

mean [miːn] *v.* 意思是，打算

picnic ['pɪknɪk] *n.* 野餐，郊游

finish ['fɪnɪʃ] *v.* 完成，结束

2. I regard that... 我认为……

对话示例

— Have you heard the news? We will take a holiday next week.	— 你听说了吗？我们下周要放假。
— Yes, but **I regard that** this seems impossible.	— 听说了，但是我认为这似乎不可能。
— Why?	— 为什么？
— The manager told me that we would have our annual meeting next week.	— 经理告诉我下周我们要开年会。
— Really? When shall we have the annual meeting?	— 真的吗？下周什么时候开年会？
— Next Friday.	— 下周五。

句型分析

I regard that... 其中 I regard 是主句，that 引导的句子是宾语从句，由主句 + 从句构成的句子是一个主从复合句。

句子示例

- **I regard that** to achieve this plan seems impossible. 我认为实现这个计划似乎是不可能的。
- **I regard that** you have made a mistake. 我认为你已经犯了一个错误。
- **I regard that** they will accomplish the work next week. 我认为他们下周就能完成。

重点单词

impossible [ɪm'pɒsəbl] *a.* 不可能的

annual ['ænjʊəl] *a.* 每年的

accomplish [ə'kʌmplɪʃ] *v.* 完成，达到

3. I believe that... 我相信……

对话示例

— Anna, you must finish it today.	— 安娜，你今天必须完成。
— What? What happened?	— 什么？发生什么事了？
— I have told you that you must get this	— 我已经告诉过你了，你必须在上周拿到这

consignment last week.	批货物。
— I am so sorry. Can you give me a chance? **I believe that** I will never let it happen again.	— 我很抱歉。你能再给我一次机会吗？我相信我再也不会让它发生了。
— Well. Don't let me down again.	— 好吧，不要再让我失望。

句型分析

I believe that... 其中主语 I 是第一人称，谓语是 believe。当主语为第三人称单数如“he, she, it”时，谓语动词 believe 要变成相应的第三人称单数形式 believes。

句子示例

- **I believe that** we can learn something new from everyone. 我相信我们能从每个人身上学到一些新东西。
- **I believe that** anyone in our company has the responsibility to maintain business interests. 我相信我们公司的任何人都有维护公司利益的责任。
- **I believe that** Jason will come back soon. 我相信杰森很快就会回来。

重点单词

consignment [kən'saɪnmənt] *n.* 装运的货物，托运

chance [tʃɑːns] *n.* 机会，机遇

responsibility [rɪˌspɒnsə'bɪlətɪ] *n.* 责任，职责

maintain [meɪn'teɪn] *v.* 保持，坚持

4. I was ready to believe that... 我坚信……

对话示例

— You look unhappy. What's wrong with you?	— 你看起来很不开心。怎么了？
— **I was ready to believe that** I could pass the French test. But I failed.	— 我坚信我能通过法语考试。但是，我没有通过。
— How come?	— 怎么会这样？
— I didn't see the title clearly before I finished the paper.	— 在完成卷子之前，我没有看清楚题目。
— I am sorry to hear that.	— 很遗憾听到这个消息。

句型分析

I was ready to believe that... 如果主句的谓语动词为一般过去时，从句要用相应的过去时态；如果主句的谓语动词是一般现在时，宾语从句中的谓语动词可根据意思的需要，使用任何一种时态。

句子示例

- **I was ready to believe that** I would achieve the sales goals this month. 我坚信我将完成这个月的销售目标。
- **I was ready to believe that** your dream would come true in the future. 我坚信你将来一定能够实现梦想。
- **I was ready to believe that** the products would meet the need of consumers. 我坚信这些产品将会满足消费者的需求。

重点单词

title ['taɪtl] *n.* 标题

achieve [ə'tʃiːv] *v.* 取得，实现

future ['fjuːtʃə] *n.* 未来，前途

consumer [kən'sjuːmə] *n.* 消费者

5. ...be confident... ……相信……

对话示例

— How are you going to spend your weekend?	— 你打算怎么过周末?
— I have no idea.	— 我不知道。
— Would you like to play basketball with us?	— 你愿意和我们一起打篮球吗?
— I'd love to. But I'm not good at basketball. I have never played basketball.	— 我很乐意。但是我不擅长打篮球。我从来没有打过篮球。
— Well. What a pity!	— 好吧，真遗憾!
— I **am confident** that you will have a good time.	— 我相信你们会玩得很开心。

句型分析

... be confident... 其中 be 动词可分为“am, is, are”，是系动词。confident 表示“有信心的”，是一个形容词，在句中作表语。

句子示例

- He **is confident** that he will become a doctor when he grows up. 他相信，他长大以后会成为一名医生。
- They **are confident** in overcoming difficulties. 他们相信能够克服困难。
- That policeman **is confident** of catching the gunman. 那个警察相信能抓住那个持枪歹徒。

重点单词

confident ['kɒnfɪdənt] *a.* 有信心的

never ['nevə] *ad.* 从不，从来没有

overcome [ˌəʊvə'kʌm] *v.* 克服，制服

6. I could never quite believe that... 我永远也不会相信……

对话示例

— Here is a gift for you. Happy birthday, Marry!	— 这是你的礼物。生日快乐，玛丽。
— Thank you for remembering my birthday.	— 谢谢你能记得我的生日。
— Look, Max is coming to your birthday party, too.	— 看，麦克斯也来你的生日派对了。
— **I could never quite believe that** he would come here.	— 我永远也不相信他也会来。

句型分析

I could never quite believe that...包含一个that引导的宾语从句，其中I是主语，could是情态动词，never是否定副词，quite是一个表示程度的副词，believe是谓语动词。

句子示例

- **I could never quite believe that** we had missed the bus. 我永远也不相信我们居然错过了公交车。
- **I could never quite believe that** she picked a winning number. 我永远也不相信她抽到了一个中奖号码。
- **I could never quite believe that** I got another chance to come here. 我永远也不相信我还有机会来这里。

重点单词

remember [rɪ'membə] *v.* 记得

birthday ['bɜ:θdeɪ] *n.* 生日

pick [pɪk] *v.* 挑选，摘

7. ... cannot believe that... ……无法相信……

对话示例

— Good morning! I have an appointment with Manager Wang at nine.	— 早上好，我和王经理约好九点见面。
— Sorry, sir. Mr. Wang is having an emergency meeting at the moment. Would you mind waiting?	— 对不起，先生。王经理正在开一个紧急会议。你能等一下吗?
— How long will it be?	— 需要多久?
— About one hour.	— 大概一个小时。
— I **cannot believe that** I must wait for one hour. I have another appointment at ten.	— 我无法相信我必须等一个小时。我在十点还有一个约会。

句型分析

... cannot believe that... 包含一个 that 引导的宾语从句，can 是情态动词，not 表示否定之意，believe 是谓语动词。

句子示例

- I **cannot believe that** she is a mother of two children. 我无法相信她是两个孩子的母亲。
- I **cannot believe that** you get married with him. 我无法相信你和他结婚了。
- We **cannot believe that** the old man likes to run marathons. 我们无法相信这个老人喜欢跑马拉松。

重点单词

appointment [ə'pɒɪntmənt] *n.* 约会，任命

emergency [ɪ'mɜ:dʒənsɪ] *a.* 紧急的

marathon ['mærəθən] *n.* 马拉松赛跑

8. I do not think... 我不认为……

对话示例

— May I help you?	— 我能帮你吗?
— I want to buy a dress for my daughter.	— 我想给我女儿买裙子。
— Which dress do you like best? How about this red one?	— 你最喜欢哪条裙子呢? 这个红色的裙子怎么样?
— **I do not think** that the red one will suit her. Maybe she prefers the pink dress.	— 我不认为这条红色的裙子适合她。或许她更喜欢粉色的。
— Well, I guess pink is your daughter's favorite color.	— 好吧，我猜粉色是你女儿最喜欢的颜色。

句型分析

I do not think... 此处 do 是助动词，not 表示否定之意，此句型中存在否定转移。在英语中，否定转移是指否定形式在谓语动词，而否定的信息焦点却在状语和表语，或否定形式在主句，而否定的信息焦点却在从句。

句子示例

- **I do not think** that we have enough time to go fishing. 我认为我们没有足够的时间去钓鱼。
- **I do not think** he is in charge of this matter. 我不认为他负责这件事。
- **I do not think** our company will establish a factory in the suburbs. 我认为我们公司不会在郊区建立一个工厂。

重点单词

charge [tʃɑ:dʒ] *v.* 索价，控诉

establish [ɪ'stæblɪʃ] *v.* 建立，创建

suburb ['sʌbɜ:b] *n.* 郊区

9. ... reckon... ……认为……

对话示例

— How old are you?	— 你多大了?
— Twenty-three.	— 23 岁。
— Why did you apply for the job?	— 为什么申请这个工作?
— Because this is my major which I have learnt in the college. I **reckon** I can do well in a short time.	— 因为这是我在大学所学的专业。我认为我能在短时间内做得很好。
— Thank you for your coming. I'll let you know as soon as possible.	— 谢谢你的到来。我会尽快通知你。

句型分析

... reckon... 其中 reckon 是一个动词，指对人或事全面“权衡”，把各方面意见考虑进去后得出结论，reckon 后也可以加 that 引导的宾语从句。

句子示例

- I **reckon** that the boy will fail the final exam this term. 我认为这个男孩本学期的期末考试将会不及格。
- He **reckons** the manager will arrive in London this afternoon. 他认为经理将于今天下午抵达伦敦。
- We **reckon** the sales task will be completed ahead of time. 我们认为销售任务将提前完成。

重点单词

reckon ['rekən] *v.* 认为，估计　　apply [ə'plaɪ] *v.* 应用，申请

ahead [ə'hed] *ad.* 向前，预先

10. I can't believe... 我真不敢相信……

对话示例

— Where would you like to go during the vacation?	— 你假期打算去哪儿?
— I have no plan. What about you?	— 我还没有计划。你呢?
— We are going to Australia. Would you like	— 我们打算去澳大利亚。你愿意和我们一起

to go with us?	去吗?
— I'd be glad to go.	— 我很乐意去。
— Really? **I can't believe** we will go together.	— 真的吗? 我真不敢相信我们会一起去。

句型分析

I can't believe... 其中 I 是主语，believe 是谓语动词，无论主语是何人称，believe 的动词形态均不发生变化，因为 can 是情态动词，情态动词后加动词原形。

句子示例

- **I can't believe** that we are on the London Eye. 我真不敢相信我们在伦敦眼上。
- **I can't believe** I have passed the French test. 我真不敢相信我通过了法语考试。
- **I can't believe** this happened to him. 我真不敢相信这件事发生在他身上。

重点单词

vacation [və'keɪʃn] *n.* 假期

together [tə'geðə] *ad.* 同时，一起

Australia [ɒ'streɪlɪə] *n.* 澳大利亚

11. I'd like to put reliance on... 我宁愿相信……

对话示例

— Mike will leave our company next week.	— 麦克下周将离开我们公司。
— Why? I think he likes to be here.	— 为什么? 我认为他很喜欢这里。
— Because he didn't pass the examination yesterday.	— 因为他没有通过昨天的入职考试。
— **I'd like to put reliance on** he has passed it. He is very hard-working.	— 我宁愿相信他已经通过了考试。他工作很努力。

句型分析

I'd like to put reliance on... 这个句型中，would like 表示“想要”，语气比 like 委婉，后可以接名词或代词，也可以接动词不定式，在此句型中 would like 后接的是不定式。

句子示例

- **I'd like to put reliance on** the reaction of consumers. 我宁愿相信消费者的反应。
- **I'd like to put reliance on** sales plans can be changed. 我宁愿相信销售计划可以改变。
- **I'd like to put reliance on** what the man said. 我宁愿相信这位男士的说法。

重点单词

reliance [rɪ'laɪəns] *n.* 依靠
examination [ɪg,zæmɪ'neɪʃn] *n.* 考试
hard [hɑ:d] *a.* & *ad.* 努力
reaction [rɪ'ækʃn] *n.* 反应

12. I think it means that... 我认为，这意味着……

对话示例

— What would you like to be in the future?	— 你将来想成为什么?
— I want to be a doctor. What about you?	— 我想成为一名医生。你呢?
— I like teaching.	— 我喜欢教书。
— Wonderful. **I think it means that** you want to be a teacher.	— 非常棒。我认为，这意味着你想成为一名老师。
— I think so.	— 我也这样认为。

句型分析

I think it means that... 包含两个宾语从句，I think it means... 有省略 that 的宾语从句，原句是 I think that it means； it means that... 含有 that 引导的宾语从句；当同时含有两个宾语从句时，第二个宾语从句的 that 不能省略。

句子示例

- **I think it means that** you can obtain your driving license. 我认为，这意味着你可以获得你的驾照。
- **I think it means that** the leader can take our company public. 我认为，这意味着领导能带领公司上市。
- **I think it means that** you have to pass the entrance exam. 我认为，这意味着你不得不通过入学考试。

重点单词

wonderful ['wʌndəfl] *a.* 精彩的

license ['laɪsns] *n.* 许可证，执照

obtain [əb'teɪn] *v.* 获得

public ['pʌblɪk] *a.* 公众的 *n.* 公共场所

13. ... trust... ……相信……

对话示例

— I am sorry. I can't take part in the party on time.	— 我很抱歉，不能准时参加聚会了。
— What happened?	— 怎么了?
— The plane is behind schedule.	— 飞机晚点了。
— I **trust** you are not on purpose. But don't worry. We will put off the dinner.	— 我相信你不是故意的。但是不要担心。我们将会推迟晚餐时间。
— I'm so terrible sorry to keep you waiting.	— 真的很抱歉，让你们久等了。
— It doesn't matter.	— 没关系。

句型分析

... trust... 是一个动词，后可以跟人表示“相信某人”；也可以跟 that 引导的宾语从句，表示“相信……”；trust in 是固定搭配，表示“信仰；信任”

句子示例

- The manager **trusts** that we will finish the task in three weeks. 我们经理相信我们将在三周之内完成任务。
- I **trust** I will achieve my dream in the future. 我相信我将实现我的梦想。
- We **trust** our leader is of justice on this matter. 我们相信我们的领导在这件事上是公正的。

重点单词

purpose ['pɜːpəs] *n.* 目的

justice ['dʒʌstɪs] *n.* 正义，公正

terrible ['terəbl] *a.* 可怕的 *ad.* 非常，很

14. In my opinion... 在我看来……

对话示例

— We intend to book an order with you.	— 我们想向贵方预订一批货。
— Thank you very much for your order.	— 感谢您的订货。
— Will you wait while I see if we have them in stock?	— 请稍等一下，我看看还有没有库存。
— OK.	— 好的。
— **In my opinion**, we've got no inventory on those products.	— 在我看来，那些产品已经没有库存了。

句型分析

In my opinion... 此句型常常用于表达自己的观点看法，该句型中的 my 是形容词性物主代词，也可由其他的形容词性物主代词代替，如：in his opinion（在他看来）。

句子示例

- **In my opinion**, this aspect is of secondary importance. 在我看来，这个方面属于第二重要的地位。
- **In my opinion**, you should appreciate your friend. 在我看来，你应该感激你的朋友。
- **In my opinion**, they just filled a very large order. 在我看来，他们刚完成了一笔很大的订单。

重点单词

inventory ['ɪnvəntrɪ] *n.* 存货清单　　secondary ['sekəndrɪ] *a.* 第二的，中等的

Unit 2 建议请求

1. What I'm suggesting here is that... 我在此提议……

对话示例

— I am glad that we have made an agreement on the merger.	— 我很高兴，我们在合并一事上达成了一致意见。
— Indeed, it took us almost two months to make the details.	— 的确，我们花了几乎两个月的时间来制定细节。
— **What I'm suggesting here is that** we should have a dinner for celebration.	— 我在此提议我们举办一个庆祝晚宴。
— I have the same idea as you.	— 我和你的想法一样。

句型分析

What I'm suggesting here is that... 包含一个以 what 引导的名词性从句作主语和一个 that 引导的表语从句，here 是副词。当“suggest”表示建议时，that 从句中的谓语动词要用虚拟语气，即 (should) + 动词原形。

句子示例

- **What I'm suggesting here is that** you take part in the game. 我在此提议你们参加比赛。
- **What I'm suggesting here is that** we toast our mother's birthday. 我在此提议为母亲的生日干杯。
- **What I'm suggesting here is that** the old buildings be kept entirely. 我在此提议这些古老的建筑应该完整地保存下来。

重点单词

merger ['mɜ:dʒə] *n.* 合并，联合

toast [təʊst] *v.* 干杯 *n.* 烤面包

2. It's best to... 最好……

对话示例

— Paul, has your scheme passed the board's resolution?	— 保罗，你们的方案通过董事会的决议了吗？
— Not yet, because the company has to pay a large sum of funds according to our scheme.	— 没有，因为根据我们的方案，公司需要支付大笔经费。
— **It's best to** work out a practical plan in this case.	— 这样的话，最好制定一个切实可行的方案。
— We are going to remove some unnecessary items.	— 我们打算把一些不必要的项目去掉。
— Just do it.	— 那就去做吧。

句型分析

It's best to... 是用 it 作形式主语的句型，真正的主语是不定式 to 后的内容，best 在此处是形容词作表语。

句子示例

- **It's best to** visit the professor at seven in the evening. 最好在晚上七点拜访这位教授。
- **It's best to** place the medicines away from the children. 最好把药物放在远离孩子的地方。
- **It's best to** fill up the car before starting out. 在出发前最好给汽车加满油。

重点单词

scheme [ski:m] *n.* 计划，策划 *v.* 谋划

resolution [ˌrezəˈlu:ʃn] *n.* 解决，决心

fund [fʌnd] *n.* 资金，基金

practical [ˈpræktɪkl] *a.* 实际的，实用的

remove [rɪˈmu:v] *v.* 去除，开除

3. I suggest that... 我建议……

对话示例

— **I suggest that** we go to climb the mountain at the weekend.	— 我建议我们周末去爬山。
— The weather forecast says there will be a heavy rain this weekend.	— 天气预报说这周末有大雨。
— Then let's play games at home.	— 那我们在家里打游戏吧。
— Well, that's what I want.	— 嗯，那就这样决定了。

句型分析

I suggest that... 是典型的主谓宾结构，但宾语是 that 引导的宾语从句，从句的谓语动词用虚拟语气，即 (should+) 动词原形。suggest 可以用 advise 和 propose 来替换。

句子示例

- **I suggest that** you use another hall. 我建议你们使用另外一个礼堂。
- **I suggest that** they save the strength at this part. 我建议他们在这一环节省力气。
- **I suggest that** the tree be planted in the right of the road. 我建议把这棵树种到道路的右边。

重点单词

forecast ['fɔ:kɑ:st] *n. & v.* 预报，预测　　strength [streŋθ] *n.* 力气，长处

4. You'd better... 你最好……

对话示例

— David, the final exam is coming. Why are you still playing?	— 戴维，马上就要期末考试了，你为什么还在玩?
— I think I've reviewed the lessons well.	— 我觉得我已经复习好了。
— **You'd better** review them again, because you may have missed much knowledge.	— 你最好再复习一遍，因为你可能漏掉了很多知识。
— Let me play for another half an hour.	— 再让我玩半个小时吧。
— No, you must begin to study.	— 不行，你必须要开始学习了。

句型分析

You'd better... 是 You had better... 的缩写，had better 是助动词，其后接动词原形，该句型与 It's best to... 的用法相似。

句子示例

- **You'd better** take good care of your younger brother. 你最好照顾好你弟弟。
- **You'd better** follow the teacher's advice. 你最好听从老师的建议。
- **You'd better** drink a cup of milk before going to bed. 你最好在睡前喝一杯牛奶。

重点单词

review [rɪ'vjuː] *v.* 评论，复习

miss [mɪs] *v.* 想念，漏掉，错过

advice [əd'vaɪs] *n.* 建议，忠告

5. It is recommended that... 有人建议……

对话示例

— Linda, what's the theme of the meeting today?	— 琳达，今天会议的主题是什么？
— **It is recommended that** the company should lay off staff.	— 有人建议公司应该裁员。
— Wow, that's so bad news.	— 哇，那可真是个坏消息。
— I don't think there's any basis for the news.	— 我认为这个消息没有任何根据。

句型分析

It is recommended that... 句型的是包含主句和从句的复合句，主句是被动语态，而 recommended 可被 suggested 和 advised 替换。在该句型的 that 从句中，谓语动词应用虚拟语气。

句子示例

- **It is recommended that** the park be open again. 有人建议这个公园应该再次开放。
- **It is recommended that** the death penalty be abolished. 有人建议死刑应该被废除。
- **It is recommended that** students have more extracurricular activities. 有人建议学生们应该有更多的课外活动。

重点单词

theme [θi:m] *n.* 主题，话题

basis ['beɪsɪs] *n.* 根基，基础

abolish [ə'bɒlɪʃ] *v.* 废除，取消

lay off 裁员

penalty ['penəltɪ] *n.* 刑罚，惩罚

extracurricular [ˌekstrəkə'rɪkjʊlə] *a.* 课外的

6. He made the suggestion that... 他建议……

对话示例

— **He made the suggestion that** the city build an amusement park.	— 他建议该市建一个娱乐公园。
— But he was not approved finally.	— 但是他的建议最终没有被采纳。
— That's because his suggestion didn't match the city's plan.	— 那是因为他的建议与城市的规划不符。
— You are right.	— 你说得对。

句型分析

He made the suggestion that... 句型中的 suggestion 是名词，作宾语，而 that 引导的是对 suggestion 作说明的同位语从句。suggestion 可用 advice 和 proposal 替换。

句子示例

- **He made the suggestion that** the air conditioner be closed. 他建议把空调关掉。
- **He made the suggestion that** the crowd disperse. 他建议人群散开。
- **He made the suggestion that** more evidence be found. 他建议找出更多的证据。

重点单词

approve [ə'pru:v] *v.* 同意，批准

evidence ['evɪdəns] *n.* 证据，明显

disperse [dɪ'spɜ:s] *v.* 散开，分散

7. On the suggestion of... 在……的建议下

对话示例

— George, you look upset. What happened?	— 乔治，你看起来很沮丧。发生了什么事?
— I bought some stocks **on the suggestion of others**, but I lost them all.	— 在别人的建议下，我买了一些股票，但是我全赔了。
— Oh, that's so unfortunate. What are you going to do now?	— 那可真不幸。你现在打算怎么办?
— I can do nothing but work hard.	— 除了努力工作，我现在什么也做不了。

句型分析

on the suggestion of... 是介词短语，在句中一般作状语修饰整个句子，of 后接名词、动名词或代词。该句型一般不构成复合句，而是简单句。

句子示例

- **On the suggestion of** my mother, my father planted many flowers. 在妈妈的建议下，爸爸种了很多花。
- He decided to give up the trip **on the suggestion of** his wife. 在妻子的建议下，他决定放弃这次旅行。
- No one would like to leave **on the suggestion of** the mayor. 在市长的建议下，没有人愿意离开。

重点单词

upset [ʌp'set] *a.* 沮丧的 *v.* 搅乱

unfortunate [ʌn'fɔːtʃənət] *a.* 不幸的

mayor [meə] *n.* 市长

8. Can I ...? 我可以……吗?

对话示例

— There are too many people here. **Can I** sit here?	— 这里的人太多了，我可以坐在这里吗?
— Help yourself. I am to leave now.	— 请随意，我马上要离开了。
— What do you think of the food of this restaurant?	— 这家餐馆的食物怎么样?
— All the food here is of light flavor, suitable for those who have no healthy stomach.	— 这里的食物都很清淡，适合肠胃不好的人。
— That's exactly what I am asking for.	— 那正是我想要的。

句型分析

Can I...? 是表示请求的疑问句型，can 是情态动词，所以谓语动词要用动词原形。Can I... 也可用于提供帮助的疑问句中。

句子示例

- **Can I** help you with the heavy box? 需要我帮助你拎这个沉重的箱子吗?
- **Can I** borrow one of your novels and return it three days later? 我可以借你的一本小说，三天后还给你吗?
- **Can I** have a talk with the manager about the investment? 我能和经理谈谈关于投资的事情吗?

重点单词

flavor ['fleɪvə] *n.* 味道，风味

manager ['mænɪdʒə] *n.* 经理，管理者

stomach ['stʌmək] *n.* 胃

investment [ɪn'vestmənt] *n.* 投资，投入

9. Shall we ...? 我们是不是应该……?

对话示例

— It's Sunday tomorrow. **Shall we** go to the cinema**?**	— 明天是周日，我们去看电影，好吗?
— But I'm afraid that in the cinema there is no movie I am interested in.	— 但是我担心电影院里没有我感兴趣的电影。
— It's easy to solve. We can check out the movies online today.	— 这很容易解决。我们今天可以在网上查查影院的排片。
— Let's go home and search the Internet now.	— 我们快回家上网吧。

句型分析

Shall we...? 是表示请求的句型，shall 是助动词，通常和第一人称连用，谓语动词要用原形。shall we 也可作 let's 句型的附加疑问句。

句子示例

- **Shall we** go to the park on a bus**?** 我们乘公交车去公园好吗?

• **Shall we** keep quiet for the baby is sleeping**?** 我们保持安静好吗？婴儿在睡觉。

• **Shall we** help the disabled men with other ways**?** 我们用其他的方式帮助残疾人好吗？

重点单词

quiet ['kwaɪət] *a.* 安静的　　disabled [dɪs'eɪbld] *a.* 残疾的

10. Will you promise me to...? 你能答应我……吗？

对话示例

— Honey, you are packing up the luggage. What are you going to do?	— 亲爱的，你在收拾行李，你要做什么？
— I will go on a business trip tomorrow for half a month. I told you yesterday.	— 我明天要出差，为期半个月。我昨天已经告诉你了。
— Oh, you made me remember. **Will you promise me to** take good care of yourself**?**	— 我想起来了。你能答应我在那里照顾好自己吗？
— Don't worry, I have checked the weather condition there and I will bring many clothes.	— 别担心，我已经查了那里的天气，还带了很多衣服。
— It seems you are well prepared.	— 看来你已经准备得很充分了。

句型分析

Will you promise me to...? 是委婉地请求对方答应做某事的句型，不定式 to 和其后的内容是非谓语结构。will 可以用 can, would, could 来替换。

句子示例

• **Will you promise me to** help me do the housework**?** 你能答应帮我做家务吗？

• **Will you promise me to** reserve a double room one day in advance**?** 你能答应我提前一天预订一间双人房吗？

• **Will you promise me to** get away from the fire**?** 你能答应我离火远一点吗？

重点单词

luggage ['lʌɡɪdʒ] *n.* 行李　　remember [rɪ'membə] *v.* 记得，记起

advance [əd'vɑːns] *a.* 预先的 *v.* 前进

11. Would you mind...? 你介意……吗?

对话示例

— Robert, I feel a little hard for breath. **Would you mind** helping me open the window**?**	— 罗伯特，我觉得呼吸有点困难。你介意帮我打开窗户吗?
— Of course not. But Lisa, I think you should go to see a doctor. You have coughed for two days.	— 当然不介意。但是，丽萨，我认为你应该去看医生。你已经咳嗽了两天。
— I have bought some medicines in the drugstore.	— 我已经在药店买了药了。
— Obviously, those medicines don't work well.	— 显然，那些药并没有很好的疗效。
— I know, I plan to go to the hospital after work.	— 我知道，我打算下了班就去医院。

句型分析

Would you mind...? 是表示请求的句型，mind 后要接动词的 -ing 形式。对这个句型的否定回答即是答应请求，肯定回答则是拒绝请求。Would you mind... 也可用 Do you mind... 替换。

句子示例

- **Would you mind** changing the seat with me**?** 你介意和我换下座位吗?
- **Would you mind** smoking in the bathroom**?** 你介意在卫生间里吸烟吗?
- **Would you mind** getting me another cup of coffee**?** 你介意为我再拿一杯咖啡吗?

重点单词

breath [breθ] *n.* 呼吸

cough [kɒf] *v.* & *n.* 咳嗽

obviously ['ɒbvɪəslɪ] *ad.* 明显地

12. Should you care to...? 你愿意……吗?

对话示例

— Carl, my car broke down on the halfway. **Should you care to** drive to pick me up**?**	— 卡尔，我的汽车在半路抛锚了。你愿意开车来接我吗?
— I'm sorry, Bill. I am on a business trip abroad now. Maybe you can ask William for help.	— 很抱歉，比尔，我正在国外出差。也许你可以求助威廉。
— I called him just now, but he didn't answer me.	— 我刚刚给他打电话，但是他没接。
— He might be sleeping at the time.	— 这个时间他可能还在睡觉。

句型分析

Should you care to...? 是请求帮助的句型，should 是情态动词，to 是不定式标志而不是介词，所以其后要接动词原形。

句子示例

- **Should you care to** borrow me some money**?** 你愿意借给我一些钱吗?
- **Should you care to** clean the yard for me**?** 你愿意帮我打扫院子吗?
- **Should you care to** go shopping with me**?** 你愿意和我去逛街吗?

重点单词

trip [trɪp] *n.* 旅途，出行

yard [jɑːd] *n.* 院子，尺码

13. Can you please...? 你能……吗?

对话示例

— What book are you looking for?	— 你在找什么书?
— A book about economics. I need it as a reference for my paper.	— 一本关于经济学的书。我要用它作论文的参考文献。
— Maybe you should ask the librarian. he must know where the book you are looking for is.	— 也许你应该问问图书管理员，他肯定知道你要找的书在哪里。

— I did, but he is busy now. **Can you please** give me a hand**?**	— 我的确问了，但是他现在在忙。你能帮帮我吗?

句型分析

Can you please...? 是礼貌地请求对方给予帮助的句型，而 Could you please... 则是比该句型更加委婉的用语，不是 Can you please... 的过去式表达。

句子示例

- **Can you please** put away the clothes for me before six**?** 你能在六点前帮我收衣服吗?
- **Can you please** attend the dancing party as my partner**?** 你能作为我的搭档参加舞会吗?
- **Can you please** sew up the buttons on the sleeves**?** 你能把袖子上的纽扣缝好吗?

重点单词

economics [ˌiːkəˈnɒmɪks] *n.* 经济，经济学

librarian [laɪˈbreərɪən] *n.* 图书管理员

sew [səʊ] *v.* 缝纫

button [ˈbʌtn] *n.* 纽扣

sleeve [sliːv] *n.* 袖子

14. Would you be kind as to...? 能否请你……?

对话示例

— You look so worried. What's the matter?	— 你看起来很着急，怎么了?
— My car is stuck in the mud, and I can't drive it out. **Would you be kind as to** help me**?**	— 我的汽车陷进泥里了，我无法开出来。能否请你帮帮我?
— No problem. I will drive my car to pull your car out.	— 没问题。我会开着我的车把你的汽车拉出来。
— It's very kind of you.	— 你真是太好了。

句型分析

Would you be kind as to...? 中的 as 是介词，不定式是非谓语结构，其中 kind 前省略了副词 so。would 也可用 could 来替换，都表示委婉的语气。

句子示例

- **Would you be kind as to** teach me something about interview tips? 能否请你教我一些面试技巧?
- **Would you be kind as to** come to my birthday party that day? 能否请你那天来参加我的生日晚会?
- **Would you be kind as to** change a bulb for us? 能否请你为我们换一个灯泡?

重点单词

stuck [stʌk] *a.* 困住的

tip [tɪp] *n.* 尖端，小费，建议

bulb [bʌlb] *n.* 电灯泡，球茎

15. I have a request... 我有个请求……

对话示例

— The office supplies in the stationery cabinet are out of stock.	— 文具柜里的办公用品快用完了。
— Mark is in charge of the purchase, but he asks for leave this week. **I have a request** that you go to the stationery supermarket nearby for a reservation and let the boss give a delivery.	— 马克负责采购，但是他这周请假了。我有个建议，你去附近的文具超市预订一些，然后让老板送到我们公司。
— Good idea, but I remember there is only a large mall nearby.	— 好主意，但是我记得这附近只有一家大型商场。
— The stationery supermarket is behind the mall. I will send the address to you.	— 那家文具超市在商场的后面，我会把地址发给你。
— I got it.	— 我知道了。

句型分析

I have a request... 后可以接介词短语和 that 引导的从句，that 在该句型中引导的是同位语从句。request 是名词，也是从句说明的对象。

句子示例

- **I have a request** about the topic. 关于这个主题我有个建议。

· **I have a request** that you should read some famous books. 我有个建议，你应该读一些名著。

· **I have a request** that the door be closed. 我有个建议，把门关上。

重点单词

stationery ['steɪʃənərɪ] *n.* 办公用品，文具

purchase ['pɜ:tʃəs] *n. & v.* 采购，购买

address [ə'dres] *n.* 地址 *v.* 称呼

16. Shall I have the honor to...? 我能荣幸地……吗?

对话示例

— Excuse me, are you Mrs. White?	— 请问你是怀特女士吗?
— I am, but I don't seem to know you.	— 我就是，但是我好像并不认识你。
— I am Sophia. I like your novels very much. **Shall I have the honor to** ask for your autograph?	— 我是索菲亚，我很喜欢你的小说。我能荣幸地要求你的签名吗?
— Thank you. I can sign the name for you now.	— 谢谢，我现在就可以给你签名。

句型分析

Shall I have the honor to...? 句型带有恭敬崇拜的语气，其中 shall 可以用 may 来替换，have 是谓语动词，honor 是宾语，不定式在这里是非谓语结构。

句子示例

· **Shall I have the honor to** invite you to attend the meeting**?** 我能荣幸地邀请您参加会议吗?

· **Shall I have the honor to** shake hands with you**?** 我能荣幸地和你握手吗?

· **Shall I have the honor to** interview you**?** 我能荣幸地采访你吗?

重点单词

autograph ['ɔ:təgrɑ:f] *n.* 手稿，亲笔签名

sign [saɪn] *v.* 签字 *n.* 符号

interview ['ɪntəvju:] *v.* 采访 *n.* 面试

17. I would appreciate it if you can... 如果你可以……，我将不胜感激。

对话示例

— Madam, do you have any luggage?	— 女士，请问你有什么行李吗？
— I have two suitcases. **I would appreciate it if you can** carry them upstairs for me.	— 我有两个行李箱。如果你能帮我把两个箱子拿到楼上，我将不胜感激。
— I'm afraid that will hold up my time.	— 那恐怕会耽误我的时间。
— I will pay you the extra fees.	— 我会支付你额外的费用。

句型分析

I would appreciate it if you can... 这是由主句和 if 引导的条件状语从句构成的复合句，would 在这里并不是 will 的过去式，而是表示委婉的语气。it 指代的是从句中提到的事情。

句子示例

- **I would appreciate it if you can** cure my pet. 如果你可以治好我的宠物，我将不胜感激。
- **I would appreciate it if you can** find the wallet for me. 如果你可以帮我找到钱包，我将不胜感激。
- **I would appreciate it if you can** tell me the truth. 如果你可以告诉我真相，我将不胜感激。

重点单词

suitcase ['su:tkeɪs] *n.* 行李箱

extra ['ekstrə] *a.* 额外的，另外的

cure [kjʊə] *v.* 治愈，治疗

18. Is it convenient for you to...? 你是否方便……？

对话示例

— **Is it convenient for you to** book an air ticket for me**?**	— 你是否方便为我订一张机票？
— Where are you going?	— 你要去哪里？
— My boss asked me to have the negotiation with the other side.	— 我的老板让我去和对方谈判。
— OK, I will do it for you now.	— 好的，我马上为你办理。

句型分析

Is it convenient for you to...? 是 it 作形式主语的句型，真正的主语是不定式后的内容，convenient 在这里是形容词作表语，for you 是介词短语作状语。

句子示例

- **Is it convenient for you to** explain the question for me**?** 你是否方便为我讲解这道题?
- **Is it convenient for you to** cook porridge for me**?** 你是否方便为我煮粥?
- **Is it convenient for you to** go for a walk with me**?** 你是否方便和我去散步?

重点单词

negotiation [nɪˌgəʊʃɪ'eɪʃn] *n.* 谈判，商谈

explain [ɪk'spleɪn] *v.* 解释，说明

19. Can you tell me...? 你能告诉我……吗?

对话示例

— **Can you tell me** what they are planning**?**	— 你能告诉我他们在计划什么吗?
— Teachers' Day is coming and they are planning to send gifts to the teachers.	— 教师节快到了，他们在计划给老师送礼物。
— Sounds great. Can I join them?	— 听起来很棒。我能加入他们吗?
— You can ask George.	— 你可以问问乔治。

句型分析

Can you tell me...? 是“主谓 + 双宾语”的结构，me 是间接宾语，me 后可接名词、代词或疑问词引导的从句作直接宾语。can 也可以被 could 替换。

句子示例

- **Can you tell me** why they have cancelled the plan**?** 你能告诉我他们为什么取消计划吗?
- **Can you tell me** where I can find some useful information**?** 你能告诉我在哪里可以找到一些有用的信息吗?
- **Can you tell me** who the man in the photo is**?** 你能告诉我照片上的这个人是谁吗?

重点单词

gift [gɪft] *n.* 天赋，礼物

cancel ['kænsl] *v.* 取消，撤消

information [ˌɪnfə'meɪʃn] *n.* 信息，消息

20. It's about time... 差不多是时候……了。

对话示例

— What is the expiration date of our auto insurance?	— 我们的汽车保险什么时候到期?
— Next month.	— 下个月。
— **It's about time** we pay the auto insurance.	— 差不多是时候交我们的汽车保险了。
— Let's handle the auto insurance next week.	— 让我们下周去办理一下吧。

句型分析

It's about time... 该句型中，主句是一个主系表结构，主语是 it，系动词是 is，表语是 time，该句型与 It's time... 用法相似。

句子示例

- **It's about time** that they join the community. 差不多是时候让他们加入社团了。
- **It's about time** we give hospitality to homeless refugees. 差不多是时候给无家可归的难民献爱心了。
- **It's about time** we maintain our car. 差不多是时候保养我们的车了。

重点单词

expiration [ˌekspə'reɪʃn] *n.* 满期，截止

community [kə'mju:nətɪ] *n.* 社区，社会团体

hospitality [ˌhɒspɪ'tælətɪ] *n.* 招待，款待

21. Maybe you should... 也许你应该……

对话示例

—What's the matter with you? You look very upset.	—怎么了？你看起来很不开心。
—I don't know how to say.	—我不知道如何说。
—**Maybe you should** tell me the truth.	—也许你应该告诉我实情。
—I fail the math exam.	—我数学考试不及格。
—Don't be discouraged. I'll always be there for you!	—别灰心。我会永远为你加油打气的。

句型分析

Maybe you should... 该句型在给别人提供自己的意见的场合使用，语气比较委婉，其用法与 You should... 用法相似。

句子示例

- **Maybe you should** draw your guest card. 也许你应该领取你的贵宾卡。
- **Maybe you should** show your exhibition certificate. 也许你应该出示你的参展证。
- **Maybe you should** have your board meeting. 也许你应该开个董事会议。

重点单词

discouraged [dɪs'kʌrɪdʒd] *a.* 灰心的，沮丧的

guest [gest] *n.* 客人

certificate [sə'tɪfɪkət] *n.* 证明书

22. Do you mind if I...? 如果我……你不介意吧？

对话示例

—My computer crashed when I was almost finishing my work.	—我就要完成作业的时候，我的电脑死机了。
—Let me check your computer. You should reinstall the system.	—让我给你检查一下。你应该重装一下系统。
—Thank you. **Do you mind if I** use your notebook?	—谢谢。如果我用一下你的笔记本你不介意吧？
—I don't mind at all.	—我一点也不介意。

句型分析

Do you mind if I... 该句型中含有一个 if 引导的虚拟条件句，Do you mind 可以与 Would you mind 互换使用，Would you mind 语气更委婉。

句子示例

- **Do you mind if I** open the window? 如果我开窗户你不介意吧?
- **Do you mind if** I check your suitcase? 如果我检查你的行李箱你不介意吧?
- **Do you mind if** I shut the door? 如果我关门你不介意吧?

重点单词

reinstall [ˌriːɪn'stɔːl] *v.* 重新设置　　suitcase ['suːtkeɪs] *n.* 手提箱

23. How about...? 你认为……怎么样?

对话示例

— How are you going to spend your weekend?	— 你周末打算做什么?
— I have no idea.	— 我不知道。
— **How about** going fishing?	— 你认为钓鱼怎么样?
— But it might rain at the weekend.	— 但是周末有可能会下雨。
— We will go to the cinema if it rains at the weekend.	— 如果下雨，周末我们就去看电影。

句型分析

How about...? 该句型作为一个常用的客套话，常常出现在向对方提出意见或请求时，其与 What about...? 用法相似。

句子示例

- **How about** working in the library? 你认为在图书馆工作怎么样?
- **How about** investing in stocks? 你认为投资股票怎么样?
- **How about** making a compromise? 你认为折中一下怎么样?

重点单词

weekend [ˌwiːk'end] *n.* 周末　　compromise ['kɒmprəmaɪz] *n.* 妥协

Unit 3 意愿希望

1. I designed to... 我原本打算……

对话示例

— I thought you were going to the mall to buy a gift for your mother today.	— 我以为你今天会去商场给你妈妈买礼物。
— **I designed to** go there.	— 我原本打算去的。
— Why didn't you go there?	— 那你为什么没去?
— The manager asked me to sort out all the receipts and invoices after work.	— 经理让我下班后整理所有的收据和发票。

句型分析

I designed to... 表示过去计划要做的事情，也就是我原本想做但没做成的事情，to 在这里表示不定式，因此后接动词原形。

句子示例

- **I designed to** go to the hospital to visit my grandpa yesterday evening. 我原本打算昨天晚上去医院看望我的爷爷。
- **I designed to** send this E-mail to the manager, but I forgot. 我本打算把这封电子邮件发给经理的，但是我忘记了。
- **I designed to** decorate the house before I rent it out. 我原本打算在房子出租之前把它装修一下。

重点单词

receipt [rɪ'siːt] *n.* 收据　　invoice ['ɪnvɔɪs] *n.* 发票
decorate ['dekəreɪt] *v.* 装饰

2. I hope to... 我希望……

对话示例

— Linda, why do you want Alice's phone number?	— 琳达，为什么你想要爱丽丝的电话号码？
— **I hope to** ask her some questions, because she's really a very capable person.	— 我希望能向她请教一些问题，因为她真的是一个工作能力很强的人。
— Indeed. I'm sure you'll gain a lot.	— 确实。我相信你会收获很多。
— Thank you.	— 谢谢。

句型分析

I hope to... 这个句型里的 to 是不定式，后接动词原形，表示“希望去做某事”，一般表示还没有做。

句子示例

- **I hope to** continue my work in this position. 我希望能继续从事这份工作。
- **I hope to** find a job I am satisfied with in a week. 我希望一周内能找到一份我满意的工作。
- **I hope to** see the play next week. 我希望下星期能看这个话剧。

重点单词

capable ['keɪpəbl] *a.* 有能力的

position [pə'zɪʃn] *n.* 职位

satisfied ['sætɪsfaɪd] *a.* 满意的

3. I don't want to... 我不想……

对话示例

— **I don't want to** travel alone. Shall we go there together?	— 我不想一个人去旅游，我们一起去好吗？
— I'd like to, but I have to work overtime this week.	— 我想去，但是我这星期要加班。
— Well, can you ask Amy for me?	— 好吧，那你能帮我邀请艾米吗？
— Sure. Maybe she's free this week.	— 当然可以。或许她这周有空。

句型分析

I don't want to... 句型中，to 在这里作不定式，后直接跟动词原形，表示“我不愿做什么事情”，这个句型是在 I want to do sth（我想做某事）的基础上加上否定词。

句子示例

- **I don't want to** leave any evidence to Tom. 我不想给汤姆留下任何的证据。
- **I don't want to** eat in such an unclean restaurant. 我不想在这么不干净的餐厅里吃饭。
- **I don't want to** bother you with this question. 我不想因这个问题打扰你。

重点单词

overtime ['əʊvətaɪm] *v.* 加班

evidence ['evɪdəns] *n.* 证据

bother ['bɒðə] *v.* 打扰

4. I am not going to... 我不打算……

对话示例

— I heard that you plan to go fishing this weekend, right?	— 我听说你计划这周末要去钓鱼，是吗?
— Yes, but **I'm not going to do** that, because I've heard that the weather is bad this weekend.	— 是的，但我不打算去了，因为我听说这周末的天气不好。
— It's a pity. I like fishing, too. Can we go together next time?	— 真遗憾。我也喜欢钓鱼。下次我们能一起去吗?
— Of course, I'll call you.	— 当然可以了，我会给你打电话。
— OK. Call me anytime.	— 好的，随时给我打电话。

句型分析

I am not going to... 这个句型是用否定形式来表示将来不打算做的事情，to 后跟动词原形，这里的 be going to 表示将来打算做的事情。

句子示例

- **I'm not going to** let her be my kid's piano teacher. 我不打算让她来当我小孩的钢琴老师。

- **I'm not going to** go climbing this week. 我不打算这周去爬山。
- **I'm not going to** invite her to my birthday party. 我不打算邀请她参加我的生日聚会。

重点单词

climb [klaɪm] *v.* 爬　　invite [ɪn'vaɪt] *v.* 邀请

5. I won't... 我不会……

对话示例

— Mike, I heard that you've been working overtime lately.	— 麦克，我听说你最近一直加班。
— Yes, I've been checking my report. **I won't** let it have a little mistake.	— 是的，我一直在检查我的报告。我不会让它有一点差错。
— You are really a serious person.	— 你真是一个严谨的人。
— Thank you. I just don't want to cause any loss to the company.	— 谢谢，我只是不想因为我给公司带来任何损失。

句型分析

I won't... 这个句型是由 will + not 构成，可知其带有将来的含义，且表示否定，也就是说某件事不在自己的考虑范围之内。

句子示例

- If the conditions are not good, **I won't** pitch a tent here. 如果条件不好，我就不在这里搭帐篷了。
- **I won't** stay here too long because I have a lot of things to do. 我不会在这里待太久，我还有很多事情要做。
- **I won't** allow you to delay your study because of the game. 我不会允许你因为游戏而耽误学习。

重点单词

mistake [mɪ'steɪk] *n.* 错误　　pitch [pɪtʃ] *v.* 搭起

tent [tent] *n.* 帐篷

6. I look forward to... 我期待着……

对话示例

— Thank you for your cooperation and understanding. Please take a rest.	— 感谢您的配合和理解。请休息一下。
— You're welcome. It's my honor.	— 不客气，这是我的荣幸。
— **I look forward to** interviewing you next week.	— 我很期待下周采访你。
— Me too. See you next week.	— 我也是。下周见。

句型分析

I look forward to... 这个句型是各类考试的万能句子，to 在这里作介词使用，后跟名词或者动名词。

句子示例

- **I look forward to** the arrival of my parents. 我期待着父母的到来。
- **I look forward to** attending a business dinner next week. 我期待着下星期去参加商务晚宴。
- **I look forward to** our meeting next month. 我期待着我们下个月的见面。

重点单词

cooperation [kəʊˌɒpəˈreɪʃn] *n.* 合作　　interview [ˈɪntəvjuː] *v.* 采访

7. I wish... 我希望……

对话示例

— I'm going to study in Melbourne this week. Is there anything you want to say to me?	— 我这周要去墨尔本学习了，你有什么想对我说的吗?
— Yeah, **I wish** you have a good time in Melbourne.	— 是的，我希望你能在墨尔本过得愉快。
— Thank you. You can tell me in advance if you have anything you want.	— 谢谢。如果你有任何想要的东西可以提前告诉我。
— OK.	— 好的。

句型分析

I wish... 这个句型的用法有很多，① wish 后面可接不定式作宾语。②可接双宾语表示祝愿。③可接 that 从句表示虚拟语气，若表示对现在的虚拟，从句动词要用过去时或者 were; 若表示对过去的虚拟，从句动词要用 had + 过去分词形式；若表示对将来的虚拟，从句动词要用 would + 动词原形。

句子示例

- **I wish** you keep fit. 我希望你保持健康。
- **I wish** he can forgive me. 但愿他能原谅我。
- **I wish** I had been with him 要是我当时在他身边就好了。

重点单词

Melbourne ['melbən] *n.* 墨尔本

forgive [fə'gɪv] *v.* 原谅

8. I am willing to... 我愿意……

对话示例

— I heard you never do housework.	— 我听说你在家里从来不做家务。
— Yes, **I am willing to** share the housework for my mom actually, but she wouldn't let me do it.	— 是的，其实我很愿意为妈妈分担家务，但是她不让我做。
— Me too. But I think we should learn how to do housework.	— 我也是。但是我认为我们应该学会如何做家务。
— Yes, it helps us to be self-reliant.	— 是的。它有助于我们学会自立。

句型分析

I am willing to... 指的是“我心甘情愿”做某事的状态，to 在这里表示不定式，后跟动词原形，这个句型是系表结构，即 be + 形容词 + to。

句子示例

- **I am willing to** collate these documents. 我愿意负责整理这些文档。
- **I am willing to** go with you tomorrow as an auditor. 我愿意明天和你一起去当旁听生。
- **I am willing to** help you with this problem. 我愿意帮你解决这个难题。

重点单词

self-reliant [ˌselfrɪ'laɪənt] *a.* 自力更生

collate [kə'leɪt] *v.* 整理

auditor ['ɔ:dɪtə] *n.* 旁听生

9. I shall ever try to... 我要永远……

对话示例

— John, please keep this secret for me.	— 约翰，帮我保守这个秘密。
— Rest assured. **I shall ever try to** hide it in my heart.	— 放心。我将永远把它藏在心里。
— Thank you. I'm really scared of people hating me.	— 谢谢。我真的很害怕别人讨厌我。
— Don't worry. No one will know it.	— 不要担心。没有人会知道的。

句型分析

I shall ever try to... 这个句型要表达的意思类似于“保证……”，to 在这里作不定式，后常跟动词原形。

句子示例

- **I shall ever try to** put you in my heart. 我要永远把你放在我的心里。
- **I shall ever try to** put evil away from my mind. 我要永远把邪恶摒弃于我的思想外。
- **I shall ever try to** treat him as a stranger. 我要永远把他当成是陌生人。

重点单词

secret ['si:krət] *n.* 秘密

evil ['i:vl] *n.* 邪恶

10. I sincerely hope you... 我真诚地希望你……

对话示例

— Jessica, **I sincerely hope you** will find a good job abroad.	— 杰西卡，我真诚地希望你能在国外找到一份好工作。
— Thank you, I will. I also hope you can recover soon.	— 谢谢，我会的。我也希望你能早日康复。
— And this is my favorite mascot. I hope it will bring you good luck.	— 此外，这个是我最喜欢的吉祥物，我希望它能给你带来好运。
— Thanks, I'll keep it all the time.	— 谢谢，我会一直保留着。

句型分析

I sincerely hope you... 这个句型可用来表示衷心“祝福、期待某件事情”，hope you 后面跟的是 do sth，构成 hope sb do sth，意为“希望某人做某事”。

句子示例

- **I sincerely hope you** can be part of our club. 我真心希望你能成为我们俱乐部的一员。
- **I sincerely hope you** will go to London with me. 我真心希望你能和我一起去伦敦。
- **I sincerely hope you** can work smoothly. 我真心希望你能工作顺利。

重点单词

abroad [ə'brɔ:d] *ad.* 在国外　　smoothly ['smu:ðlɪ] *ad.* 顺利地

11. May you... 祝你……

对话示例

— You look very happy today!	— 你今天看起来很高兴！
— Yes, I'm going to Europe with my uncle tomorrow.	— 是的，明天我就要和我叔叔去欧洲了。
— **May you** have a good time.	— 祝你玩得愉快！
— Thanks. I will bring a gift to you.	— 谢谢！回来我会给你带礼物的。

句型分析

May you... 是用来表示“祝愿”，可构成 May + you + 动词原形，这个句型中的 may 不在主语后，而用于句子开头，后面紧跟祝愿的内容。

句子示例

- **May you** live as you want. 愿你活成自己想要的样子。
- **May you** and your family be healthy and happy. 愿你和你的家人都健康幸福。
- **May you** succeed in next week's negotiation. 愿你在下周的谈判中取得成功。

重点单词

negotiation [nɪˌgəʊʃɪ'eɪʃn] *n.* 谈判

succeed [sək'si:d] *v.* 成功，继承

12. If only... 真希望……

对话示例

— Our flight has taken off. Amy did not catch up with it.	— 我们的航班已经起飞了，艾米最终还是没有赶上。
— Just three minutes. She should have got up earlier.	— 只晚了三分钟，她应该早点起床的。
— That's right. **If only** she had arrived in time.	— 没错。要是她能及时赶到就好了。
— Yeah.	— 是的。

句型分析

If only... 这个句型表达的是一种与事实相反的假设。这个句型的中心词是从属连词 if，副词 only 只是为了加强 if 的语气，所以其主要用在虚拟语气中，常译为“但愿、要是……该多好”。

句子示例

- **If only** my racket weren't missing. 要是我的球拍没有丢失该多好。
- **If only** he could come to the meeting. 要是他能来参加会议就好了。
- **If only** there were two tickets for the concert. 要是有两张演唱会门票就好了。

重点单词

racket ['rækɪt] *n.* 球拍

concert ['kɒnsət] *n.* 演唱会

13. How I wish... 我多么希望……

对话示例

— Mike, I go to play basketball with John first.	— 麦克，我先和约翰去打篮球了。
— All right. **How I wish** I did my homework.	— 好吧。我多希望我的作业做完了。
— It's okay. We'll be waiting for you at the basketball court.	— 没事的，我们会一直在篮球场等你的。
— All right, I'll be ready in twenty minutes.	— 好的，我会在二十分钟内完成。

句型分析

How I wish... 这个句型的后面要跟从句来引导虚拟语气，表示与事实相反的情况或者不太可能实现的愿望。表示对现在情况的虚拟，从句动词用过去式"did"（be 动词一般用 were）；对过去情况的虚拟，从句动词常用"had + 过去分词"；表示对将来情况的虚拟，从句动词用"could / would + 动词原形"。

句子示例

- **How I wish** I had a new sports car. 我多么希望我有一辆最新款的跑车。
- **How I wish** I had gone to the mall yesterday. 我多希望我昨天去商场了。
- **How I wish** I could go surfing with you. 我多希望能和你一起去冲浪。

重点单词

court [kɔ:t] *n.* 球场，院子，法院

surf [sɜ:f] *v.* 冲浪

14. I wish I could ... 我希望我能……

对话示例

— Linda, we had a wonderful performance yesterday.	— 琳达，我们昨天的演出非常精彩。
— Yes, I've heard. **I wish I could** watch it.	— 是的，我听说了。我希望我能去观看。
— Never mind. I brought you the video.	— 没关系，我给你带来了视频。
— Wonderful!	— 太棒了！

句型分析

I wish I could... 这个句型所表达的愿望一般是实现不了的，wish 引导的是虚拟语气，could 后跟动词原形。

句子示例

- **I wish I could** eat fresh vegetables every day. 我希望我每天都能吃到新鲜的蔬菜。
- **I wish I could** be in the play. 我希望我能参演这个话剧。
- **I wish I could** take a parachute. 我希望我能带一个降落伞。

重点单词

parachute ['pærəʃu:t] *n.* 降落伞　　performance [pə'fɔ:məns] *n.* 表演，表现

15. I hope that... 我希望……

对话示例

— You're going to have an exam tomorrow. **I hope that** you will pass it.	— 明天你就要考试了，我希望你能通过这次考试。
— Thanks. Let's play the game after I finish the exam, shall we?	— 谢谢，等我考完试我们一起去玩游戏吧，好吗?
— Sure, I will be waiting for you at the school gate.	— 可以，我会在学校门口等着你。
— Okay.	— 好的。

句型分析

I hope that... 这个句型所表示的是可能实现的事情，其所希望的事情通常指的是好事。这里的 that 可以省略，引导宾语从句。

句子示例

- **I hope that** you can be the leader of your company. 我希望你能成为你们公司的佼佼者。
- **I hope that** our reports will be adopted. 我希望我们的报告会被采用。
- **I hope that** everyone can express his or her view. 我希望每个人都能发表自己的意见。

重点单词

express [ɪk'spres] *v.* 发表　　adopt [ə'dɒpt] *v.* 采用，收养

16. I would rather... 我愿意……

对话示例

— Can I turn on the air conditioner to make the classroom cooler?	— 我能打开空调让教室更凉爽吗?
— No, **I would rather** you didn't. I still have a little cold.	— 不，我想你最好别开。我的感冒还没好。
— Well. Shall I open the window?	— 好吧。那我把窗户打开可以吗?
— Of course.	— 当然可以。

句型分析

I would rather... 这个句型后面可接从句，构成虚拟语气。用一般过去时表示“我愿意某人现在或将来做某事”；用过去完成时表示“我愿意某人过去做某事”，引导从句的 that 常省略。would rather 后还可直接跟动词原形，表示“宁愿……，宁可……”。would rather 后若跟动词的完成时则表示“我愿意做某事，但是我没有做成”。

句子示例

- **I'd rather** he went to work at the company now. 我宁愿他现在就去公司加班。
- **I would rather** write proposals in the office. 我宁愿在办公室写策划书。
- **I would rather** have left this letter on his desk. 我本想把这封信留在他的桌子上。

重点单词

conditioner [kən'dɪʃənə] *n.* 调节器

proposal [prə'pəʊzl] *n.* 提议，建议

17. I do expect to... 我非常希望……

对话示例

— John, **I do expect to** work with you in a company.	— 约翰，我非常希望能和你在一个公司工作。
— But your company is only hiring secretaries. You know, I just want to be a manager.	— 但是你们公司现在只招秘书。你知道，我只想当经理。
— Yes, but I heard that a manager in our company has resigned.	— 是的，但我听说我们公司有一个经理已经辞职了。
— Okay, I'll send my resume to your company right now.	— 好，那我立即向你们公司投递简历。

句型分析

I do expect to... 这个句型中的 do 表示强调，表示“确实，真的”，这里的 to 作不定式使用，后跟动词原形，意为“我确实希望能做某事”。

句子示例

- **I do expect to** have some free time tomorrow. 我非常希望明天能有空闲的时间。
- **I do expect to** visit these children in the poor areas. 我确实希望去看望这些贫困地区的孩子。
- **I do expect to** see a lot of young people join our team. 我非常希望看到很多年轻的面孔加入我们的团队。

重点单词

resume [rɪ'zjuːm] *n.* 简历

resign [rɪ'zaɪn] *v.* 辞职

18. I want to... 我想……

对话示例

— What's wrong, Jason?	— 杰森，怎么了?
— **I want to** ask you some questions about accounting.	— 我想向你请教一些关于会计的问题。
— Sure, but I'm only available at night.	— 可以，但是我只有晚上才有空。
— Okay, I'll see you tomorrow night.	— 好的，我明天晚上就去找你。

句型分析

I want to... 这个句型在英语中很常用， to 后跟动词原形，表示我做某事的意愿，I 作主语，want 作谓语，to 后的内容作宾语。

句子示例

- **I want to** discuss this plan with you. 我想要和你商量一下这个方案。
- **I want to** make full use of this information. 我想要充分利用一下这份资料。
- **I want to** travel around the world and understand the customs of every country. 我想要环游世界，了解各个国家的风俗。

重点单词

accounting [ə'kaʊntɪŋ] *n.* 会计　　available [ə'veɪləbl] *a.* 有空的

19. We call on...to... 我们呼吁……

对话示例

— I heard that you've been collecting money for a child with anemia recently.	— 我听说你们最近一直在为一个患有贫血症的儿童募捐。
— Yes, **we call on** more people **to** donate money for him.	— 是的，我们呼吁更多的人为他捐款。
— Count me in.	— 算我一个。
— Thank you for your support.	— 谢谢你的支持。

句型分析

We call on...to... 这个句型中的 call on 和 to 之间缺少的是 sb，也就是要呼吁的对象，这里的 to 是不定式，后面要跟动词原形。

句子示例

- **We call on** more countries **to** participate in this program. 我们呼吁更多的国家参与到这个计划当中。
- **We call on** more people **to** protect the earth's environment. 我们呼吁更多的人来保护地球的环境。
- **We call on** the international fund **to** pay attention to the poor children. 我们呼吁国际基金组织关注那些贫困儿童。

重点单词

participate [pɑːˈtɪsɪpeɪt] *v.* 参与

donate [dəʊˈneɪt] *v.* 捐赠

20. I'm dying to... 我急切地渴望……

对话示例

— When will Jack come back from business?	— 杰克什么时候出差回来?
— He will be back next Wednesday.	— 他下周三就会回来。
— **I'm dying to** meet with him.	— 我急切地渴望见到他。
— Why?	— 为什么?
— Because he helps me to buy perfume at the duty free store.	— 因为他帮我在免税店里买了香水。

句型分析

I'm dying to... 该句型常常在表示渴望做某事时使用，I'm dying to 后加动词原形，此用法与 be eager to do sth 用法相似。

句子示例

- **I'm dying to** establish the cooperate relation. 我急切地渴望建立合作关系。
- **I'm dying to** receive your inquiry. 我急切地渴望接受你的询问。
- **I'm dying to** discuss terms of payments. 我急切地渴望讨论一下付款条件。

重点单词

duty ['djuːtɪ] *n.* 职责，责任

inquiry [ɪn'kwaɪərɪ] *n.* 调查，询问

establish [ɪ'stæblɪʃ] *v.* 建立，创建

21. I've always wanted to... 我一直都想……

对话示例

— I am concerned about the present environment problems.	— 我很担心目前的环境问题。
— Water and air pollution is becoming more and more serious.	— 水和空气污染变得越来越严重了。
— I miss the sky when I was a child in my hometown.	— 我很怀念小时候故乡的天空。
— **I've always wanted to** visit my hometown again.	— 我一直想再回故乡看看。

句型分析

I've always wanted to... 该句型的时态是现在完成时，现在完成时的结构是 have/has+ 过去分词，I've always wanted to 后加动词原形。

句子示例

- **I've always wanted to** go Vancouver. 我一直都想去温哥华。
- **I've always wanted to** find an ideal job. 我一直都想找到理想的工作。
- **I've always wanted to** take a vacation. 我一直都想去度假。

重点单词

pollution [pə'luːʃn] *n.* 污染

ideal [aɪ'dɪːəl] *a.* 理想的，完美的

Vancouver [væn'kuːvə] *n.* 温哥华

Unit 4 感谢道歉

1. Thank you for... 谢谢你……

对话示例

— **Thank you for** helping me to move.	— 谢谢你帮我搬家。
— You're welcome. We are good friends.	— 不客气，我们是好朋友。
— I'd like to treat you a dinner tonight to express my thanks.	— 我想今晚请你吃饭，表达我的谢意。
— I'm afraid I can't promise you because I have to pick up my son.	— 恐怕我不能答应你，因为我要接我儿子。

句型分析

Thank you for... 句型后接的是名词或动名词，thank 是及物动词，for 是介词，Thank you for 也可用 Thanks for 来替换。

句子示例

- **Thank you for** your donation to this charity activity. 感谢你对这次慈善活动的捐赠。
- **Thank you for** reminding me to bring a charger. 谢谢你提醒我带充电器。
- **Thank you for** telling us the news. 谢谢你告知我们的消息。

重点单词

donation [dəʊ'neɪʃn] *n.* 捐赠

charity ['tʃærətɪ] *n.* 慈善

charger ['tʃɑ:dʒə] *n.* 充电器，委托者

2. I truly appreciate... 我真心地感激……

对话示例

— I heard you were in trouble yesterday.	— 我听说你们昨天遇到麻烦了。
— Yes, we met the snow storm yesterday on the mountain.	— 是的，我们昨天在山上遇到了暴风雪。
— How did you get rid of the trouble?	— 你们怎么解决的呢?
— **I truly appreciate** the guide who guided us down the mountain quickly.	— 我真心地感激导游，是他带领我们快速下了山。

句型分析

I truly appreciate... 句型中的 truly 是副词，修饰及物动词 appreciate，truly 也可用其他副词来替换。appreciate 后可接名词、代词或 that 从句。

句子示例

- **I truly appreciate** that they gave me a ride. 我真心感激他们让我搭了便车。
- **I truly appreciate** him making a remark at this point in the book. 我真心感激他在书的这处做了标记。
- **I truly appreciate** the money that saved his life. 我真心感激这笔救了他性命的钱。

重点单词

remark [rɪ'mɑːk] *n.* 标记 *v.* 评论　　point [pɒɪnt] *n.* 点 *v.* 指向

3. I would appreciate... 我会感激……

对话示例

— David, are you free this weekend?	— 大卫，你周末有时间吗?
— Do you want me to do anything?	— 你想让我做什么事吗?
— **I would appreciate** it very much if you can accompany me to the museum.	— 如果你可以陪我去博物馆，我会非常感激。
— Let me see. I won't seem to be busy on that day.	— 让我想想。我那天好像没什么要忙的。
— Then we settled, OK?	— 那我们就说定了，好吗?

句型分析

I would appreciate... 句型中的 would 是情态动词，该句型后一般接形式宾语 it，然后再接 if 引导的条件状语从句。would 在这里并不是 will 的过去式，而是表示更委婉的语气。

句子示例

- **I would appreciate** it if you can invite him to join us. 如果你能邀请他加入我们，我会非常感激。
- **I would appreciate** it if my friends can lend me some money. 如果我的朋友可以借给我一些钱，我会非常感激。
- **I would appreciate** it if John can help me with the contract. 如果约翰能帮我解决合同问题，我会非常感激。

重点单词

accompany [ə'kʌmpənɪ] *v.* 陪伴，附加

contract ['kɒntrækt] *n.* 合同，协议

4. I'm grateful for... 我很感谢……

对话示例

— What happened to you?	— 你发生了什么事？
— My throat was in great pain, and the hospital advised me to accept a surgery.	— 我的嗓子特别难受，医院建议我做手术。
— Did you get the surgery?	— 你做手术了吗？
— No, Dr. White told me that I didn't need a surgery as long as I took his medicines. I am in fear of the surgery, so **I'm grateful for** Dr. White's decision.	— 没有，怀特医生告诉我只要我服用他的药，就无需做手术。我害怕做手术，所以我很感激怀特医生的决定。
— Taking medicine is indeed easier than accepting a surgery.	— 吃药的确比做手术更简单。

句型分析

I'm grateful for... 句型后可接名词或动名词。grateful 在这里是形容词作表语，for 是介词，其引导的介词结构在该句型中作状语。

句子示例

- **I'm grateful for** him to carry the luggage for me. 我很感激他帮我搬行李。
- **I'm grateful for** the teacher's advice. 我很感激老师的建议。
- **I'm grateful for** you being so kind to my pet. 我很感激你对我的宠物如此友善。

重点单词

surgery ['sɜːdʒərɪ] *n.* 手术，手术室　　medicine ['medsn] *n.* 药物，医学

5. I'd like to thank... 我想谢谢……

对话示例

— Do you know where Paul is, Catherine?	— 凯瑟琳，你知道保罗在哪里吗?
— He must be in the factory and have a meeting now. Why do you want to find him?	— 他现在肯定在工厂里开会。你为什么想找他?
— **I'd like to thank** him for recommending me to the manager.	— 我想谢谢他向经理推荐了我。
— You can make a call to him.	— 你可以给他打电话。

句型分析

I'd like to thank... 句型中的 would like 可用 want 来代替，该句型后一般接名词或代词，在名词和代词后可接非谓语动词。

句子示例

- **I'd like to thank** the professor who guided me. 我想谢谢那位指导我的教授。
- **I'd like to thank** her buying a dress for my daughter. 我想谢谢她给我女儿买了一条裙子。
- **I'd like to thank** the program which helped me find the right way. 我想谢谢这个节目帮我找到了正确方向。

重点单词

recommend [ˌrekə'mend] *v.* 推荐　　program ['prəʊgræm] *n.* 节目，程序

6. I'd like to express my gratitude to... 我想表达对……的感激。

对话示例

— **I want to express my gratitude to** a stranger who helped me.	— 我想表达对一位陌生人的感谢，他帮助了我。
— How did he help you?	— 他怎么帮助你了？
— He helped me catch the thief who stole my wallet.	— 他帮我抓住了偷我钱包的小偷。
— Oh, he is a good guy.	— 噢，他是一个好人。

句型分析

I want to express my gratitude to... 句型是主谓 + 双宾语结构，gratitude 可用 thanks 来替换，to 后接名词或代词，而名词或代词常与修饰词或定语从句搭配。

句子示例

- **I want to express my gratitude to** the nurse who took good care of my mother. 我想表达对这位护士的感谢，她把我母亲照顾得很好。
- **I want to express my gratitude to** the machine which helped me a lot with the housework. 我想表达对这台机器的感谢，它帮助我做了很多家务。
- **I want to express my gratitude to** the director who made me play the lead role. 我想表达对这位导演的感谢，他让我演了主角。

重点单词

steal [stiːl] *v.* 偷盗，偷窃　　director [dəˈrektə] *n.* 主任，导演

role [rəʊl] *n.* 角色，作用

7. Please forgive... 请原谅……

对话示例

— Why didn't you go to the park to meet me yesterday?	— 昨天你为什么没有来公园和我见面？
— **Please forgive** me standing you up. But	— 请原谅我的失约，但是我妈妈昨天生病了，

my mother was ill yesterday and I was taking care of her all the time.	我一直在照顾她。
— Thus ... how does your mother feel?	— 这样……那你妈妈好点了吗?
— Much better, or I can't come to work today.	— 好多了，否则我今天就不能来上班了。

句型分析

Please forgive... 句型后一般接名词或代词，也可接从句。forgive 是及物动词，宾语后常接补足语来使句子完整。

句子示例

- **Please forgive** that we didn't notice the announcement. 请原谅我们没有注意到公告。
- **Please forgive** them for being late. 请原谅他们迟到了。
- **Please forgive** the dog that dirtied the sofa. 请原谅小狗把沙发弄脏了。

重点单词

notice ['nəʊtɪs] *v.* 注意到 *n.* 通知

announcement [ə'naʊnsmənt] *n.* 通告，公告

8. It was...to blame. 这是……的错。

对话示例

— What are they discussing about?	— 他们在讨论什么?
— Who should be to blame for the project's failure?	— 谁应该为项目的失败负责?
— In my opinion, **it was** the supplier **to blame** because they broke the contract first.	— 在我看来，这是供应商的错，因为他们首先违背了合约。
— I think so.	— 我也是这么想的。

句型分析

It was ... to blame. 句型是主动语态表示被动含义，含有强调意味，blame 没有被动形式，blame 后常接 for 引导的介词结构或状语从句。

句子示例

- **It was** the road failure **to blame** for the slow speed. 车速缓慢是道路破败的过错。
- **It was** the bad weather **to blame** for the delayed flight. 航班延误是天气恶劣的过错。
- **It was** the father's behavior **to blame** for his son's rebellion. 儿子叛逆是父亲行为的过错。

重点单词

supplier [sə'plaɪə] *n.* 供应者，供货商

behavior [bɪ'heɪvjə] *n.* 行为

rebellion [rɪ'beljən] *n.* 叛逆，叛乱

9. I must apologize for... 我必须为……道歉。

对话示例

— Linda, what are you worrying about?	— 琳达，你在烦恼什么？
— I was supposed to have an appointment with Bob yesterday, but I forgot. I stayed at home for all the day.	— 昨天我本来要和鲍勃约会，但是我忘记了。我在家里待了一整天。
— Didn't Bob call you?	— 难道鲍勃没有给你打电话吗？
— He might be angry. I think **I must apologize for** my behavior.	— 他可能生气了。我想我必须为自己的行为道歉。
— That's what you should do now.	— 你现在的确应该这样做。

句型分析

I must apologize for... 句型后接名词或动名词，apologize 是不及物动词，其后不能直接接宾语，要和介词连用。for 后接表示道歉事由的宾语。

句子示例

- **I must apologize for** being late again. 我必须再次为迟到道歉。
- **I must apologize for** the mistake during the experimental process. 我必须为实验过程中的失误道歉。
- **I must apologize for** not attending the event. 我必须为没有出席活动而道歉。

重点单词

experimental [ɪkˌsperɪ'mentl] *a.* 实验的　　process ['prəʊses] *n.* 过程，程序

10. I'm sorry to... 对于……我很抱歉。

对话示例

— Dear, **I'm sorry** not **to** buy the celery you want.	— 亲爱的，我没有买到你要的芹菜。
— It doesn't matter. Maybe I can replace it with something else.	— 没关系，也许我可以用其他的菜来代替。
— I didn't have celery, but I bought some mushrooms. What about cooking a mushroom soup?	— 虽然我们没有买到芹菜，但是我买了一些蘑菇。做一个蘑菇汤怎么样?
— That's a good idea.	— 那是个好主意。

句型分析

I'm sorry to... 句型的主干是主系表结构，sorry 是形容词作表语，to 后接动词原形，不定式作主语的补足语。

句子示例

- **I'm sorry to** break your cup. 打碎你的杯子，我很抱歉。
- **I'm sorry to** come too late to meet you. 我很抱歉来得太晚而没有见到你。
- **I'm sorry to** know my son fought with your son. 知道我儿子和你儿子打架了，我很抱歉。

重点单词

celery ['selərɪ] *n.* 芹菜　　replace [rɪ'pleɪs] *v.* 代替，替换

fight [faɪt] *v.* 打架，战斗

11. Please excuse me for... 请原谅我……

对话示例

— **Please excuse me for** interrupting your work, but I have something important to tell you.	— 请原谅我打扰你工作，但是我有些重要的事情要告诉你。
— What's up?	— 什么事?
— Mr. Smith and his negotiating team have come to our company.	— 史密斯先生和他的谈判团队已经到我们公司了。
— You should arrange them to the reception hall. I'll be there soon.	— 你先把他们安排到会客厅，我马上就到。

句型分析

Please excuse me for... 句型一般用于较为正式的场合，其包含的道歉意味比较弱，更侧重为一种礼貌用语。for 后接名词或动名词。

句子示例

- **Please excuse me for** visiting you in a wrong time. 请原谅我在一个不合时宜的时间来拜访您。
- **Please excuse me for** my offence. 如果我有冒犯之处，请您体谅。
- **Please excuse me for** occupying your few minutes. 请原谅我占用您几分钟时间。

重点单词

reception [rɪ'sepʃn] *n.* 接待，招待　　offence [ə'fens] *n.* 冒犯，攻击

12. I've got to apologize for... 我得为……道歉。

对话示例

— Cathy, **I've got to apologize for** my behavior.	— 凯西，我得为我的行为道歉。
— What did you do?	— 你做了什么?
— I draw a cat on the cover of your new book.	— 我在你的新书封面上画了一只猫。
— You are really naive, but it doesn't matter. That won't stop me reading.	— 你可真幼稚，不过没关系，那并不妨碍我阅读。

句型分析

I've got to apologize for... 句型中的 for 是介词，其后接名词或动名词。该句型还可以被 I have to apologize for... 替换。

句子示例

- **I've got to apologize for** making a trouble for you. 给你添了麻烦，真是抱歉。
- **I've got to apologize for** my abruptness. 我为我的唐突向你道歉。
- **I've got to apologize for** misunderstanding you. 我为误解你向你道歉。

重点单词

naive [naɪ'i:v] *a.* 天真的，幼稚的

abruptness [ə'brʌptnəs] *n.* 唐突，鲁莽

13. Please accept...apology 请接受……的歉意

对话示例

— **Please accept** our **apology** for your loss.	— 请接收我们对贵方的损失表示的歉意。
— We hope you can lower the price as compensation.	— 我公司希望贵方降低价格作为补偿。
— Sir, we agree to reduce by 3% on the basis of the original price.	— 先生，我们同意在原有价格的基础上降低3%。
— In this case, we hope you can bear all the freight.	— 这样的话，我们希望贵方承担所有运费。

句型分析

Please accept ... apology 句型中的 apology 前一般为形容词性物主代词或其他修饰词，apology 后常接介词 for 的结构。

句子示例

- **Please accept** my sincere **apology** for not giving you a hand. 没能向您伸出援手，请接受我诚挚的道歉。
- **Please accept** my **apology** for the loss caused by my work. 对于我的工作给您带来的损失，请接受我的道歉。

• He had to say, "**Please accept** my **apology** for the improper speech." 他不得不表示："对于我不合适的言论，请接受我的道歉。"

重点单词

loss [lɒs] *n.* 损失，丢失

freight [freɪt] *n.* 运费

improper [ɪm'prɒpə] *a.* 不正确的，不恰当的

compensation [ˌkɒmpen'seɪʃn] *n.* 赔偿，补偿

sincere [sɪn'sɪə] *a.* 真诚的，真挚的

14. I'm sorry to tell you that I can't... 对于我不能……，我表示抱歉

对话示例

— **I'm sorry to tell you that I can't** go to pick you up at the airport.	— 我不能去机场接你，我很抱歉。
— That's all right. I will take a taxi to your apartment directly.	— 没关系，我会乘坐出租车直接去你的公寓。
— OK. My wife is at home and she will receive you. I won't go back until around eight.	— 好的，我妻子在家，她会招待你的。我到 8 点左右才能回去。
— I got it.	— 我知道了。

句型分析

I'm sorry to tell you that I can't... 句型是 I'm sorry to... 的延伸，是主句和宾语从句构成的复合句。to tell you 是非谓语结构作主语的补足语，that 从句作 tell 的宾语从句。

句子示例

• **I'm sorry to tell you that I can't** come according to the appointed time. 对于我不能按照约定的时间前来，我表示很抱歉。

• **I'm sorry to tell you that I can't** go to the cinema with you. 对于不能和你一起看电影，我表示很抱歉。

• **I'm sorry to tell you that I can't** finish the task in time. 对于我不能及时完成任务，我表示很抱歉。

重点单词

apartment [ə'pɑ:tmənt] *n.* 公寓，住所

task [tɑ:sk] *n.* 任务，工作

15. I sincerely hope you can understand that... 我真心地希望你能理解……

对话示例

— George, could you come to host the party tomorrow evening?	— 乔治，明天晚上你能来主持晚会吗？
— **I sincerely hope you can understand that** I can't attend the party tomorrow evening, because I have to write the paper.	— 我真心地希望你能理解我明晚不能参加晚会，因为我要写论文。
— Well, do you know whether Lisa is free or not tomorrow evening?	— 好吧，你知道丽萨明晚是否有空吗？
— Sorry, I don't know. You can ask her on the phone.	— 抱歉，我不知道。你可以打电话问她。

句型分析

I sincerely hope you can understand that... 句型是复合句型，sincerely 是副词，修饰及物动词 hope，that 在该句型中引导的是宾语从句，that 可省略。

句子示例

- **I sincerely hope you can understand that** he had to refuse your invitation. 我真心地希望你能理解他不得不拒绝你的邀请。
- **I sincerely hope you can understand that** I don't have much time to spare. 我真心地希望你能理解，我无法挪出很多时间。
- **I sincerely hope you can understand that** we will use the money to pay the house rent. 我真心地希望你能理解我们要用这笔钱支付房租。

重点单词

refuse [rɪ'fju:z] *v.* 拒绝

rent [rent] *n.* 房租，租金 *v.* 出租

16. I hope you will excuse me for... 我希望你可以原谅我……

对话示例

— Emily, I heard you would go abroad for further study.	— 艾米丽，我听说你要去国外深造了。
— That's true. I will leave for America next week. **I hope you will excuse me for** not traveling with you.	— 那是真的。下周我就要出发前往美国了。我希望你可以原谅我，我不能和你一起旅行了。
— That's all right. We can meet in America.	— 没关系，我们可以在美国见面。
— I will send you a letter from America.	— 我会从美国给你寄信的。

句型分析

I hope you will excuse me for... 句型中的excuse可被forgive替换。for是介词，后接名词或动名词。you will excuse me for 是省略了 that 的宾语从句。

句子示例

- **I hope you will excuse me for** not buying beer for you. 我希望你能原谅我没有给你买啤酒。
- **I hope you will excuse me for** picking up a flower of your garden. 我希望你能原谅我摘了你花园里的一朵花。
- **I hope you will excuse me for** not replying to your letter in time. 我希望你能原谅我没有及时给你回信。

重点单词

beer [bɪə] *n.* 啤酒　　reply [rɪ'plaɪ] *v.* 回复，回答

17. It is...that should apologize. 应该道歉的人是……

对话示例

— We should not quarrel. **It is** the monitor who didn't allocate the resources well **that should apologize.**	— 我们不应该吵架，应该道歉的人是班长，他没有分配好资源。
— I don't think you are right. The monitor	— 我认为你的想法是不对的。班长不应该为

should not be responsible for this matter.	这件事情负责。
— Let's ask the teacher how to solve it in this case.	— 既然这样，我们去问问老师应该怎么解决。
— All the teachers are in the meeting.	— 老师们现在都在开会。

句型分析

It is ... that should apologize. 是典型的强调句型，强调的一般是人，that 也可用 who 来替换。但是如果强调的是非人的事物，that 不能被替换。

句子示例

- **It is** the person who caused the accident **that should apologize.** 造成事故的人应该道歉。
- **It is** the pet's owner **that should apologize.** 应该道歉的是宠物的主人。
- **It is** the man who fought first **that should apologize.** 先打架的人应该道歉。

重点单词

allocate ['æləkeɪt] *v.* 分配，指派

resource [rɪ'sɔːs] *n.* 资源

responsible [rɪ'spɒnsəbl] *a.* 负责的

18. I do apologize for you, because... 我向你道歉，因为……

对话示例

— **I do apologize for you, because** I broke your bike yesterday.	— 我向你道歉，因为我昨天把你的自行车弄坏了。
— It doesn't matter. I'm going to repair it anyway.	— 没关系，反正我要修理它了。
— So how do you go to school, by bus?	— 那么你怎么去上学呢？乘公交车吗？
— My father drives me every day now.	— 我爸爸现在每天开车送我。

句型分析

I do apologize for you, because... 是复合句型，包含主句和一个原因状语从句。因为从句与主句用逗号隔开了，所以 because 也可以用 for 来替换。

句子示例

- **I do apologize for you, because** the sound of my playing the game has disturbed you. 我向你道歉，因为我打游戏的声音吵到你了。
- **I do apologize for you, because** I have left your book at my home. 我向你道歉，因为我把你的书落在我家里了。
- **I do apologize for you, because** I forgot to bring some food for you. 我向你道歉，因为我忘记给你带食物了。

重点单词

anyway [ˈenɪweɪ] *ad.* 无论如何，反正

disturb [dɪˈstɜːb] *v.* 打扰，扰乱

19. You should apologize to... 你应该向……道歉。

对话示例

— Mark, you shouldn't apologize to us. **You should apologize to** the dog's owner.	— 马克，你不应该向我们道歉，你应该向小狗的主人道歉。
— But I don't know where the dog's owner is.	— 但是我不知道小狗的主人在哪里。
— You should wait here for a while, and its owner may come to look for it.	— 你应该在这里等一会儿，它的主人可能过一会儿会回来找它。
— Well, I will follow your advice.	— 好吧，我听你的。

句型分析

You should apologize to... 句型中，to 后多接名词或代词，也可在复合宾语后加 for 引导的介词短语作为附加信息。

句子示例

- **You should apologize to** the disabled man whom you discriminated against. 你应该向这位你歧视的残疾人道歉。
- **You should apologize to** those who are harmed by your decision. 你应该向那些被你的决定伤害了的人道歉。
- **You should apologize to** your parents you cheated. 你应该向被你欺骗的父母道歉。

重点单词

discriminate [dɪˈskrɪmɪneɪt] *v.* 歧视，分辨

cheat [tʃiːt] *v.* 欺骗

Unit 5 态度想法

1. I am inclined to... 我倾向于……

对话示例

— What do you think of the idea of the purchasing department?	— 你认为采购部的想法怎么样?
— I think it's a little extreme.	— 我认为有一点儿极端。
— How could you think so? I think this idea is very good.	— 你怎么会这样认为呢? 我觉得这个想法挺好的。
— **I am inclined to** support the marketing department.	— 我倾向于支持市场部。
— Maybe everyone's thoughts on this matter are different.	— 可能每个人对这件事的想法不一样吧。

句型分析

I am inclined to... 该句型中 to 后面必须跟动词原形。该句型可用于表示自己的态度和想法。be inclined to do sth，意为“倾向于做某事”，incline 的其他用法有：incline one's head，意为“点头”；incline one's ear to，意为“倾听”。

句子示例

- **I am inclined to** read some classic literature books. 我倾向于读一些经典的文学书。
- **I am inclined to** hire the boy whom I am interested in. 我倾向于雇用那位让我感兴趣的男孩。
- **I am inclined to** buy the black jacket which my father is fond of. 我倾向于买我父亲喜欢的那件黑色夹克。

重点单词

incline [ɪn'klaɪn] *v.* 倾向，同意，倾斜

extreme [ɪk'stri:m] *a.* 偏激的，极端的 *n.* 极端

department [dɪ'pɑ:tmənt] *n.* 部门，车间

classic ['klæsɪk] *a.* 经典的，传统的 *n.* 文学著作

literature ['lɪtrətʃə] *n.* 文学，名著

hire ['haɪə] *v.* 雇用 *n.* 佣金

2. There is no need to... 没有必要去……

对话示例

— You look unhappy. What's wrong with you?	— 你看起来不高兴。怎么了?
— I didn't pass the English exam. English is too difficult for me.	— 我英语考试不及格，英语对我来说简直太难学了。
— **There is no need to** lose confidence. I will help you learn the grammar.	— 没有必要失去信心。我会帮助你学习语法知识的。
— With your help, my English will improve soon.	— 在你的帮助下，我的英语肯定很快就会提高。
— Let's make an appointment to study together tomorrow afternoon.	— 那我们约定明天下午一起学习吧。
— OK.	— 好的。

句型分析

There is no need to... 句型中 to 后面必须跟动词原形。此句型可用于表示没有必要去做某事。

句子示例

- **There is no need to** buy some expensive luxuries. 没有必要去买一些昂贵的奢侈品。
- **There is no need to** award scholarships for them. 没有必要授予他们奖学金。
- **There is no need to** care for those who are lazy. 没有必要去关心那些好吃懒做的人。

重点单词

improve [ɪm'pru:v] *v.* 改善，提高

scholarship ['skɒləʃɪp] *n.* 奖学金

luxury ['lʌkʃərɪ] *a.* 奢侈的，豪华的 *n.* 奢侈品

lazy ['leɪzɪ] *a.* 懒的，慢的

3. They ought to... 他们应该……

对话示例

— What's wrong with the light? It is too dark to see anything in the room.	— 灯是怎么回事？房间里太黑了以至于什么也看不见。
— There is no electricity in our building.	— 我们这栋楼停电了。
— Did you call the maintenance department?	— 你给维修部门打电话了吗？
— Yes, I did. But the number is busy.	— 打过了。但是电话占线。
— **They ought to** repair it right away after the power cut.	— 他们应该在停电之后立刻来修。

句型分析

They ought to... 本句型中 ought to do sth 相当于 should do sth，意为“应该做某事”。本句型可用于表示他们应该做某事。

句子示例

- **They ought to** take good care of their parents. 他们应该照顾好他们的父母。
- **They ought to** help those poor children. 他们应该帮助那些贫困儿童。
- **They ought to** pay off the loan on time. 他们应该按时还清贷款。
- **They ought to** keep in touch with each other. 他们应该互相保持联系。

重点单词

electricity [ɪˌlek'trɪsətɪ] *n.* 电，电流

maintenance ['meɪntənəns] *n.* 维修，维护，保持

repair [rɪ'peə] *v.* 修理，恢复

loan [ləʊn] *n.* 贷款 *v.* 借

4. We have to... 我们必须……

对话示例

— **We have to** hand in the design scheme now.	— 我们现在必须上交设计方案了。
— Take it easy. We have a little time to amend.	— 别着急。我们还有一点的时间去修改。
— But I'm afraid that the manager will rebuke us.	— 但是我担心经理会斥责我们。
— Don't worry. The manager is not that kind	— 放心吧。经理不是那种不明智的人。

of people who is unwise.	
— OK. Let's begin.	— 好吧。那我们现在开始修改吧。

句型分析

We have to... 本句型中 to 后面必须跟动词原形。have to do sth = must do sth，意为“必须做某事”。

句子示例

- **We have to** obey the traffic rules. 我们必须遵守交通规则。
- **We have to** take an active part in the community activities. 我们必须积极参加社团活动。
- **We have to** leave before it gets dark. 我们必须在天黑之前离开。
- **We have to** book a standard room. 我们必须预订一个标准间。

重点单词

scheme [ski:m] *n.* 方案，计划

rebuke [rɪ'bju:k] *v.* 斥责，指责

standard ['stændəd] *a.* 标准的 *n.* 标准

amend [ə'mend] *v.* 修改，改正

community [kə'mju:nətɪ] *n.* 社区，社团

5. I feel that I should... 我觉得我应该……

对话示例

— I am too fat to walk very slowly. **I feel that I should** lose weight.	— 我太胖了以至于走路很慢。我觉得我应该减肥了。
— You finally want to lose weight.	— 你终于想减肥了。
— Do you have any good suggestions?	— 你有什么好的建议吗?
— I suggest that you do exercise every day. And remember not to overeat.	— 我建议你每天都做运动。还有，记得不要暴饮暴食。
— Oh, my dear! I don't like doing exercise.	— 哦，我的天哪！我不喜欢做运动。

句型分析

I feel that I should... 本句型中 should 后面必须跟动词原形，可用于表示自己应该做某事。也可在 should 后面加 not，再加动词原形，表示不应该做某事。

句子示例

- **I feel that I should** give him a surprise. 我觉得我应该给他一个惊喜。
- **I feel that I should** cook a superb dinner for them. 我觉得我应该为他们做一顿丰盛的晚餐。
- **I feel that I should** not touch those toxic chemicals. 我觉得我不应该碰那些有毒的化学用品。

重点单词

overeat [ˌəʊvər'iːt] *v.* 吃得太多
superb [suː'pɜːb] *a.* 丰盛的，很好的
toxic ['tɒksɪk] *a.* 有毒的
chemical ['kemɪkl] *n.* 化学用品 *a.* 化学的

6. It's not fair to... ……是不公平的。

对话示例

— The construction company doesn't allow us to build a school near the village.	— 建筑公司不让我们在农村附近建学校。
— Why did they say that?	— 他们为什么会那样说呢?
— Because they think there are few students in the villiage.	— 因为他们认为农村的学生很少。
— **It's not fair to** do that. I will complain about the company.	— 这样做是不公平的。我要投诉这家公司。
— It's no use to do it.	— 你这样做是没有用的。

句型分析

It's not fair to... 该句型中 to 后面要用动词原形。该句型可用于表达自己认为某事是不公平的。not fair = unfair，意为“不公平的”。

句子示例

- **It's not fair to** let him know the answer ahead of time. 让他提前知道答案是不公平的。
- **It's not fair to** divide them into three groups. 把他们分成三组是不公平的。
- **It's not fair to** treat the disabled like this. 像这样对待残疾人是不公平的。
- **It's not fair to** win the prize in this way. 用这种方式赢得奖励是不公平的。

重点单词

fair [feə] *a.* 公平的，公正的，合理的

complain [kəm'pleɪn] *v.* 投诉，抱怨

prize [praɪz] *n.* 奖励，奖品

construction [kən'strʌkʃn] *n.* 建筑，建筑物

disabled [dɪs'eɪbld] *a.* 残疾的，残废的

7. I shall... 我要……

对话示例

— How is everything going?	— 你最近怎么样?
— I've been under too much pressure lately.	— 我最近压力太大了。
— You must relax yourself. What about going swimming on Sunday?	— 你必须让自己放松。星期天去游泳怎么样?
— Sorry. **I shall** have a rest at home.	— 对不起。我只想在家好好休息。
— OK. Let's make an appointment next time.	— 好吧。那我们下次再约吧。

句型分析

I shall... 本句型中 shall 为情态动词，后面必须跟动词原形。shall 的过去式为 should。

句子示例

- **I shall** come up with a good idea in fifteen minutes. 我要在十五分钟之内想出一个好主意。
- **I shall** buy a pair of gloves because it is too cold. 我要买一双手套，因为天气太冷了。
- **I shall** study history at the museum. 我要在博物馆学习历史。

重点单词

lately ['leɪtlɪ] *ad.* 最近，近来

museum [mju'zi:əm] *n.* 博物馆

history ['hɪstrɪ] *n.* 历史，历史学

8. We just need to... 我们只需要……就可以。

对话示例

— When will Steven come to work?	— 史蒂文什么时候来上班?
— He fell off his bicycle the day before yesterday, and the wound has not healed.	— 他前天从自行车上摔下来了，伤口还没有痊愈。
— Shall we go to the hospital to see him?	— 我们要不要去医院看看他?
— **We just need to** wait for him to come back.	— 我们只需要在这儿等他回来就好了。
— I am looking forward to his return.	— 我期待他的归来。

句型分析

We just need to... 本句型中 to 后面要跟动词原形。need to do sth，意为“需要做某事”。本句型用于表达“我们只需要做某事”。

句子示例

- **We just need to** light the candles. 我们只需要点燃蜡烛就可以了。
- **We just need to** know what he is doing. 我们只需要知道他正在干什么就行了。
- **We just need to** cheer for athletes. 我们只需要为运动员喝彩就可以了。
- **We just need to** defeat the enemies. 我们只需要打败那些敌人就好。

重点单词

heal [hi:l] *v.* 恢复，痊愈

candle ['kændl] *n.* 蜡烛，烛光

athlete ['æθli:t] *n.* 体育家，运动员

cheer [tʃɪə] *v.* 欢呼，加油，喝彩

enemy ['enəmɪ] *n.* 敌人，敌军

9. What I'm suggesting here is that... 我在此提议……

对话示例

— The manager denied my proposal just now.	— 经理刚才否定了我的提案。
— **What I'm suggesting here is that** the leaders shouldn't ignore the staff's opinions.	— 我在此提议，领导不应该忽视员工的想法。
— I will tender my resignation after finishing	— 我会在这个项目完成之后递交辞呈。

this project.	
— Are you too hasty?	— 你是不是太草率了?
— I can't stand the manager.	— 我真的忍受不了经理了。

句型分析

What I'm suggesting here is that... 本句型中 that 引导的从句要用陈述句的语序。本句型可用于表达自己的态度和想法。

句子示例

- **What I'm suggesting here is that** we pay more attention to the disabled. 我在此提议，我们要更加关注残疾人士。
- **What I'm suggesting here is that** we should forget the unhappy things in the past. 我在此提议，我们应该忘记过去那些不开心的事情。
- **What I'm suggesting here is that** raising money for the underprivileged is essential to the charity. 我在此提出，为穷人募捐对于慈善机构来说是必须的。

重点单词

tender ['tendə] *v.* 正式提出，递交

hasty ['heɪstɪ] *a.* 草率的，匆忙的

charity ['tʃærətɪ] *n.* 慈善机构，仁爱

resignation [ˌrezɪg'neɪʃn] *n.* 辞职，辞职信

essential [ɪ'senʃl] *a.* 必须的，基本的

10. I guess I can... 我想我可以……

对话示例

— Oh, my God! My purse has gone!	— 哦，我的天哪！我的钱包丢了！
— What is it?	— 怎么回事?
— It seemed like a thief had walked by me. I have no money to take the bus.	— 刚才好像有个小偷从我身边走过。我没有钱去坐公交车了。
— **I guess I can** help you.	— 我想我可以帮助你。
— Thank you very much!	— 非常感谢！

句型分析

I guess I can... 本句型中 can 后面必须跟动词原形。本句型用于表达自己的一种想法或者推测。

句子示例

- **I guess I can** increase the sales. 我想我可以提高销售额。
- **I guess I can** persuade him not to smoke. 我想我可以说服他不要抽烟。
- **I guess I can** move the heavy box. 我想我可以搬走那个很重的箱子。
- **I guess I can** help those who have difficulty in studying English. 我想我可以帮助那些在英语学习方面有困难的人。

重点单词

purse [pɜ:s] *n.* 钱包

sale [seɪl] *n.* 销售，销售额

increase [ɪn'kri:s] *v.* 增加，提高

difficulty ['dɪfɪkəltɪ] *n.* 麻烦，困难

11. It is dangerous... ……是很危险的。

对话示例

— How do you like your new job?	— 你觉得你的新工作怎么样?
— I think I can't work under such great pressure.	— 我认为我不能在这么大的压力下工作。
— You should learn how to relieve stress.	— 你应该学会怎样缓解压力。
— I want to quit.	— 我想要辞职。
— **It is dangerous** for you to do that.	— 你这么做是很危险的。
— I don't care.	— 我不在乎。

句型分析

It is dangerous ... 本句型可用于表达“做某事很危险”。

句子示例

- **It is dangerous** for people to get near wild animals. 人们靠近野生动物是很危险的。
- **It is dangerous** for the little girl is to walk in the middle of the road. 那个小女孩走在马路中间是很危险的。

• **It is dangerous** for the baby to be left at home alone. 让婴儿独自在家是很危险的。

重点单词

crisis ['kraɪsɪs] *n.* 危机，紧要关头

relieve [rɪ'li:v] *v.* 缓解，解除

alone [ə'ləʊn] *a.* 独自地，单独地

pressure ['preʃə] *n.* 压力，气压

wild [waɪld] *a.* 野生的

12. You are wicked to... 你……真是太卑鄙了。

对话示例

— What do you think of the new colleague?	— 你认为那个新同事怎么样?
— I don't like him at all.	— 我一点也不喜欢他。
— Why?	— 为什么?
— I think he is a total flatterer.	— 我认为他完全就是一个奉承者。
— **You are wicked to** say that.	— 你这样说真是太卑鄙了。

句型分析

You are wicked to... 本句型中 to 后面必须跟动词原形。本句型可用于指责某人。

句子示例

• **You are wicked to** steal food to survive. 你靠偷食物生存真是太卑鄙了。

• **You are wicked to** quarrel with your mother. 你和你母亲吵架真是太卑鄙了。

• **You are wicked to** break her vase. 你打碎她的花瓶真是太卑鄙了。

• **You are wicked to** throw the rubbish everywhere. 你到处扔垃圾真是太卑鄙了。

重点单词

wicked ['wɪkɪd] *a.* 卑鄙的，缺德的，邪恶的

steal [sti:l] *v.* 偷

flatterer ['flætərə] *n.* 奉承者

survive [sə'vaɪv] *v.* 生存，幸存

13. We are all for... 我们都赞成……

对话示例

— What did the manager say at the meeting yesterday morning?	— 经理昨天早晨在会上说了什么?
— He said we have to have a summary every day. **We are all for** his saying.	— 他说我们每天要有一个总结。我们都赞成他说的话。
— I think it will waste our time.	— 我认为这样会浪费我们的时间。
— Do you have any good advice?	— 那你有什么好的建议吗?
— We can summarize once a week.	— 我们可以每周总结一次。
— Good idea!	— 好主意!

句型分析

We are all for... 本句型中 for 后面要跟名词或者动名词，be for 意为“赞同，支持”。本句型可用于表示赞同某人的想法或者观点。

句子示例

- **We are all for** your suggestion that the meeting should be cancelled. 我们都赞同你的建议，这次会议应该被取消。
- **We are all for** your idea that we should fly to America next week. 我们都赞同你的想法，我们应该下周飞往美国。
- **We are all for** your saying that he shouldn't be fired. 我们都赞成你说的话，他不应该被解雇。

重点单词

summary ['sʌmərɪ] *n.* 总结，概括

waste [weɪst] *v.* 浪费，损耗 *n.* 浪费，废品

summarize ['sʌməraɪz] *v.* 总结

14. I totally agree... 我完全同意……

对话示例

— Undoubtedly, English is widely used all over the world.	— 毫无疑问，英语在全世界被广泛使用。

— **I totally agree** with you. English is becoming more and more important in our daily life.	— 我完全同意。英语在我们的日常生活中变得越来越重要。
— So my mother always asks me to read English magazines in my leisure time.	— 所以我妈妈总是要求我在业余时间看英文杂志。
— How is your English now?	— 那现在你的英语怎么样?
— Just so so.	— 一般般。

句型分析

I totally agree... 本句型中 totally 为副词，修饰 agree。agree 后面可以跟 with sb 或者 that 从句。

句子示例

- **I totally agree** with your opinion. 我完全同意你的观点。
- **I totally agree** with him on the importance of studying. 关于学习的重要性，我完全同意他的看法。
- **I totally agree** that books are our best lifelong companions. 我完全同意，书籍是我们最好的终生伴侣。
- **I totally agree** that environment is very important to us. 我完全同意，环境对我们很重要。

重点单词

totally ['təʊtəlɪ] *ad.* 全部，完全

leisure ['leʒə] *a.* 业余的，空闲的

undoubtedly [ʌn'daʊtɪdlɪ] *ad.* 毫无疑问地，毋庸置疑地

companion [kəm'pænɪən] *n.* 同伴，伴侣

15. I decide to... 我决定……

对话示例

— How is your life going on?	— 你过得怎么样?
— Not so good. I was dismissed for my blunder in the work.	— 不是很好。我因为工作中的失误被解雇了。
— I am sorry to hear that. Have you found a new job?	— 听到这个我感觉很抱歉。那你找到新工作了吗?
— Not yet. **I decide to** find a job in another city.	— 还没有。我决定去另外一个城市找工作。

句型分析

I decide to... 本句型中 to 后面要跟动词原形，decide to do sth 意为“决定做某事”， make up one's mind to do sth 意为“下定决心做某事”，二者可以互换。

句子示例

- **I decide to** take a course in psychology. 我决定修一门心理学课程。
- **I decide to** go to church on Sunday. 我决定星期天去教堂做礼拜。
- **I decide to** catch the last train. 我决定乘坐末班火车。
- **I decide to** make friends with the little girl. 我决定和那个小女孩交朋友。

重点单词

blunder ['blʌndə] *n.* 错误，失误 *v.* 弄错，出错

psychology [saɪ'kɒlədʒɪ] *n.* 心理，心理学

church [tʃɜ:tʃ] *n.* 教堂

16. He claimed that... 他声称……

对话示例

— John is really arbitrary.	— 约翰真是太霸道了。
— Why did you say that?	— 你为什么这样说?
— **He claimed that** we won't have bonuses this month.	— 他声称我们这个月没有奖金。
— Really? I'm going to negotiate with him now.	— 真的吗? 我现在就去找他谈判。
— I hope that he can accept your opinion.	— 我希望他会接受你的意见。

句型分析

He claimed that... 本句型中 claim 意为“声称，断言”， assert 和它意思相同，二者可以替换。本句型可用于表达某人的观点或者态度。

句子示例

- **He claimed that** he had seen some foreigners. 他声称他看到了一些外国人。
- **He claimed that** he would be responsible for this matter. 他声称他会对这件事负责。

• **He claimed that** everyone should have the privacy right. 他声称每个人都应该有隐私权。

重点单词

claim [kleɪm] *v.* 断言，声称 *n.* 声称

negotiate [nɪˈɡəʊʃɪeɪt] *v.* 协商，谈判

privacy [ˈprɪvəsɪ] *n.* 秘密，隐私

arbitrary [ˈɑːbɪtrərɪ] *a.* 霸道的，任性的

foreigner [ˈfɒrənə] *n.* 外国人

right [raɪt] *a.* 右边的，正确的 *n.* 右方，权利 *ad.* 立刻

17. I am anxious to... 我很想……

对话示例

— What can I do for you?	— 有什么我可以帮你的吗?
— **I am anxious to** know whether there is an electric shaver. I want to buy it for my father.	— 我很想知道你这里有没有电动剃须刀。我想给我父亲买一个。
— Sure. We have many different brands of electric shavers.	— 有的。我们有很多不同品牌的电动剃须刀。
— Let me have a look.	— 让我看一看。
— Here you are.	— 给你。

句型分析

I am anxious to... 本句型中 to 后面必须跟动词原形，be anxious to do sth 意为“渴望做某事”。本句型可用于表达“我很想做某事”。

句子示例

• **I am anxious to** know when they can marry. 我很想知道他们什么时候能结婚。

• **I am anxious to** go to Japan to see the cherry blossoms. 我很想去日本看樱花。

• **I am anxious to** know why he doesn't keep in touch with others. 我很想知道他为什么不和其他人保持联系。

• **I am anxious to** plant a tree in the yard. 我很想在院子里种一棵树。

重点单词

anxious [ˈæŋkʃəs] *a.* 渴望的，着急的

blossom [ˈblɒsəm] *n.* 花 *v.* 开花，绽放

shaver [ˈʃeɪvə] *n.* 剃须刀，理发师

yard [jɑːd] *n.* 院子，场地

18. I think highly of ... 我对……高度评价

对话示例

— I am going to the theater to see the actor's performance. Would you like to go with me?	— 我要去剧院看那位演员的表演。你要和我一起去吗?
— What is the actor's name?	— 那位演员叫什么名字?
— I forgot it. But **I think highly of** his acting.	— 我忘记了。但是我很欣赏他的演技。
— Sorry. I have no time, because I will attend a lecture.	— 对不起。我没有时间，因为我要去参加一个讲座。
— What a pity!	— 真遗憾!

句型分析

I think highly of... 本句型中 of 后面可以跟名词或者代词，但是不能直接跟从句。本句型可用于表达对某人或者某事的高度评价。

句子示例

- **I think highly of** this kind of unified spirit. 我高度评价这种团结的精神。
- **I think highly of** your work. You're the most responsible person I've ever met. 我非常看重你的工作。你是我见过的最有责任心的人。
- **I think highly of** what you have done for me. I will remember your kindness and diligence. 我高度评价你为我所做的一切。我会记住你的善良和勤奋。

重点单词

acting ['æktɪŋ] *n.* 演技，表演

lecture ['lektʃə] *n.* 演讲，讲座

unified ['ju:nɪfaɪd] *a.* 统一的，团结的

spirit ['spɪrɪt] *n.* 精神，心灵

19. I set my mind... 我下定决心……

句型分析

— I heard that the examination results came out.	— 我听说考试成绩出来了。
— Do you know my score?	— 你知道我的分数吗?

— Sorry. You didn't pass the exam.	— 很抱歉。你考试不及格。
— From now on, **I set my mind to** study hard.	— 从现在起，我下定决心努力学习。
— Come on, boy!	— 加油吧，少年！

句型分析

I set my mind ... 本句型后面跟动词不定式。set one's mind to do sth，意为“下定决心做某事”，可以和 make up one's mind to do sth 互换。

句子示例

- **I set my mind to** buy an expensive computer. 我下定决心去买一台昂贵的电脑。
- **I set my mind to** travel abroad. 我下定决心去国外旅行。
- **I set my mind** to clean this vacant room. 我下定决心去打扫这个空房间。

重点单词

result [rɪ'zʌlt] *n.* 结果

score [skɔ:] *n.* 分数，得分

vacant ['veɪkənt] *a.* 空的，空缺的

20. I assent to... 我同意……

对话示例

— Tomorrow is Saturday. What do you want to do?	— 明天是星期六。你想去干什么？
— Our teacher suggests that we should participate in some public welfare activities.	— 老师建议我们应该参加一些公益活动。
— **I assent to** the teacher's suggestion.	— 我同意老师的建议。
— Let's go to the welfare house tomorrow.	— 那我们明天去福利院吧。
— OK. See you tomorrow.	— 好的。明天见。

句型分析

I assent to... 本句型中 to 后面跟名词或者动名词。本句型可用于表达自己的观点和想法。

句子示例

- **I assent to** such a reasonable demand. 我同意这个合理的要求。
- **I assent to** what he said. 我同意他说的话。
- **I assent to** the monitor's plan. 我同意班长的计划。

重点单词

assent [ə'sent] *v.* 同意，赞成 *n.* 赞成　　welfare ['welfeə] *n.* 福利
demand [dɪ'mɑ:nd] *n.* 要求，需求 *v.* 要求，请求

21. It matters little... ……不重要

对话示例

— Yesterday, our sports meeting was very wonderful. Do you know which class won the first?	— 昨天，我们的运动会特别精彩。你知道哪个班级赢得了第一吗?
— **It matters little** who is number one. Because I heard Bill was injured in the race.	— 谁是第一并不重要。因为我听说比尔在赛跑中受伤了。
— Was he sent to the hospital?	— 他被送去医院了吗?
— Yes. He is being treated now.	— 是的，他现在正在被治疗。
— Let's go to the hospital to see him after school.	— 放学后我们一起去医院看他吧。
— OK.	— 好的。

句型分析

It matters little... 本句型中 little 后面通常跟特殊疑问词引导的从句，从句必须用陈述句的语序。本句型可用于表达某人做某事不重要。

句子示例

- **It matters little** whether he was interested in volleyball. 他对排球是否感兴趣，并不是很重要。
- **It matters little** when she will have a chance for promotion. 她什么时候有机会升职，并不是很重要。
- **It matters little** how you lose your weight. 你是怎么减肥的并不重要。
- **It matters little** why you were angry with me. 你为什么生我的气并不重要。

重点单词

race [reɪs] *n.* 赛跑，比赛，竞赛

treat [tri:t] *v.* 招待，治疗 *n.* 招待，乐趣

volleyball ['vɒlɪbɔ:l] *n.* 排球

22. I endeavored to... 我为……努力奋斗

对话示例

— I carried a torch for a girl two years ago.	— 两年前我暗恋一个女孩。
— Have you confessed your love for her?	— 你向她表白了没有?
— No. I had no job at that time, but **I endeavored to** give her a happy life. So she's my girlfriend now.	— 没有。那时候我没有工作，但是我为了能给她一个幸福的生活而努力奋斗。所以她现在是我的女朋友了。
— Congratulations!	— 恭喜!

句型分析

I endeavored to... 本句型中 to 后面必须跟动词原形。本句型可用于表达为了做某事而努力奋斗。endeavor to do sth，意为“努力做某事”。

句子示例

- **I endeavored to** realize my dream at that time. 那时候，我为了实现我的梦想而努力奋斗。
- **I endeavored to** buy the expensive make-up. 我为了买那件昂贵的化妆品而努力奋斗。
- **I endeavored to** win the gold medal. 我为了赢得那块金牌而努力奋斗。
- **I endeavored to** improve my oral English. 我为了提高我的口语而努力奋斗。

重点单词

endeavor [ɪn'devə] *v.* 努力，尝试

confess [kən'fes] *v.* 承认，坦白

realize ['ri:əlaɪz] *v.* 实现，意识到

gold [gəʊld] *a.* 金的，金色的 *n.* 金色，黄金

medal ['medl] *n.* 奖牌，奖章

23. It was necessary that... 有必要……

对话示例

— Did you put these data into your computer?	— 你把这些数据输入电脑里了吗?
— No. I was arranged to leave for a business trip yesterday, so I had no time to do it.	— 还没有。昨天我临时被安排出差，所以没时间去做。
— **It was necessary that** you do that now because the manager will check these data after fifteen minutes.	— 你现在有必要去做。因为经理十五分钟以后就要检查这些数据。
— OK. Thank you for your reminding.	— 好的。谢谢你的提醒。
— You are welcome.	— 不客气。

句型分析

It was necessary that... 本句型中 that 引导的从句中要用 should + 动词原形，should 可以省略。本句型可用于表示“某人做某事很有必要”。

句子示例

- **It was necessary that** he should say goodbye to us. 他有必要向我们道个别。
- **It was necessary that** you should apologize to her. 你有必要向她道歉。
- **It was necessary that** they should drive to work, because there was not enough time. 他们有必要开车去上班，因为时间不充裕了。

重点单词

necessary ['nesəsərɪ] *a.* 必要的，必须的　　arrange [ə'reɪndʒ] *v.* 安排，整理，分类

24. It wasn't very civil of you to... 你……真不礼貌。

对话示例

— Your performance is the worst this week. Do you know what the reason is?	— 这星期你的表现是最差的。你知道原因是什么吗?
— I don't know. I am really confused.	— 我不知道。我真的很困惑。
— **It wasn't very civil of you to** say some rude	— 你对客户说一些粗鲁的话真不礼貌。

words to the customers.

— Sorry. I won't do it again.
— 对不起，下次我不会这样了。

— I hope you can remember what you said.
— 我希望你记住你说的话。

句型分析

It wasn't very civil of you to... 本句型中 to 后面必须跟动词原形，civil 在此意为“有礼貌的，文明的”，本句型可用于责备某人做某事不礼貌。

句子示例

- **It wasn't very civil of you to** make faces to the teachers. 你对老师做鬼脸真不礼貌。
- **It wasn't very civil of you to** mess up the baby's toys. 你把那个婴儿的玩具弄乱真不礼貌。
- **It wasn't very civil of you to** quarrel with your grandfather. 你和爷爷吵架真不礼貌。

重点单词

civil ['sɪvl] *a.* 公民的，文明的，有礼貌的

customer ['kʌstəmə] *n.* 客户，顾客

mess [mes] *v.* 弄乱，弄脏

25. We look up to... 我们尊敬……

对话示例

— Our head teacher is going to Germany next week.
— 我们的班主任下周要去德国了。

— Will you miss her?
— 你们会想念她吗？

— Of course. In fact, **we look up to** her because she is very friendly and erudite.
— 当然会。事实上，我们更加尊敬她，因为她对我们特别友好，而且博学多才。

— Unfortunately, I have not seen your head teacher yet.
— 遗憾的是，我还没见过你们的班主任。

— We can send her to the airport next week.
— 下周我们可以一起送她去机场。

句型分析

We look up to... 本句型中 to 为介词，后面要跟名词、动名词，或者代词。本句型可用于表达对某人或某事的崇敬和敬仰之情。look up to，意为“尊敬，敬仰，赞美”。

句子示例

- **We look up to** her because she has a kind heart. 我们尊敬她是因为她有一颗善良的心。
- **We look up to** the man who likes to help others. 我们尊敬那个爱帮助别人的人。
- **We look up to** the man who is very earnest. 我们尊敬那个非常真挚的人。
- **We look up to** the woman who devotes her lifetime to the career. 我们尊敬那个把她的一生都奉献给事业的女人。

重点单词

erudite ['erʊdaɪt] *a.* 博学的，有才的

devote [dɪ'vəʊt] *v.* 奉献

career [kə'rɪə] *n.* 事业，职业

earnest ['ɜːnɪst] *a.* 真挚的，热心的 *n.* 真挚，热心

unfortunately [ʌn'fɔːtʃənətlɪ] *ad.* 遗憾地，不幸运地

26. You're better off... 你……会更好。

对话示例

— I'd like to have a chance of pay raise.	— 我想加薪。
— Tell me your reason.	— 说说你的理由。
— My salary isn't enough to support me and my family.	— 我的工资都不够养我和家人。
— Let me think about it, and tell you later.	— 让我考虑一下，晚点告诉你。
— **You're better off** replying as soon as possible.	— 你尽快告诉我会更好。

句型分析

You're better off... 该句型常常在给别人提供自己的想法时使用，You're better off 后加动词的 -ing 形式。

句子示例

- **You're better off** running in the morning. 你早上跑步会更好。

- **You're better off** filling the request form for taking the day off. 你填一张请假申请单会更好。
- **You're better off** coming tomorrow morning. 你明天早上来会更好。

重点单词

pay [peɪ] *v.* 付款，偿还　　request [rɪ'kwest] *v.* & *n.* 要求，请求

27. I never took you for... 我从来没有把你当做……

对话示例

— What's come over you?	— 你怎么了?
— I haven't seen my parents for a year. I am a foreigner here.	— 我一年没有见到我的父母了。我在这里只是一个外国人。
— **I never took you for** a foreigner.	— 我从来没有把你当做一个外国人。
— Thank you very much.	— 谢谢你。
— You will see your parents in the summer vacation.	— 你在暑假就能见到你的父母了。

句型分析

I never took you for... 该句型中，主语是 I，谓语是 took（take 的过去式），宾语是 you，for 之后可跟名词或名词短语。

句子示例

- **I never took you for** a thief. 我从来没有把你当做小偷。
- **I never took you for** my stepmother. 我从来没有把你当做我的继母。
- **I never took you for** a business associate of mine. 我从来没有把你当做生意上的伙伴。

重点单词

thief [θi:f] *n.* 小偷　　stepmother ['stepmʌðə] *n.* 继母，后母

associate [ə'səʊʃɪeɪt] *n.* 合伙人

28. What I mean is... 我的意思是……

对话示例

— Excuse me. I think you are Mr. Brown.	— 对不起，打扰一下，我想您一定是布朗先生吧。
— Yes.	— 是的。
— Welcome to London. I'm here to meet you.	— 欢迎来到伦敦。我是过来接你的。
— I don't understand why you say that.	— 我不明白你的意思。
— **What I mean is** I am appointed as your accompaniment during your stay in London.	— 我的意思是我受委派担任您在伦敦期间的陪同。

句型分析

What I mean is... 该句型中，含有一个主语从句 What I mean，所谓主语从句就是指一个句子在整个句子中充当主语，What I mean 在句中充当主语，谓语是 is。

句子示例

- **What I mean is** that this matter is unbelievable. 我的意思是这件事情难以置信。
- **What I mean is** a group of six can finish the task effectively. 我的意思是六人一组能有效地完成这项任务。
- **What I mean is** we want a better return. 我的意思是我们想要一个更好的回报。

重点单词

accompaniment [əˈkʌmpənɪmənt] *n.* 伴随物，陪同人员

unbelievable [ˌʌnbɪˈliːvəbl] *a.* 不可相信的

effectively [ɪˈfektɪvlɪ] *ad.* 有效地

29. Let's just say... 就这么说吧……

对话示例

— Mr. Green has pushed us several times.	— 格林先生已经催我们好几次了。
— What happened?	— 什么事?
— He wants to deliver goods as soon as	— 他想要尽快发货。我不知道如何回复他。

possible. I don't know how to reply him.	
— **Let's just say** I will call them back soon.	— 就这么说吧，我会尽快给他打电话。

句型分析

Let's just say... 该句型中，Let's 是 let us 的缩写，let 引导的是第一人称和第三人称的祈使句。此句型中的 just 是一个副词，表示“刚才，仅仅，只是”。

句子示例

- **Let's just say** that we are too young and naive to handle everything. 就这么说吧，我们又年轻又天真，搞不定所有事情。
- **Let's just say** I need a change of scenery. 就这么说吧，我想换一种生活环境。
- **Let's just say** we are too busy to bother with such details. 就这么说吧， 我们太忙顾不上那么琐碎的事。

重点单词

deliver [dɪ'lɪvə] *v.* 发表，投递，传送　　　naive [naɪ'i:v] *a.* 幼稚的，天真的

30. That means... 那意味着……

对话示例

— Do you finish your annual report?	— 你完成你的年终报告了吗?
— Yes, I finally completed the annual report yesterady.	— 是的，我终于在昨天完成了。
— How long have you finished it?	— 你用了多久完成的?
— About one week.	— 大约一周。
— **That means** I don't have enough time to do it.	— 那意味着我没有足够的时间完成了。

句型分析

That means... 该句型中的 mean 是一个动词，表示“意思是”，mean to do sth，表示“打算做某事”，mean doing sth，表示“意味着做某事”，该句型中 That means 之后可接一个宾语从句。

句子示例

- **That means** we have to indent for the office requirements well in advance. 那意味着我们得提前申请办公用品。
- **That means** we will share the technology with you. 那意味着我们将和贵公司分享技术。
- **That means** your products are very poor in quality. 那意味着你们的产品质量太差。

重点单词

indent [ɪn'dent] *v.* 切割……使呈锯齿状，缩进排版 *n.* 订单，订购

quality ['kwɒlətɪ] *n.* 品质，质量

Unit 6 假设

1. What if...? 如果……该怎么办?

对话示例

— Would you want to take part in the basketball match?	— 你想参加篮球比赛吗?
— I'd love to.	— 我很乐意。
— You can sign up on the website of our company.	— 你可以在我们公司网站上报名参加。
— Okay. **What if** it would rain that day?	— 好的。如果那天下雨该怎么办?
— Don't worry! The basketball match will be held in the gym.	— 不要担心！篮球比赛将会在体育馆举行。

句型分析

What if...? 用于提出假设时，其后的句子如果是对现在情况的假设，就用一般现在时；对过去、将来的假设，需要用虚拟语气。

句子示例

- **What if** I don't have enough money to travel? 如果我没有足够的钱去旅游，该怎么办?
- **What if** the consumers prefer those products? 如果消费者更喜欢那些产品，该怎么办?
- **What if** the manager doesn't accept my apology? 如果经理不接受我的道歉，该怎么办?

重点单词

sign [saɪn] *v.* 签名 *n.* 符号

gym [dʒɪm] *n.* 体育馆

apology [ə'pɒlədʒɪ] *n.* 道歉

2. What choices do we have if...? 如果……我们能有什么选择?

对话示例

— Hello, Nancy. Where are you going?	— 你好，南茜。你准备去哪里?
— I am going to the Bali with my family.	— 我打算和我家人去巴厘岛。
— Really? We also go there. But our plane was behind schedule.	— 真的吗? 我们也去那里。但是我们的飞机竟然晚点了。
— Yes. **What choices do we have if** we want to go there early?	— 是的。如果想早点去那里，我们能有什么选择?
— I have no idea.	— 我也不知道。

句型分析

What choices do we have if... 此句型中 What choices do we have 是主句，if 引导的是从句，表示假设；如果主句是一般将来时，从句用一般现在时，即所谓的“主将从现”。

句子示例

- **What choices do we have if** we won't achieve the goal on time? 如果没有准时完成目标，我们能有什么选择?
- **What choices do we have if** the delivery date will be postponed? 如果交货时间推迟，我们能有什么选择?
- **What choices do we have if** we cannot pass the examination? 如果没有通过考试，我们能有什么选择?

重点单词

schedule [ˈʃedjuːl] *n.* 时刻表

early [ˈɜːlɪ] *ad.* 早，先前

postpone [pəˈspəʊn] *v.* 延缓，延期，推迟

3. I shall never...if... 如果……我绝不会……

对话示例

— What's the matter with you, Lena?	— 你怎么了，丽娜?
— The manager tells me that I must finish the sales task this week. But I have no	— 经理告诉我这周必须得完成销售任务。但是我还没有头绪。

idea.	
— Don't worry! I believe you can do it.	— 不要担心！我相信你可以做到的。
— Thank you, Nina. **I shall never** be a loser **if** I come across setbacks.	— 谢谢你，妮娜。如果我遇到挫折，我绝不会成为一个失败者。

句型分析

I shall never...if... 在此句型中 I shall never... 是主句，其中 I 是主语；if 引导的是条件状语从句，表示说话人的某种假设。

句子示例

- **I shall never** give up you **if** all of the people do not believe you. 如果所有人都不相信你，我也绝不会放弃你。
- **I shall never** miss the opportunity **if** the professor does not see my letter. 如果教授不看我写的信，我也绝不会错过这个机会。
- **I shall never** go there **if** I have another choice. 如果我没有别的选择，我也绝不会去那里。

重点单词

setback ['setbæk] *n.* 挫折，阻碍
opportunity [ˌɒpə'tju:nətɪ] *n.* 机会，条件
professor [prə'fesə] *n.* 教授，讲师

4. If you want..., you have to... 如果你想……就必须……

对话示例

— Tina, why are you late for work again?	— 缇娜，为什么上班又迟到了？
— I am so sorry. One of the elevators was broken this morning.	— 我很抱歉。今天早上有一台电梯坏了。
— I don't think this is a good excuse. **If you want** to work on time, **you have to** be earlier next time.	— 我不认为这是一个好借口。如果你想准时上班，你下次就必须早点过来。
— I think you are right. I must correct this bad habit.	— 我认为你是正确的。我必须纠正这个坏习惯。
— You can do that.	— 你可以做到的。

句型分析

If you want..., you have to... 此句型中 if 引导的是条件状语从句，you have to... 是主句，其中 you 是主语，have to 表示“不得不”，后加动词原形。

句子示例

- **If you want** to be a successful man, **you have to** make effort. 如果你想成功，就必须付出努力。
- **If you want** to travel all over the world, **you have to** get enough money. 如果你想环游全世界，就必须有足够的钱。
- **If you want** respect, **you have to** give respect. 如果你想获得尊重，就必须尊重别人。

重点单词

elevator ['elɪveɪtə] *n.* 电梯

effort ['efət] *n.* 努力，尝试

correct [kə'rekt] *v.* 纠正，改正

5. I will..., even if... 我会……即便……

对话示例

— So many things in our office.	— 我们办公室有好多东西。
— Yes, and you need to put away these things.	— 是的，你需要把它们收拾起来。
— I have a lot of work to do. I can't finish it today.	— 我有很多工作要做。今天完不成。
— Don't worry! **I will** help you, **even if** I won't sleep tonight.	— 放心吧！我会帮助你的，即使今晚我不睡觉。
— I really don't know how to express my gratitude to you.	— 我真不知道该如何感激你。

句型分析

I will..., even if... 此句型中 I will... 是主句，even if... 引导的是让步状语从句，该从句往往表示假设，有时还可以用虚拟语气。

句子示例

- **I will** always be your partner, **even if** we are not together. 我永远是你的伙伴，即便我们不在一起了。
- **I will** go there, **even if** it is windy or rainy. 我会去那里，不管刮风还是下雨。
- **I will** overcome the difficulty, **even if** no one helps me. 我会克服困难，即便没有人帮助我。

重点单词

express [ɪk'spres] *v.* 表达，表示
gratitude ['grætɪtju:d] *n.* 感激，感谢
partner ['pɑ:tnə] *n.* 伙伴，同伙，同伴

6. It's all for nothing if... 如果……一切都是空想。

对话示例

— What will you do if you have enough money?	— 如果你有足够的钱，你会做什么？
— I will buy my wife a big house. What about you?	— 我会给我妻子买一个大房子。你呢？
— I will build a school in my hometown. This is my dream.	— 我会在我家乡建立一所学校。这是我的梦想。
— Wonderful!	— 很棒！
— **It's all for nothing if** we don't have enough money.	— 如果没有足够的钱，一切都是空想。

句型分析

It's all for nothing if... 此句型中 It's all for nothing 是主句，其中 nothing 是不定代词；if 引导的是条件状语从句。

句子示例

- **It's all for nothing if** you don't consider the customer benefits. 如果你不考虑客户的利益，一切都是空想。
- **It's all for nothing if** they amend the contract. 如果他们修改了合同，一切都是空想。
- **It's all for nothing if** bad weather prevented some from parading. 如果由于天气原因一些人没有来参加，一切都是空想。

重点单词

hometown ['həʊmtaʊn] *n.* 家乡，故乡

amend [ə'mend] *v.* 修改，修订

consider [kən'sɪdə] *v.* 考虑，认为

parade [pə'reɪd] *v.* 游行，接受检阅

7. I shall not..., unless... 我不会……，除非……

对话示例

— Our company will travel abroad next week.	— 我们公司下周会出国旅游。
— That sounds great. Would you want to go with us?	— 听起来很不错。你会跟我们一起去吗?
— **I shall not** come, **unless** I finish the listing report.	— 我不会去，除非我完成了上市报告。
— I hope you can finish it. I really want to go with you.	— 我希望你能完成。我真想跟你一起去。
— Thank you for your inviting.	— 谢谢你的邀请。

句型分析

I shall not..., unless... 此句型中，I shall not... 是主句，是一个否定句；unless 引导条件状语从句，含有否定之意，相当于 if 条件状语从句的否定形式。

句子示例

- **I shall not** agree with your proposal, **unless** absolutely compelled. 我不会同意你的提议，除非万不得已。
- **I shall not** promise the plan, **unless** you decide to change the plan. 我不会允许这项计划，除非你决定改变这项计划。
- **I shall not** answer his questions, **unless** he realizes his mistakes. 我不会回答这些问题，除非他意识到他的错误。

重点单词

listing ['lɪstɪŋ] *n.* 列表，名单

promise ['prɒmɪs] *v.* 允诺，许诺

absolutely ['æbsəlu:tlɪ] *ad.* 绝对地，完全地

8. If I were you, I would... 如果我是你，我会……

对话示例

— The shop windows are beautifully decorated. **If I were you, I would** not do that.	— 商店的橱窗里布置得很漂亮。如果我是你，我做不到。
— Thank you for your encouragement. I still have a lot of things to prepare.	— 谢谢你的鼓励。我仍然有很多要准备的。
— What can I do for you?	— 我能为你做些什么呢？
— Can you book some flowers for me?	— 你能给我预订一些花吗？
— It's my pleasure.	— 我很乐意。

句型分析

If I were you, I would... 此句型中，if 引导的是虚拟语气，表示说话人的某种假设，if 引导的从句谓语用一般过去时，主句谓语用“助动词 should/would+ 动词原形”表示与现在 / 将来事实相反的假设。

句子示例

- **If I were you, I would** accept the improvement plan. 如果我是你，我会接受这项改进计划。
- **If I were you, I would** open a bookstore. 如果我是你，我会开一家书店。
- **If I were you, I would** marry at the end of the year. 如果我是你，我会在年底结婚。

重点单词

encouragement [ɪn'kʌrɪdʒmənt] *n.* 鼓励，支持

prepare [prɪ'peə] *v.* 准备，预备

improvement [ɪm'pru:vmənt] *n.* 改进，改善，改良

9. If I were as...as..., I shall not... 如果我和……一样……，我不会……

对话示例

— You look so sad. What's the matter with you?	— 你看起来很伤心，怎么了？
— I fail the math exam.	— 我数学考试没有及格。
— How could it? You are good at math.	— 怎么可能？你很擅长数学。

— **If I were as** careful **as** you, **I shall not** fail the math exam.	— 如果我和你一样细心，我不会通不过数学考试。
— That is a pity.	— 真遗憾。

句型分析

If I were as...as..., I shall not... 此句型中If引导的是虚拟条件句，其中as...as表示“与……一样”；I shall not... 是主句表示否定。

句子示例

- **If I were as** clever **as** you, **I shall not** fail to understand this book. 如果我和你一样聪明，我不会读不懂这本书。
- **If I were as** strong **as** the man, **I shall not** be unable to lift the box. 如果我和那个男人一样强壮，我不会举不起那个箱子。
- **If I were as** rich **as** you, **I shall not** fail to buy the car. 如果我和你一样有钱，我不会买不起那辆车。

重点单词

fail [feɪl] *v.* 失败，不及格

careful ['keəfl] *a.* 仔细的，小心的

unable [ʌn'eɪbl] *a.* 不能的，无能力的

10. What would have happened if...? 如果……，会发生什么事情?

对话示例

— I met a car accident in the morning.	— 我早上遇到了一起车祸。
— Oh, my god. Are you OK?	— 我的天呐！你还好吗?
— It's fortunate that I was not in the car when the accident happened.	— 幸运的是事故发生时我不在车里。
— Thank God.	— 真是谢天谢地。
— **What would have happened if** I were in the car?	— 如果我当时在车里，会发生什么事情呢?
— I dare not wish to go on.	— 我不敢想下去了。

句型分析

What would have happened if...? 是 what 引导的特殊疑问句，在这个特殊疑问句中包含一个 if 引导的虚拟条件句，表示假设。

句子示例

- **What would have happened if** I hadn't acted quickly? 如果我没有反应那么快，会发生什么事情呢?
- **What would have happened if** we didn't acknowledge the shortcomings? 如果我们没有承认这些缺点，会发生什么事情呢?
- **What would have happened if** they didn't sell the stocks? 如果他们没有卖出股票，会发生什么事情呢?

重点单词

accident ['æksɪdənt] *n.* 事故

acknowledge [ək'nɒlɪdʒ] *v.* 承认

fortunate ['fɔːtʃənət] *a.* 幸运的

11. If you..., what would you do? 如果你……，你会怎么做?

对话示例

— **If you** had a million dollars, **what would you do?**	— 如果你有一百万美元，你会怎么做?
— I would help the children who can't go to school. How about you?	— 我会帮助不能上学的那些孩子们。你呢?
— Sounds great. I would build a school for the children.	— 听起来很不错。我将给那些孩子们建一所学校。
— But everything depends on "if".	— 但是所有的事情都依靠“如果”。

句型分析

If you..., what would you do? 本句型中，主句 what would you do 用的是“would+ 动词原形”结构，因此 If 引导的虚拟条件句要用一般过去时。

句子示例

- **If you** were the boy, **what would you do?** 如果你是这个男孩，你会怎么做?

- **If you** had the key to the door, **what would you do?** 如果你有这扇门的钥匙，你会怎么做？
- **If you** went to the Paris, **what would you do?** 如果你去巴黎了，你会怎么做？

重点单词

million ['mɪljən] *n.* 百万

depend [dɪ'pend] *v.* 依靠，依赖

key [ki:] *n.* 钥匙

12. The same result would follow if... 如果……，结果也是一样的。

对话示例

— Have you placed the order for the coming year?	— 你已经为接下来一年订过货了吗？
— Not yet.	— 还没有。
— Why? I worry about the delay on delivery of goods.	— 为什么？我很担心会延迟交货。
— **The same result would follow if** we placed our order in advance.	— 如果提前订货，结果也是一样的。

句型分析

The same result would follow if... 此句型中主句是 The same result would follow，其中 would 用于第二和第三人称中，本句中的 the same result 属于第三人称。

句子示例

- **The same result would follow if** we carried out this measure. 如果执行这项措施，结果也是一样的。
- **The same result would follow if** the manager didn't agree with you. 如果经理不同意，结果也是一样的。
- **The same result would follow if** you went there by subway. 如果你们乘地铁去那里，结果也是一样的。

重点单词

advance [əd'vɑ:ns] *v.* 提前，预付

measure ['meʒə] *n.* 措施

13. It would be an accommodation to me if... 如果……我会比较方便一些。

对话示例

— Can I book a hotel here?	— 我能在这里预订酒店吗?
— I am glad to reserve the public house for you.	— 我很高兴为你预订酒店。
— I want to book a presidential suite and three standard rooms.	— 我想预订一个总统套房和三个标准间。
— Anything else?	— 还有其他的吗?
— No. **It would be an accommodation to me if** you could inform me in advance.	— 没有了。如果你能提前通知我，我会比较方便。

句型分析

It would be an accommodation to me if... 此句型中，主句是 It would be an accommodation to me，是主系表结构，其中主语是 it，系动词是 be，表语是 an accommodation。

句子示例

- **It would be an accommodation to me if** you could give me some help. 如果给我帮助，我会比较方便一些。
- **It would be an accommodation to me if** it didn't rain. 如果没有下雨，我会比较方便一些。
- **It would be an accommodation to me if** you could abide the rules. 如果你能遵守规则，我会比较方便一些。

重点单词

presidential [ˌprezɪ'denʃl] *a.* 总统的　　suite [swi:t] *n.* 套件

standard ['stændəd] *a.* 标准，规格　　inform [ɪn'fɔ:m] *v.* 通知

14. If you..., I'd be happy to... 如果你……，我会很乐意……

对话示例

— You look tired. What's wrong with you?	— 你看起来很累。怎么了?
— I have a terrible headache.	— 我头很疼。
— Do you have a fever?	— 你发烧了吗?
— Yes. I want to go to see the doctor.	— 是的。我想去看医生。
— **If you** want to go to the hospital, **I'd be happy to** be with you.	— 如果你想去医院的话，我会很乐意陪你去。

句型分析

If you..., I'd be happy to... 此句型中，if 引导的是条件状语从句，是真实条件句，用陈述语气，假设的情况有可能发生；其中 happy 可以用 glad 替换。

句子示例

- **If you** want to cooperate with us, **I'd be happy to** introduce our new products. 如果你想继续和我们合作，我会很乐意介绍我们的新产品。
- **If you** have an opportunity to join the party, **I'd be happy to** welcome your coming. 如果你有机会参加聚会，我会很乐意欢迎你的到来。
- **If you** could enter our company, **I'd be happy to** help out. 如果你能来我们公司，我会很乐意帮忙。

重点单词

headache ['hedeɪk] *n.* 头疼

enter ['entə] *v.* 进入，开始

15. If you had..., we should have... 如果你……我们应该……

对话示例

— Which plan should I choose? I can't make up my minds.	— 我应该选择哪个计划? 我做不了决定。
— Both of them are good plans. But I suppose we can get a better plan.	— 两个都是好计划。但是我认为我们可以有更好的计划。
— **If you had** a better plan, **we should have**	— 如果你有更好的计划，我们应该听从你的。

obeyed you.	
— Let me introduce the details of the plan.	— 让我来介绍这个计划的详细内容。

句型分析

If you had..., we should have... 此句型含 if 引导的虚拟条件句，从句谓语用的是一般过去时，主句谓语用的是 should+ 动词原形，should 通常用于第一人称。

句子示例

- **If you had** some good proposals, **we should have** obeyed your command. 如果你有更好的提议，我们应该听从你的指挥。
- **If you had** enough time, **we should have** made another sales plan. 如果你有足够的时间，我们应该制定另一个销售计划。
- **If you had** not answered us, **we should have** found you. 如果你没有回应我们，我们应该去找你。

重点单词

choose [tʃu:z] *v.* 选择

detail ['di:teɪl] *n.* 详细内容

command [kə'mɑ:nd] *n.* 指挥，命令

16. If so, I fear... 如果是这样，恐怕……

对话示例

— I have been offered two new jobs.	— 我得到了两份新工作。
— Congratulations. Which job do you want to choose?	— 祝贺你。你想选择哪一份工作?
— I want to choose the bigger company. **If so, I fear** the work is challenging.	— 我想选择这个更大的公司。如果是这样，恐怕工作很有挑战性。
— I support you. You can get a higher salary, too.	— 我支持你。你也可以得到一个更高的工资。
— I have to think about it.	— 我好好考虑一下。

句型分析

If so, I fear... 此句型中，if so 是省略了主谓的 if 状语从句，表示对前面所说事情的肯定，完整的句子应该是 if that is so 或者 if it is so。

句子示例

- **If so, I fear** to pursue a different strategy. 如果是这样，恐怕我要采取不同的策略。
- **If so, I fear** he will misunderstand me. 如果是这样，恐怕他会误解我。
- **If so, I fear** we will meet a big challenge. 如果是这样，恐怕我们会面临巨大的挑战。

重点单词

congratulation [kənˌɡrætʃʊ'leɪʃn] *n.* 祝贺，恭喜

salary ['sælərɪ] *n.* 薪水

strategy ['strætədʒɪ] *n.* 策略，战略

17. Whatever comes, I'll... 无论发生什么事，我都会……

对话示例

— Your spoken English is really good.	— 你的口语真的很好。
— Thank you.	— 谢谢。
— I thought I was speaking English well. Now I'm not sure.	— 我原本以为我英语说得不错。现在我不确定了。
— There is nothing wrong with your English. Just believe in yourself.	— 你的英语没有问题。要相信自己。
— Don't worry. **Whatever comes, I'll** believe in myself.	— 别担心。无论发生什么事，我都会相信自己的。

句型分析

Whatever comes, I'll... 此句型中，whatever 引导的是让步状语从句，主句是 I'll...，I'll 是 I will 的缩写，I'll 后跟动词原形。

句子示例

- **Whatever comes, I'll** finish it by myself. 无论发生什么事，我都会靠自己去完成它。
- **Whatever comes, I'll** come up with you. 无论发生什么事，我都会追赶上你。

• **Whatever comes, I'll** not lose my heart. 无论发生什么事，我都不会灰心。

重点单词

whatever [wɒt'evə] *a. & pron.* 不管怎样；无论如何

believe [bɪ'li:v] *v.* 相信，信任

lose [lu:z] *v.* 失去，错过

18. It may be some time before... 也许要过一段时间之后……

对话示例

— Could you effect an earlier shipment by the end of the month?	— 你们能否早一点在月底之前发货?
— The date of shipment has to delay because of the storm.	— 因为暴风雨装运日期不得不推迟。
— How long should it take?	— 这应该需要多长时间?
— **It may be some time before** the storm ends.	— 也许要在暴风雨结束之后过一段时间。

句型分析

It may be some time before... 此句型中，it 是主语，may 是情态动词，be 是系动词，some time 是表语，before 既可作介词或副词用，也可作从属连词用。

句子示例

• **It may be some time before** the diffusion of new technology. 新技术也许要过一段时间之后才能普及。

• **It may be some time before** we get a new idea. 也许要过一段时间之后我们才能有新想法。

• **It may be some time before** he returns to his college. 也许要过一段时间之后他才能重返大学。

重点单词

shipment ['ʃɪpmənt] *n.* 装运，装货

delay [dɪ'leɪ] *v.* 延期，推迟

diffusion [dɪ'fju:ʒn] *n.* 扩散，传播

19. It would do no harm if... 如果……也没有什么坏处。

对话示例

— Is there any sales promotion in your shop?	— 你们店里有促销活动吗?
— In order to celebrate the new business, our company holds the activity.	— 为了庆祝开张，我们公司推出促销活动。
— What about this one and that one?	— 这个和那个产品怎么样?
— Both of them are really good. This product is a high grade product.	— 两个都很不错。这个是我们的高端产品。
— But I prefer that one.	— 但是我更喜欢那个。
— **It would do no harm if** you chose that one. That one is cheaper.	— 如果你选择那个产品，也没有什么坏处。那个更便宜些。

句型分析

It would do no harm if... 此句型中主句是 It would do no harm，主句用的是 would+ 动词原形，if 引导的从句要用过去时。

句子示例

- **It would do no harm if** we could stay as vigorous as we were at twelve. 如果我们像 12 岁那样精力充沛，也没有什么坏处。
- **It would do no harm if** I bought this car. 如果我买这辆车，也没有什么坏处。
- **It would do no harm if** they went to see a film. 如果他们去看场电影，也没有什么坏处。

重点单词

promotion [prə'məʊʃn] *n.* 促进，增进 vigorous ['vɪgərəs] *a.* 精力充沛的

20. If I were in your place, I should not... 如果我处于你的境地，我不会……

对话示例

— I heard you would travel extensively with varied business interests.	— 我听说你因为各种生意需要频繁出差。
— Yeah, I feel very tired.	— 是啊，我感到很累。

— I think you need relax as much as possible.	— 我认为你需要尽可能多的放松。
— But I have no time to relax.	— 但是我没有时间。
— **If I were in your place, I should not** be strong like you.	— 如果我处于你的境地，我不会像你那么坚强的。

句型分析

If I were in your place, I should not... 此句型中，if 引导的是虚拟条件句，I should not... 是主句，主句中的主语 I 是第一人称，所以用 should。

句子示例

- **If I were in your place, I should not** come up with her. 如果我处于你的境地，我不会赶上她。
- **If I were in your place, I should not** take part in the party. 如果我处于你的境地，我不会参加这个聚会。
- **If I were in your place, I should not** accept the advice. 如果我处于你的境地，我不会接受这个建议。

重点单词

extensively [ɪk'stensɪvlɪ] *ad.* 广泛地

possible ['pɒsəbl] *a.* 可能的，合理的

varied ['veərɪd] *a.* 各种各样的

21. If I knew..., I would... 如果我知道……，我会……

对话示例

— Our manager asked me to come to meet you.	— 我们经理让我替他来接你。
— Thank you very much. Why didn't your manager come?	— 谢谢你。为什么经理没有来?
— Some business held him back.	— 因为他公务太忙。
— I suddenly remember I forgot to book a hotel.	— 突然想起来我忘记订酒店了。
— **If I knew** it, **I would** book you a hotel in advance.	— 如果我知道，我会提前给你预订酒店的。

句型分析

If I knew..., I would... 此句型中包含一个 if 引导的虚拟条件句，谓语动词 knew 用的是过去式，因此主句应该用 would/should+ 动词原形。

句子示例

- **If I knew** English, **I would** read the book in the original. 如果我懂英语，我会看这本书的原版。
- **If I knew** you will come, **I would** pick you up at the airport. 如果我知道你会来，我会去机场接你。
- **If I knew** the truth, **I would** tell you. 如果我知道真相，我会告诉你。

重点单词

hold [həʊld] *v.* 拿住，握住

original [ə'rɪdʒənl] *a.* 最初的，原始的

airport ['eəpɔ:t] *n.* 机场

Chapter 4
叙述用语句型

Unit 1 描述
Unit 2 比较
Unit 3 转折
Unit 4 强调
Unit 5 重复省略
Unit 6 否定

Unit 1 描述

1. I say to you that... 我要和你们说的是……

对话示例

— Do you know the vice manager of the marketing department?	— 你认识市场部的副经理吗?
— Yes, I know him. What's wrong?	— 是的，我认识。怎么了?
— **I say to you that** he had a car accident last night.	— 我跟你说，他昨天晚上出车祸了。
— Oh, my god. Is it serious?	— 天啊。严重吗?
— I am not clear. He fainted and was sent to the hospital.	— 我也不清楚。他昏了过去，然后被送到了医院。

句型分析

I say to you that... 包含一个 that 引导的宾语从句，其中 I 是主语，say 是谓语动词，that 从句是直接宾语，you 是间接宾语。

句子示例

- **I say to you that** he received a court summons. 我跟你们说，他昨天收到了法院的传票。
- **I say to you that** the head teacher asks for a leave today. 我跟你说，班主任今天请假了。
- **I say to you that** John resigned this morning. 我跟你说，约翰上午辞职了。

重点单词

summons ['sʌmənz] *n.* 传票，传唤

vice [vaɪs] *n.* 恶习，缺陷 *a.* 副的，代替的

2. All you had to do was... 你只需要……

对话示例

— You are late for work. What's wrong?	— 你上班迟到了。怎么回事?
— Sorry, I worked overtime in the company last night, so I went to bed too late.	— 对不起，我昨天晚上在公司加班，所以睡得很晚。
— Why did you work overtime?	— 你为什么加班?
— Because I can't use the printer in our office.	— 因为我不会使用我们办公室的打印机。
— **All you had to do was** to read the instructions.	— 你只需要读一下说明书就好了。
— Thank you for your suggestion. It is very useful for me.	— 好的。谢谢你的建议。它对我非常有用。

句型分析

had to，意为“必要，只要”，原形为 have to，was 是 is 的过去式，was 后面必须跟动词不定式。本句型通常用于告诉或者提醒对方只需要做某件事就可以了。

句子示例

- **All you had to do was** to divide them into two groups. 你只需要把他们分成两组。
- **All you had to do was** to check the bill. 你只需要核对一下账单。
- **All you had to do was** to follow the rules. 你只需要遵守规则就好。
- **All you had to do was** to clean the room. 你只需要把房间打扫干净就好。

重点单词

company ['kʌmpənɪ] *n.* 公司　　instructions [ɪn'strʌkʃənz] *n.* 说明书，使用说明

check [tʃek] *v.* 检查，核对　　bill [bɪl] *n.* 账单，钞票

3. I close in saying that... 最后，我要讲的是……

对话示例

— I know you are not satisfied with the new interns.	— 我知道你对新来的实习生不满意。
— Yes, they are always careless with the	— 是的，他们在工作上很粗心。

work.	
— Anything else?	— 还有其他的吗?
— They also chat at work time. **I close in saying that** I will fire them.	— 他们还在工作时间聊天。最后，我要讲的是我将解雇他们。

句型分析

I close in saying that 包含的是一个 that 引导的宾语从句，I 在句子中做主语，that 引导的宾语从句是直接宾语。close in 意为“迫近，逼近”。

句子示例

- **I close in saying that** you need to get these data together. 最后，我要讲的是你需要把这些数据汇集到一起。
- **I close in saying that** I'll be on a business trip tomorrow. 最后，我要讲的是明天我要出差。
- **I close in saying that** you must let these people obey your orders. 最后，我要讲的是你必须让这些人服从你的命令。

重点单词

intern [ɪn'tɜ:n] *n.* 实习生 *v.* 扣留，关押

fire ['faɪə] *v.* 解雇，燃烧 *n.* 火，燃烧物

order ['ɔ:də] *n.* 命令，规则 *v.* 命令，订购，整理

careless ['keələs] *a.* 粗心的，无忧无虑的

data ['deɪtə] *n.* 数据，资料

obey [ə'beɪ] *v.* 服从，遵守

4. I know... 我知道……

对话示例

— The singer is famous for her voice.	— 这个歌手因她的嗓音而出名。
— Yes, her voice is very unique. We all like her.	— 是的，她的声音非常独特，我们大家都很喜欢她。
— **I know** she has experienced a lot of frustration.	— 我知道她经历了很多挫折。
— Because of this, she can become a good singer.	— 正因为如此，她才能成为一名好歌手。
— So, we must cherish everything now.	— 所以，我们一定要珍惜现在的一切。

句型分析

I know 后面跟的是 that 引导的一个宾语从句，that 可以省略。I 是句子的主语，know 是谓语，宾语从句是宾语。

句子示例

- **I know** he is used to drinking milk before going to bed. 我知道他习惯在睡觉之前喝牛奶。
- **I know** his bike was stolen by the thief. 我知道他的自行车被小偷偷走了。
- **I know** you like her innocence. 我知道你喜欢她的天真无邪。
- **I know** this movie is your favorite. 我知道这部电影是你的最爱。

重点单词

unique [jʊ'nɪ:k] *a.* 仅有的，唯一的，独特的

innocence ['ɪnəsns] *n.* 天真，清白，没有罪的人

experience [ɪk'spɪərɪəns] *n.* 经验，经历 *v.* 经历，感受

cherish ['tʃerɪʃ] *v.* 珍惜，爱护

thief [θi:f] *n.* 盗贼，小偷

5. He began to... 他开始……

对话示例

— John did not like to talk to his classmates before.	— 约翰以前不喜欢和同学们说话。
— He always looks very shy. And he looks like a kid.	— 他看起来总是很害羞，而且看起来像个小孩子。
— But **he began to** talk to me actively yesterday.	— 但是昨天开始他积极主动地和我说话了。
— Really? This is really good news.	— 真的吗？这真是个好消息。
— I also think so.	— 我也这样认为。

句型分析

he 是句子的主语，began 是 begin 的过去式，to 后面要跟动词原形。begin to do sth = start to do sth，意为“开始做某事”。

句子示例

- **He began to** take an interest in western culture. 他开始对西方文化感兴趣了。
- **He began to** help his mother clean the room. 他开始帮助他妈妈打扫房间了。
- **He began to** prepare for the graduation party. 他开始为毕业晚会做准备了。
- **He began to** take part in outdoor activities. 他开始参加户外活动了。

重点单词

shy [ʃaɪ] *a.* 害羞的，胆小的

interest ['ɪntrəst] *n.* 兴趣，利益 *v.* 使有兴趣，使有关系

prepare [prɪ'peə] *v.* 准备

graduation [ˌgrædʒʊ'eɪʃn] *n.* 毕业

6. Presently it occurred to him that... 他突然想到……

对话示例

— Where is Paul going? I can't find him.	— 保罗去哪里了？我找不到他了。
— He went back to the classroom.	— 他回教室去了。
— Why?	— 为什么？
— **Presently it occurred to him that** he left the key in the classroom.	— 他突然想到，他把钥匙放在教室了。
— What a careless boy!	— 真是个粗心的男孩！
— He should change his carelessness.	— 他应该改掉粗心的毛病。

句型分析

Presently it occurred to him that... 此句型包含一个 that 引导的宾语从句，宾语从句的时态要根据句意而定。

句子示例

- **Presently it occurred to him that** he can solve the problem for us. 他突然想到，他可以为我们解决这个问题。
- **Presently it occurred to him that** he can let his daughter go abroad to study. 他突然想到，他可以让他的女儿出国留学。
- **Presently it occurred to him that** he can build a photography studio. 他突然想到，他可以建立一间摄影工作室。

· **Presently it occurred to him that** he can accept the teacher's advice. 他突然想到，他可以接受老师的建议。

重点单词

presently ['prezntlɪ] *ad.* 目前，不久，马上　　photography [fə'tɒgrəfɪ] *n.* 照片，摄影

studio ['stjʊ:dɪəʊ] *n.* 工作室，画室

7. There are some who say that... 有人说……

对话示例

— This professor is particularly authoritative.	— 这位教授特别有权威。
— **There are some who say that** he received a lot of international awards.	— 有人说，他获得了很多国际奖项。
— We have met such an excellent teacher.	— 我们竟然遇见了一位这么优秀的老师。
— How lucky we are!	— 我们真是太幸运了！
— Then, we have to study hard.	— 这样的话，我们也必须努力学习。

句型分析

There are some who say that... 此句型包含一个 that 引导的宾语从句，本句型可用于表示某人说了什么话。

句子示例

· **There are some who say that** he comes from a poor village. 有人说，他来自一个贫困的乡村。

· **There are some who say that** the policeman used to be a lawyer. 有人说，这个警察以前是一名律师。

· **There are some who say that** she will not have mercy on the poor. 有人说，她不会怜悯那些穷人。

· **There are some who say that** he is the chairman of a company. 有人说，他是一家公司的董事长。

重点单词

particularly [pə'tɪkjələlɪ] *ad.* 特别，尤其　　authoritative [ɔ:'θɒrətətɪv] *a.* 权威的，有权力的

award [ə'wɔ:d] *n.* 奖品，奖励，判决 *v.* 授予，奖励，判定

excellent ['eksələnt] *a.* 优秀的，卓越的　　mercy ['mɜ:sɪ] *n.* 怜悯，宽容，可怜

chairman ['tʃeəmən] *n.* 主席，董事长

8. ...be used to... ……是被用来……

对话示例

— Would you like to go shopping with me tomorrow?	— 明天和我一起去购物吧?
— Yes, I'd love to. What do you want to buy?	— 好啊，我很乐意。你想买什么?
— I want to buy a towel, which **is used to** clean the floor.	— 我想买一条毛巾，用来擦地板。
— OK. See you at the bus station tomorrow.	— 好的，那我们明天在公交车站见。

句型分析

...be used to... 本句型中主语一般是一些没有生命的物体。注意不能与 used to do sth“过去常常做某事”和 be used to doing sth“习惯于做某事”混淆。

句子示例

- The scissors can only **be used to** cut paper. 这把剪刀只能用来剪纸。
- The box **is used to** package toys. 这个箱子是用来装玩具的。
- Letters **are used to** keep in touch with others. 信件是用来和他人保持联系的。

重点单词

towel ['taʊəl] *n.* 毛巾，纸巾

scissors ['sɪzəz] *n.* 剪刀

9. It is natural that... ……是很自然的。

对话示例

— We have a new classmate in our class.	— 我们班有一个新同学。
— I know her name is Emma. She comes from America.	— 我知道她叫艾玛，来自美国。
— I heard that she learned well, especially English.	— 我听说她学习很好，尤其很擅长英语。

— **It is natural that** she should speak English fluently.	— 她说英语很流利是理所应当的。
— I am really envious of her.	— 我真的很羡慕她。

句型分析

It is natural that... 这个句型中，it 是形式主语，用来表示后面从句的内容，that 后面要跟 should + 动词原形。

句子示例

- **It is natural that** he should pass the final exam. 他通过期末考试是理所应当的。
- They are 30 years old, and **it is natural that** they should have a baby. 他们 30 岁了，有个小孩是理所应当的。
- She was born in a poor family, and **it is natural that** she should live such a simple life. 她出生在一个贫穷的家庭，她过着如此简朴的生活是理所应当的。

重点单词

natural ['nætʃrəl] *a.* 天生的，自然的 *n.* 自然的事

fluently ['flu:əntlɪ] *ad.* 流利地，流畅地

simple ['sɪmpl] *a.* 简单的，朴素的

especially [ɪ'speʃəlɪ] *ad.* 尤其地，主要地

envious ['envɪəs] *a.* 羡慕的，妒忌的

10. It seems that... 某事看起来似乎……

对话示例

— Yesterday you asked for leave, and we had a meeting.	— 昨天你请假，我们开了一个会。
— What did the boss say at the meeting?	— 会上老板都说什么了？
— He said the designer's design is not realistic.	— 他说那个设计师的设计方案不符合实际。
— **It seems that** the boss is right.	— 老板似乎是对的。
— But I think the boss is too straightforward.	— 但是我认为老板说话太直接了。

句型分析

It seems that... 句型中 it 是形式主语，真正的主语是 that 后面的从句。it seems = it appears，两者可以互换。

句子示例

- **It seems that** Lucy told the truth. 露西说的似乎是事实。
- **It seems that** it is going to snow. 似乎要下雪。
- **It seems that** Marry has decided to divorce. 玛丽似乎已经决定要离婚了。
- **It seems that** he has already figured out the answer. 他似乎已经想到答案了。

重点单词

realistic [ˌriːəˈlɪstɪk] *a.* 现实的，实际的　　truth [truːθ] *n.* 真理，事实，真相

straightforward [ˌstreɪtˈfɔːwəd] *a.* 直接的，坦率的 *ad.* 坦率地，直接地

divorce [dɪˈvɔːs] *v.* 离婚，分离 *n.* 离婚，分离

11. It was not until...that... 直到……才……

对话示例

— Jane has been in a bad mood recently.	— 简最近心情很不好。
— What's wrong with her?	— 她怎么了?
— She failed the TOEFL, so she can't study abroad.	— 她托福考试不及格，因此她不能出国留学了。
— What a pity! And I saw her go to the bar last night.	— 真遗憾！我看见她昨天晚上去酒吧了。
— Yes. **It was not until** midnight **that** she went home.	— 是的。她直到半夜才回家。
— We should communicate with her more often.	— 我们应该多和她交流。

句型分析

It was not until...that... 句型中 until 后跟某个时间点，that 后跟从句，从句要用一般过去时。

句子示例

It was not until the weekend **that** John finished the task. 约翰直到周末才把任务完成。

It was not until last year **that** she found a job. 她直到去年才找到工作。

It was not until last Saturday **that** Tina got married. 直到上个星期六蒂娜才结婚。

It was not until last month **that** he came back. 他直到上个月才回来。

重点单词

mood [mu:d] *n.* 心情，语气，气氛

pity ['pɪtɪ] *n.* 同情，遗憾，怜悯

recently ['ri:sntlɪ] *ad.* 最近

task [tɑ:sk] *n.* 工作，任务

12. Occasionally one could see... 偶尔可以看到……

对话示例

— Have you been to Prague?	— 你去过布拉格吗?
— I have never been there, but I know Prague is the capital of the Czech Republic and is a historic city in Europe.	— 我从来没去过，但是我知道布拉格是捷克共和国的首都，而且在欧洲是一座历史名城。
— Yes, and in Prague Square there are a lot of people every day. **Occasionally one could see** someone taking wedding photos in Prague Square.	— 是的，布拉格广场每天都有很多人。偶尔可以看到一些人在布拉格广场拍婚纱照。
— That scene must be beautiful. I can not wait to go there.	— 那种场景一定很美。我都迫不及待想去那里了。
— It is the best time to go there in September.	— 九月是去那里的最佳时间。

句型分析

Occasionally one could see... 句型中 see 后面用动词的 ing 形式，构成 see sb doing sth，意为“看到某人正在做某事”。

句子示例

• **Occasionally one could see** the old man playing chess in the park. 偶尔可以看到那个老人在公园下棋。

- **Occasionally one could see** him drinking coffee in the evening. 偶尔可以看到他在晚上喝咖啡。
- **Occasionally one could see** her reading the newspaper carefully. 偶尔可以看到她在认真地看报纸。
- **Occasionally one could** see him dancing for joy. 偶尔可以看到他高兴地跳起来。

重点单词

occasionally [əˈkeɪʒnəlɪ] *ad.* 偶尔，有时

chess [tʃes] *n.* 棋，国际象棋

square [skweə] *n.* 广场，正方形，平方

scene [si:n] *n.* 场面，风景

capital [ˈkæpɪtl] *n.* 首都，资本，大写字母 *a.* 首都的，资本的

13. ... be said to... ……据说是……

对话示例

— Tom went to Thailand for vacation.	— 汤姆去泰国度假了。
— Yes. I heard that he often travels abroad.	— 是的。我听说他经常出国旅行。
— He **is said to** build a company on his talent.	— 据说他靠自己的才华建立了一家公司。
— Yes, because he works very hard and often works overtime until midnight.	— 是的，因为他工作特别努力，而且经常加班到半夜。

句型分析

... be said to... 本句型中 to 后面必须跟动词原形。类似的句型还有 be estimated to...，意为"……据估计……"。

句子示例

- He **is said to** be a billionaire. 据说他是个亿万富翁。
- Mr. Hunter **is said to** be over 90. 据说亨特先生已经超过 90 岁了。
- The young lady **is said to** be married. 据说这位年轻的女士已经结婚了。

重点单词

Thailand [ˈtaɪlænd] *n.* 泰国

talent [ˈtælənt] *n.* 天才，才能

billionaire [ˌbɪljəˈneə] *n.* 亿万富翁

14. ... be thought to... ……被认为……

对话示例

— Do you know who will win the best prize in the football match?	— 你知道谁会赢得这次足球比赛的最佳奖项吗?
— Mike, of course. He **was thought to** be the best man to play football on our team.	— 当然是麦克了。他被认为是我们球队中踢足球最棒的人。
— I don't think so. I think John is very good.	— 我不这样认为。我觉得约翰很不错。
— I bet Mike will win.	— 我敢打赌，一定是麦克会赢。
— I'm looking forward to this football match. It must be wonderful.	— 我很期待这次足球比赛。一定会很精彩。

句型分析

... be thought to... 本句型和 ... said to ... 类似，to 后面必须跟动词原形。本句型可用于表达某人或者某事被认为怎么样。

句子示例

- He **is thought to** be a model worker. 他被认为是一名模范工作者。
- Miss. Wang **is thought to** be a conscientious teacher. 王女士被认为是一位认真负责的老师。
- The little girl **was thought to** act like a dancer in the party. 大家认为这个小女孩在派对上像个舞蹈家一样。

重点单词

match [mætʃ] *n.* 比赛，火柴

bet [bet] *v.* 打赌，确信 *n.* 打赌，赌注，赌博

model ['mɒdl] *n.* 模特，模型，模范

conscientious [ˌkɒnʃɪ'enʃəs] *a.* 认真负责的，谨慎的

15. ... be reported to... 据报道……

对话示例

— The traffic accident **was reported to** happen on this road yesterday.	— 据报道，这条路上昨天发生了一场车祸。
— Did anyone get hurt?	— 那有没有人受伤呢?

— Only one person was sent to the hospital, and now in the intensive care unit.	— 只有一个人被送去了医院，现在在重症监护室里。
— What about the others?	— 其他人怎么样了？
— They were not hurt, but the insurance company compensated their mental loss.	— 他们都没有受伤，但是保险公司赔偿了他们精神损失费。

句型分析

... be reported to... 本句型中 to 后面要跟动词原形。本句型可用于表示“据报道某人或者某事如何”。

句子示例

- The medicine **was reported to** contain harmful chemical components. 据报道，这种药含有有害的化学成分。
- The road in the city centre **is reported to** be crowded. 据报道，市中心的那条道路特别拥挤。
- The infectious disease **was reported to** cause about 20 people to be dead. 据报道，那个传染病造成了大约 20 个人死亡。

重点单词

report [rɪ'pɔ:t] *v.* 报道 *n.* 报告

intensive [ɪn'tensɪv] *a.* 强烈的，加强的

insurance [ɪn'ʃʊərəns] *n.* 保险

compensate ['kɒmpenseɪt] *v.* 赔偿，补偿

16. It is the general rule that... 通常情况下……

对话示例

— There are many shortcomings in this project.	— 这个项目有很多不足之处。
— Do you know who manages this project?	— 你知道是谁在管理这个项目吗？
— **It is the general rule that** Henry should manage all the projects personally. But recently he was sick and didn't come to work.	— 通常情况下，应该是亨利管理所有的项目。但是他最近生病了，没来上班。
— It is up to you to manage it.	— 那就由你来管理吧。
— OK. I will try my best to do it.	— 好的，我会尽我最大的努力去做的。

句型分析

It is the general rule that... 句型中 it 是形式主语，that 后面的从句必须是陈述句的语序。

句子示例

- **It is the general rule that** he is the first in our class. 通常情况下，他是我们班的第一名。
- **It is the general rule that** the boss likes diligent employees. 通常情况下，老板喜欢勤奋的员工。
- **It is the general rule that** the teacher will say something about the details before the exam. 通常情况下，老师会在考试之前说一些详细情况。

重点单词

manage ['mænɪdʒ] *v.* 经营，管理

personally ['pɜ:sənəlɪ] *ad.* 亲自地，个人地，私自地

diligent ['dɪlɪdʒənt] *a.* 勤奋的，努力的

employee [ɪm'plɔɪi:] *n.* 职工，员工

detail ['di:teɪl] *n.* 叙述，细节 *v.* 解释，详述

general ['dʒenrəl] *a.* 一般的，总体的，普遍的 *n.* 一般，普遍

17. There be... ……有……

对话示例

— Wow! How beautiful your house is!	— 哇！你家真漂亮！
— Thank you.	— 谢谢。
— Can you show me around your house?	— 可以带我参观一下你家吗？
— OK, my pleasure. **There are** four bedrooms, a living room, a kitchen, and a bathroom in my house.	— 好的，我很乐意。我家有四间卧室，一个客厅，一间厨房，和一间浴室。
— Oh, there is a garden here.	— 这儿还有一个花园。
— Yes, my mother often grows flowers and plants here.	— 是的，我妈妈经常在这里种一些花花草草。

句型分析

There be... 本句型是很常用的一种句型，常用于表达某地存在某人或者某物。

句子示例

- **There are** three little girls sitting on the lawn. 有三个小女孩坐在草坪上。
- **There are** 5 gouache paintings on the wall. 墙上有 5 张水粉画。
- **There are** a lot of notebooks on the desk. 课桌上有很多笔记本。

重点单词

lawn [lɔːn] *n.* 草坪，草地

gouache [gʊ'ɑːʃ] *n.* 水粉画

18. We scheduled... 我们安排了……

对话示例

— Are you ready for tomorrow's Halloween party?	— 明天的万圣节派对你们都准备好了吗?
— Yes, everything is OK.	— 是的，一切都准备好了。
— Can you tell me what your arrangement is?	— 你能告诉我你们的安排是什么吗?
— We have made a lot of pumpkin lights and **we scheduled** John to act like a ghost.	— 我们已经做了很多南瓜灯，然后我们安排约翰扮演一个鬼。

句型分析

We scheduled... 本句型中 scheduled 后面可以直接跟名词。也可以是 schedule sb to do sth，意为“安排某人做某事”。

句子示例

- **We scheduled** the young man to deliver the goods, because he was strong. 我们安排了这个年轻人去送货，因为他比较强壮。
- **We scheduled** a sales promotion. 我们安排了一场促销活动。
- **We scheduled** a press conference. 我们安排了一场新闻发布会。

重点单词

schedule ['ʃedjuːl] *v.* 安排 *n.* 时刻表

ghost [gəʊst] *n.* 鬼

deliver [dɪ'lɪvə] *v.* 传送，传递

conference ['kɒnfərəns] *n.* 会议

19. I feel like... 我感觉像是……

对话示例

— How about your computer skills?	— 你的电脑技术怎么样?
— I majored in computer science in the university.	— 我大学时主修计算机科学专业。
— That's great. I don't know how to create a form to record the results.	— 那太好了。我不知道如何制作表格记录结果。
— I can teach you. In fact, it's very easy.	— 我可以教你。事实上，很简单。
— Thank you very much. **I feel like** a student.	— 谢谢你。我感觉自己像是一个学生。

句型分析

I feel like...该句型中含有feel like，意为“感觉……，想要……”，其用法是feel like 后加名词表示“感觉像是……”；feel like doing sth，表示“想要……”之意。

句子示例

- **I feel like** a superhero at the moment. 我现在感觉自己像是一个超级英雄。
- **I feel like** a stranger. 我感觉自己像是一个陌生人。
- **I feel like** having a walk with him. 我想和他去散步。

重点单词

major ['meɪdʒə] *v.* 主修，专攻

superhero ['su:pəhɪərəʊ] *n.* 超级英雄

stranger ['streɪndʒə] *n.* 陌生人

Unit 2 比较

1. The boy is as... as... 那个男孩和……一样……

对话示例

— Look, the boy on the silver bicycle is Max.	— 看，在银色自行车上的男孩是麦克斯。
— I know him. He is Nancy's nephew.	— 我认识他。他是南茜的侄子。
— Max is very tall.	— 麦克斯很高。
— **The boy is as** tall **as** Nancy's son.	— 这个男孩和南茜的儿子一样高。
— They are both very handsome.	— 他们都很英俊。

句型分析

The boy is as... as... 该句型中的 as...as 是同级相比较，as+ 形容词 / 副词 +as 表示“和……一样……”，如：as beautiful as，“和……一样漂亮”。

句子示例

- **The boy is as** handsome **as** that boy. 这个男孩和那个男孩一样英俊。
- **The boy is as** clever **as** his uncle. 这个男孩和他的叔叔一样聪明。
- **The boy is as** powerful **as** his father. 这个男孩和他爸爸一样有力量。

重点单词

silver ['sɪlvə] *n.* 银，银色 *a.* 银色的

bicycle ['baɪsɪkl] *n.* 自行车

handsome ['hænsəm] *a.* 英俊的

powerful ['paʊəfl] *a.* 强大的，有效的

2. Bill walks as... as... 比尔走路和……一样……

对话示例

— Do you know Bill, the manager of our department?	— 你知道比尔吗？我们部门的经理。
— Yeah. What's the matter?	— 知道。怎么了？
— **Bill walks as** handsome **as** a model.	— 比尔走路和模特一样帅气。
— I heard he was a model before he came into our company.	— 我听说他在来我们公司之前就是一个模特。
— That was a wonderful experience for him.	— 那对他来说真是一段很精彩的经历。

句型分析

Bill walks as... as... 其中 Bill 是主语，谓语动词是 walks，因为主语 Bill 是第三人称单数，所以动词 walk 要变第三人称单数形式。

句子示例

- **Bill walks as** quickly **as** Jerry. 比尔走路和杰瑞一样快。
- **Bill walks as** slowly **as** an old man. 比尔走路和老人一样慢。
- **Bill walks as** elegant **as** a lady. 比尔走路和女士一样优雅。

重点单词

experience [ɪk'spɪərɪəns] *n.* 经验，经历

elegant ['elɪgənt] *a.* 优雅的

3. ... not as well as... 没……好

对话示例

— Can you balance on a ball like me?	— 你能像我一样在球上保持平衡吗？
— Let me try.	— 让我试一试。
— OK. Here you are. You must pay attention to the safety.	— 可以，给你。你必须注意安全。
— I am **not as well as** you.	— 我没你做的好。
— You had better try more than once. And you can find the tricks.	— 你最好多试几次。然后你就能找到其中的诀窍。

句型分析

...not as well as... 本句型中 as well as 表示“和……一样好”，它的否定形式是 not as well as，意为“没有……一样好”。

句子示例

- The green apple is **not as well as** the red apple. 绿苹果没有红苹果好。
- The new edition of the book is **not as well as** the original book. 这本新版书没有原版书好。
- This new advertisement is **not as well as** the old one. 这个新广告没有旧的好。

重点单词

balance ['bæləns] *v.* & *n.* 平衡；使平衡

attention [ə'tenʃn] *n.* 注意，注意力

trick [trɪk] *n.* 戏法，诀窍

edition [ɪ'dɪʃn] *n.* 版本，版次

4. Peter...as ... as ever. 彼得像往常一样……

对话示例

— How are you all keeping these days?	— 你们这些天还好吗？
— Very well. How about you?	— 很好。你们呢？
— Not bad. Look at the photo which we took in Australia last month.	— 还不错。看看上个月我们在澳大利亚拍的这张照片。
— Very beautiful. **Peter** is **as** happy **as ever**.	— 很漂亮。彼得像往常一样开心。
— Yeah, he is always happy.	— 是啊，他总是开开心心的。

句型分析

Peter...as ... as ever. 此句型中，Peter 是主语，as...as 表示“和……一样”，ever 是副词，表示“曾经，以前”。

句子示例

- **Peter** is **as** romantic **as ever**. 彼得像往常一样浪漫。
- **Peter** is **as** funny **as ever**. 彼得像往常一样滑稽。
- **Peter** is **as** humorous **as ever**. 彼得像往常一样幽默。

重点单词

always ['ɔ:lweɪz] *ad.* 总是，老是

romantic [rəʊ'mæntɪk] *a.* 浪漫的

humorous ['hju:mərəs] *a.* 幽默的

5. The more..., the more... 越……就越……

对话示例

— Which subject do you like best?	— 你最喜欢哪个学科?
— I like English. What about you?	— 我喜欢英语。你呢?
— I am good at math. But I am useless at English. I think English is the most difficult language in the world.	— 我擅长数学。但我不擅长英语。我认为英语是这个世界上最难的语言。
— Don't think like that! **The more** you practice, **the more** progress you will make.	— 别那样想！你练习越多，进步就越大。

句型分析

The more..., the more... 该句型常表示“越……就越……”，是一个复合句，其中前面的句子是状语从句，后面的句子是主句。

句子示例

- **The more** you work hard, **the more** money you will make. 你工作越努力，赚的钱就越多。
- **The more** you get, **the more** you want. 得到的越多，想要的就越多。
- **The more** he learns, **the more** he wants to learn. 他学到的知识越多，就越想学习。

重点单词

subject ['sʌbdʒɪkt] *n.* 主题，学科，科目

useless ['ju:sləs] *a.* 无用的，无效的

practice ['præktɪs] *v.* 练习，实践

6. ... be more... than... ……比……更……

对话示例

— How many people are there in your family?	— 你家里有几口人?
— Four. My father, my mother, my sister, and I.	— 四口，我爸爸，我妈妈，我姐姐，还有我。
— Wow, what a big family! I once met your sister. She is very beautiful.	— 哇，真是一个大家庭。我曾经见过你姐姐。她很漂亮。
— Yes. And now, she **is more** beautiful **than** my mother.	— 是的。现在，她比我妈妈更漂亮。

句型分析

... be more... than... 此句型是含有比较级的句型：A+ be 动词 + 比较级 +than +B，此句型仅用于两者进行比较。

句子示例

- The steak **is more** delicious **than** the chicken. 牛排比鸡肉更美味。
- This question **is more** difficult **than** that one. 这道题比那道题更难。
- The story book **is more** interesting **than** the comic book. 故事书比漫画书更有趣。

重点单词

once [wʌns] *ad.* 一次

delicious [dɪ'lɪʃəs] *a.* 美味的

steak [steɪk] *n.* 牛排

comic ['kɒmɪk] *a.* 连环画的 *n.* 连环漫画

7. He is the most...of all. 他是最……的。

对话示例

— Do you remember the Professor Wang in our university?	— 你还记得我们大学时代的王教授吗?
— Yeah, I remember him.	— 我记得他。
— He will attend our ten-year reunion this year.	— 他今年将会出席我们十周年的同学会。

— That's great. I really miss him.	— 那太好了。我真的很想念他。
— **He is the most** knowledgeable professor **of all.**	— 他是知识最渊博的教授。

句型分析

He is the most...of all. 该句型是含有最高级的句型：A +the+ 最高级 +of all，最高级通常是三者或三者以上进行比较，最高级前加 the。

句子示例

- **He is the most** important person **of all.** 他是最重要的人。
- **He is the most** intelligent student **of all.** 他是最聪明的学生。
- **He is the most** interesting marketing director **of all.** 他是最有趣的市场总监。

重点单词

university [ˌjuːnɪˈvɜːsətɪ] *n.* 大学

knowledgeable [ˈnɒlɪdʒəbl] *a.* 知识渊博的

8. She is a most...woman. 她是一个非常……的女人。

对话示例

— A new president will take over our company next week.	— 下周，新总裁将会接管我们公司。
— I heard the new president is a woman.	— 我听说这个新总裁是位女士。
— Really? I think it's impossible.	— 真的吗？我认为那是不可能的。
— I'm not fooling you. Our manager says **she is a most** capable **woman.**	— 我没有骗你。我们经理说她是一个非常有能力的女人。

句型分析

She is a most...woman. 该句型是一个简单的主系表结构，其中 she 是主语，is 是系动词，a most...woman 作表语。

句子示例

She is a most beautiful **woman**. 她是一个非常漂亮的女人。

She is a most different **woman**. 她是一个非常不同的女人。

She is a most experienced **woman**. 她是一个非常有见识的女人。

重点单词

president ['prezɪdənt] *n.* 总统，总裁，校长

capable ['keɪpəbl] *a.* 有能力的

experienced [ɪk'spɪərɪənst] *a.* 有见识的

9. He is the last person... 他是最不可能……的人。

对话示例

— I need a person who can help me to make the formal tender.	— 我需要一个人帮我制作一份正式的招标书。
— I think Jason is qualified for the job.	— 我认为杰森能胜任这项工作。
— Why?	— 为什么?
— Because he has a high sales performance record.	— 因为他有很高的销售业绩记录。
— But Jason is careless. **He is the last person** to be fit for the job.	— 但是杰森很粗心。他是最不适合这份工作的人。

句型分析

He is the last person... 该句型中 he 是主语，is 是系动词，the last person 是表语，此句型的后面可以跟一个定语从句，修饰 the last person。

句子示例

- **He is the last person** I want to trust. 他是我最不想信任的人。
- **He is the last person** to do such things. 他是最不可能做这些事的人。
- **He is the last person** whom they would have suspected. 他是最不可能引起他们怀疑的人。

重点单词

qualified ['kwɒlɪfaɪd] *a.* 有资格的

suspect [sə'spekt] *v.* 怀疑，不信任

10. ...is the last thing that I want to do. ……是我最不想做的事。

对话示例

— What are you going to do on the weekend?	— 你们周末打算做什么?
— We will go to the Disneyland. Would you want to go with us?	— 我们打算去迪士尼乐园。你愿意跟我们一块去吗?
— That sounds great. I think the most exciting thing is the Roller Coaster.	— 那听起来很不错。我觉得最兴奋的事就是坐过山车。
— Riding on the Roller Coaster **is the last thing that I want to do**.	— 坐过山车是我最不想做的事。

句型分析

...is the last thing that I want to do. 该句型中 that 是引导定语从句，先行词是 the last thing，这个句子里面的 that 作宾语，可以省略。

句子示例

- Learning math **is the last thing that I want to do**. 学习数学是我最不想做的事。
- Dancing **is the last thing that I want to do**. 跳舞是我最不想做的事。
- Bungee jumping **is the last thing that I want to do**. 蹦极是我最不想做的事。

重点单词

Disneyland ['dɪznɪlænd] *n.* 迪士尼乐园

roller ['rəʊlə] *n.* 滚筒

bungee ['bʌndʒɪ] *n.* 蹦极

11. Of the two..., I prefer the latter. 在两个……中，我更喜欢后者。

对话示例

— What a beautiful dress! Can I try it on?	— 多么漂亮的裙子！我能试一试吗?
— Sure. Here you are.	— 当然。给你。
— Thanks. But I think that green dress is more suitable for me.	— 谢谢。但是我认为那条绿色的更适合我。
— Both of them are fit for you. Which one do	— 两条都很适合你。你更喜欢哪一个呢?

you like better?	
— **Of the two** dresses, **I prefer the latter**.	— 在两条裙子中，我更喜欢后者。

句型分析

Of the two..., I prefer the latter. 该句型中，I 是主语，prefer 是谓语，the latter 是宾语，of the two... 是状语。

句子示例

- **Of the two** English dictionaries, **I prefer the latter**. 在两本英语字典中，我更喜欢后者。
- **Of the two** refrigerators, **I prefer the latter**. 在两个冰箱中，我更喜欢后者。
- **Of the two** roles, **I prefer the latter**. 在两个角色中，我更喜欢后者。

重点单词

suitable ['su:təbl] *a.* 合适的，适当的

dictionary ['dɪkʃənərɪ] *n.* 字典

role [rəʊl] *n.* 角色，作用

12. On one hand..., on the other hand... 一方面……，另一方面……

对话示例

— Do you like shopping online?	— 你喜欢网上购物吗?
— Yes, I think shopping online is the best way to save money.	— 喜欢，我认为网上购物是省钱的最佳途径。
— Shopping online is very popular among young people.	— 网上购物很受年轻人的青睐。
— **On one hand** shopping online is beneficial to us; **on the other hand**, it can assist us in saving money.	— 一方面，网上购物对我们是有利的，另一方面，它可以帮助我们节省金钱。

句型分析

On one hand..., on the other hand... 这个句型往往是指事物有两（多）个方面，但不一定是相对立的。

句子示例

- **On one hand** we have a lot of work to do, **on the other hand** we must attend the meeting.
  一方面我们有很多工作要做，另一方面我们必须得出席这个会议。
- **On one hand** you must clean up the office, **on the other hand** you must prepare the materials.
  一方面你必须打扫干净办公室，另一方面你必须准备好资料。
- **On one hand** it has lots of advantages, **on the other hand** there are some defects that cannot be ignored. 一方面它具有巨大的优势，另一方面也存在一些不能忽视的缺陷。

重点单词

popular ['pɒpjələ] *a.* 流行的　　assist [ə'sɪst] *v.* 帮助，援助
ignore [ɪg'nɔ:] *v.* 忽视

13. ... is one thing, ... is another. ……是一回事，……又是另一回事。

对话示例

— Tom promised me to finish the homework before our dinner.	— 汤姆答应我晚饭前会完成作业。
— To say **is one thing**; to do **is another**.	— 说是一回事，而做又是另一回事。
— Why did you say that?	— 为什么你会这样说？
— Because Tom is playing basketball with his friends at the moment.	— 因为此时此刻汤姆正和他的朋友们打篮球。
— You must be joking!	— 你一定是在跟我开玩笑吧！

句型分析

... is one thing, ... is another. 该句型中，用 one...another 不确定范围中的人或物中的“一个……另一个”。

句子示例

- To read the book **is one thing**, to teach **is another**. 读书是一回事，教学又是另一回事。
- Listening to the music **is one thing**, understanding the music **is another**. 听音乐是一回事，理解音乐又是另一回事。
- Job creation **is one thing**, who gains from it **is another**. 创造就业机会是一回事，谁从中受益又是另一回事。

重点单词

another [ə'nʌðə] *a. & pron.* 又一个，另一个

moment ['məʊmənt] *n.* 片刻，瞬间

creation [krɪ'eɪʃn] *n.* 制造，创造

14. Some..., and the others... 一些……，而另一些……

对话示例

— Is our company going to hold a trade fair at the conference and exhibition center?	— 我们公司要在会展中心开一个贸易展销会吗?
— Yes, we have been preparing for a very long time.	— 是的，我们已经准备很久了。
— Have you prepared the exhibits for the exhibition?	— 这次展览的展示品都已经准备好了吗?
— Of course. **Some** are in the meeting room, **and the others** are in the warehouse.	— 当然。一些在会议室里，而另一些在仓库里。

句型分析

Some..., and the others... 该句型中，some 指“一些”，the others 指“剩下的另一些”，注意 some 加上 the others 一定能涵盖全体。

句子示例

- **Some** are dancing, **and the others** are watching TV. 一些人在跳舞，而另一些人在看电视。
- **Some** are from the organizer, **and the others** are from the organizing committee. 一些人来自主办方，而另一些人来自组委会。
- **Some** are reference samples, **and the others** are sealed samples. 一些是参考样品，而另一些是密封样品。

重点单词

conference ['kɒnfərəns] *n.* 会议

committee [kə'mɪtɪ] *n.* 委员会

reference ['refrəns] *n.* 参考，涉及

15. Some..., and some... 一些……，而另一些……

对话示例

— There are so many people in the market.	— 商场里的人好多。
— Yeah, many markets cut prices just before Christmas in an attempt to spur sales.	— 是啊，许多商场在圣诞节前降价，试图刺激销售。
— Do they all come here for the discounted products?	— 他们都是来这里买打折商品的吗?
— Not really. **Some** are coming for the discounted products, **and some** will go to see a film.	— 不全是。一些人是来买打折商品的，而另一些是来看电影的。

句型分析

Some..., and some... 此句型中，两个 some 均表示的是“一些”，此处的“一些”不是特指哪一部分，仅是简单的陈述。

句子示例

- **Some** students will take part in the outing, **and some** students will go to the holiday camp. 一些学生会参加郊游，而另一些会去营地。
- **Some** are responsible for selling products, **and some** are in charge for packing the products. 一些人负责销售产品，而另一些负责包装产品。
- **Some** books are in the library, **and some** are in the classroom. 一些书在图书馆里，而另一些在教室里。

重点单词

attempt [ə'tempt] *v.* & *n.* 尝试

discount ['dɪskaʊnt] *v.* 折扣

outing ['aʊtɪŋ] *n.* 远足，郊游

16. ... be far away from... ……离……很远。

对话示例

— What's the matter with you?	— 你怎么了?
— I have a bad cold.	— 我得了重感冒。
— Have you seen the doctor?	— 你看过医生了吗?
— Yes, the doctor says I should stay in bed and stay away from the rich food and alcoholic drink.	— 看过了，医生让我卧床休息，远离油腻的食物和含酒精的饮料。
— One last thing. You should **be far away from** smoking.	— 最后补充一点。你应该远离吸烟。

句型分析

... be far away from... 此句型表示“离……很远”，只表示距离；类似的句型 be far from...，除了表示距离“远离”，还有“远远不，完全不”之意。

句子示例

- If you want to be healthy, you should **be far away from** tobaccos. 如果你想健康，你应该远离烟草。
- The company **is far away from** my hometown. 公司离我家乡很远。
- Children should **be far away from** this medicine. 儿童应该远离这种药品。

重点单词

alcoholic [ˌælkəˈhɒlɪk] *a.* 含酒精的　　　　tobacco [təˈbækəʊ] *n.* 烟草

17. ... be no more ...than... ……和……一样不……

对话示例

— Can you find the way to the Eiffel Tower?	— 你能找到去埃菲尔铁塔的路吗?
— I think we are lost.	— 我想我们迷路了。
— Perhaps, we can ask the local people, but I can't speak French.	— 或许，我们可以问问当地人，但是我不会说法语。
— I **am no more** able to speak French **than** you are.	— 和你一样，我也不会说法语。

句型分析

... be no more ...than... 该句型常用于比较两种事物，no more ... than 表示对两者都否定，相当于 neither ... nor。

句子示例

- She **is no more** a teacher **than** an accountant. 她不是老师，也不是会计。
- Your final decision **is no more** here **than** there. 你的最终决定根本就不重要。
- He **is no more** diligent **than** you. 你不勤奋，他也不勤奋。

重点单词

perhaps [pə'hæps] *ad.* 或许，也许

accountant [ə'kaʊntənt] *n.* 会计

diligent ['dɪlɪdʒənt] *a.* 勤奋的

18. ... be no less ...than... ……和……一样……

对话示例

— We will have a standard meeting on Friday at 10:00 a.m.	— 周五上午十点我们会开例会。
— I will let the secretary to inform them immediately.	— 我会让秘书立刻通知他们。
— Please inform Linda start the meeting on time.	— 请通知琳达准时开会。
— She **is no less** punctual **than** you are.	— 她和你一样很守时。
— Don't let anybody interrupt us at that time, please.	— 开会期间请不要让任何人打扰我们。

句型分析

... be no less ...than... 该句型是英语中的比较句型，常常用于比较两种事物，no less ...than 表示对两者都有肯定之意。

句子示例

- This person **is no less** diligent **than** he used to be. 这个人和从前一样勤奋。

• Her mind **is no less** alert **than** mine. 她的思路和我一样敏捷。

• The manager **is no less** careful **than** his secretary. 经理和他的秘书一样细心。

重点单词

immediately [ɪ'mi:dɪətlɪ] *ad.* 立刻地，马上

punctual ['pʌŋktʃʊəl] *a.* 守时的，准时的

19. ... be...times as...as... ……是……的……倍

对话示例

— I am conducting a market research.	— 我正在做一个市场调研。
— I made the previous market research. It took me seven days to finish it.	— 之前的那个市场调研是我做的。它花费了我 7 天时间。
— It's not too long. The time I spend on this market research **is** two **times as** much **as** yours.	— 那还不算太长。我在市场调研上所花费的时间是你的两倍。
— The market situation is better than we expected.	— 市场情况比我们预料的要好。

句型分析

... be...times as...as... 该句型常常用于倍数的表达，其结构为：主 +be+ 数词 +times+ as+ 形容词 +as，表示“……是……的……倍”。

句子示例

• The number of my toys **is** three **times as** many **as** yours. 我的玩具数量有你的三倍那么多。

• The distance from home to the park **is** two **times as** far **as** the distance from company. 从家到公园的距离是公司到公园距离的两倍。

• The time he takes **is** five **times as** much **as** yours. 他花的时间是你的五倍。

重点单词

research [rɪ'sɜ:tʃ] *n.* 研究，调查

situation [ˌsɪtʃʊ'eɪʃn] *n.* 情况，形式，局面

distance ['dɪstəns] *n.* 距离，路程

20. I bought... and..., but I prefer the former. 我买了……和……，但我更喜欢前者。

对话示例

— What did you buy in the market on the weekend?	— 你周末在商场买了什么？
— I bought a dress and a pair of shoes. What about you?	— 我买了一条连衣裙和一双鞋子。你呢？
— **I bought** a story book **and** an English book, **but I prefer the former**.	— 我买了一本故事书和一本英语书，但我更喜欢前者。
— Why do you like the story book?	— 为什么你喜欢故事书？
— Because it's very interesting.	— 因为它很有趣。

句型分析

I bought... and..., but I prefer the former. 此句型用于将购买的东西进行比较时，该句型是 but 引导的表示转折的并列句；prefer 表示“更喜欢”，其后可跟名词、动名词，以及动词不定式。

句子示例

- **I bought** a sports car and a commercial vehicle, **but I prefer the former**. 我买了一辆跑车和一辆商务车，但我更喜欢前者。
- **I bought** a bouquet of lilies and a bouquet of roses, **but I prefer the former**. 我买了一束百合花和一束玫瑰花，但我更喜欢前者。
- **I bought a** desktop computer and a laptop, **but I prefer the former**. 我买了一台台式电脑和一台笔记本电脑，但我更喜欢前者。

重点单词

commercial [kəˈmɜːʃl] *a.* 商业的，贸易的

vehicle [ˈviːəkl] *n.* 车辆，交通工具

bouquet [bʊˈkeɪ] *n.* 花束

Unit 3 转折

1. He is not so much...as... 与其说他是……，不如说他是……

对话示例

— Look at that man, his face very pale and his lips colorless.	— 看那个男人，他面色苍白，嘴唇发青。
— He must be freezing. He is staring at the window.	— 他一定很冷。他一直盯着窗户看。
— **He is not so much** cold **as** he wants to close the window.	— 与其说他很冷，不如说他想关窗户。
— Let us help him to close the window.	— 让我们帮他把窗户关上吧。

句型分析

He is not so much...as... 该句型中，not so much...as 是一个常用的并列连词，其含义相当于 rather than，意为“与其说是……倒不如说是……”；和其他连接词一样，它可以连接词与词，短语与短语，以及句子与句子。

句子示例

- **He is not so much** angry **as** disappointed. 与其说他是生气，不如说他是失望。
- **He is not so much** a journalist **as** an artist. 与其说他是新闻工作者，不如说他是艺术家。
- **He is not so much** hungry **as** thirsty. 与其说他是饿了，不如说他是渴了。

重点单词

pale [peɪl] *a.* 苍白的
colorless ['kʌləlɪs] *a.* 无色的
stare [steə] *v.* 盯着看

2. She likes... more than... 她喜欢……胜过……

对话示例

— What's your hobby?	— 你的兴趣爱好是什么?
— I am interested in collecting stamps. What's your favorite pastime?	— 我对收集邮票感兴趣。你最喜欢的业余爱好是什么?
— I like playing the piano, but my sister doesn't.	— 我喜欢弹钢琴，但是我妹妹不喜欢。
— She must like drawing. I have seen her pictures.	— 她一定喜欢画画。我见过她画的画。
— But **she likes** dancing **more than** drawing.	— 但她喜欢跳舞胜过画画。

句型分析

She likes... more than... 常常用于两者进行比较时，主语 she 是第三人称单数，谓语动词要用第三人称单数形式 likes。

句子示例

- **She likes** playing basketball **more than** playing football. 她喜欢打篮球胜过踢足球。
- **She likes** apples **more than** bananas. 她喜欢苹果胜过香蕉。
- **She likes** physics **more than** chemistry. 她喜欢物理胜过化学。

重点单词

pastime ['pɑ:staɪm] *n.* 消遣，娱乐

physics ['fɪzɪks] *n.* 物理

chemistry ['kemɪstrɪ] *n.* 化学

3. Even if ..., we... 即使明天……，我们也会……

对话示例

— The local college will hold a Halloween party on Monday.	— 当地的大学本周一将会举行万圣节聚会。
— That's great. I really want to go. Would you want to go with us?	— 那太好了。我真的很想去。你们愿意跟我一起去吗?

— We'd love to. But I don't prepare the costume for the party.	— 我们很想去。但是我们还没有准备好万圣节的服装。
— Let's prepare together. You must be going to the party.	— 让我们一起准备吧。你们必须要来参加。
— **Even if** it rains, **we** will attend the party on time.	— 即使会下雨，我们也会准时到那里。

句型分析

Even if..., we... 该句型中包含 even if 引导的让步状语从句，even though 和 even if 均可用于引导让步状语从句，even if 引导从句往往是假设性的，而 even though 引导的从句内容往往是真实的。

句子示例

- **Even if** you don't succeed, **we** will stand by you. 即使你不成功，我们也会支持你。
- **Even if** it rains tomorrow, **we** will keep on running. 即使明天下雨，我们也会坚持跑步。
- **Even if** he doesn't support us, **we** won't change our plan. 即使他不支持我们，我们也不会改变计划。

重点单词

Halloween [ˌhæləʊ'i:n] *n.* 万圣节前夜

costume ['kɒstju:m] *n.* 服装，演出服

succeed [sək'si:d] *v.* 成功，继承

4. Though..., you... 即使……，你……

对话示例

— Where is the key to the meeting room?	— 会议室的钥匙在哪里?
— I don't know. You can ask Mary.	— 我不知道。你可以问问玛丽。
— But Mary asked for leave to rest. Can you help me to find it?	— 但是玛丽请假休息了。你能帮我找一下吗?
— I am so sorry. I have much work to do.	— 很抱歉。我有很多工作要做。
— **Though** it's not your job, **you** should offer your help.	— 即使这不是你的工作，你也应该提供帮助。

句型分析

Though..., you... 该句型中含有 though 引导的让步状语从句，表示“虽然”， although 和 though 两者大致同义，可替换，但是 although 比 though 更为正式。

句子示例

- **Though** you are poor, **you** are still happy. 即使你很穷，你也依然很快乐。
- **Though** the boy is very naughty, **you** should control yourself. 即使这个男孩很淘气，你也应该控制好自己。
- **Though** you don't know him, **you** should clap for him. 即使你不认识他，你也应该为他鼓掌。

重点单词

though [ðəʊ] *conj.* 虽然，尽管

offer ['ɒfə] *v.* 提供，给予

naughty ['nɔ:tɪ] *a.* 顽皮的，淘气的

5. He... instead of... 他不是……而是……

对话示例

— How long have you been swimming?	— 你游泳多长时间了?
— About two years.	— 大约两年。
— Wow, you must be good at swimming. I am learning swimming these days.	— 哇，你一定很擅长游泳。我这些天一直在学游泳。
— Who teaches you?	— 谁教你的?
— My father. **He** is a very strict trainer **instead of** a fond father.	— 我爸爸。他不是一位慈祥的父亲，而是一个严格的教练。

句型分析

He... instead of... 该句型中包含一个介词短语 instead of，意为“代替”，其后可跟名词、代词、动名词，以及从句等。

句子示例

- **He** spends more time traveling **instead of** working. 他不是花更多的时间工作，而是旅游。
- **He** went to borrow a book **instead of** buying one. 他去借了一本书，而不是买了一本书。

• **He** must make up his mind **instead of** losing his heart. 他不是失去信心，而是下定决心。

重点单词

fond [fɒnd] *a.* 喜欢的，溺爱的
spend [spend] *v.* 花钱
borrow ['bɒrəʊ] *v.* 借钱

6. Although..., I will... 尽管……，我也会……

对话示例

— Are you learning ballet recently?	— 你最近在学习芭蕾舞吗?
— Learning ballet is just an avocation with me.	— 学习芭蕾舞只不过是我的一项业余爱好。
— I think learning ballet must be hard work.	— 我认为学习芭蕾舞很辛苦。
— **Although** it's hard work, **I will** stick with it.	— 尽管很辛苦，我也会一直坚持下去。

句型分析

Although..., I will... 该句型中含有 although 引导的让步状语从句，although 引导的从句不能与 but，however 连用，但可与 yet, still 连用。

句子示例

• **Although** there are many difficulties, **I will** try my best to make greater achievements. 尽管有很多困难，我也会尽全力取得更大的成就。
• **Although** I fail the exam, **I will** never give up. 尽管我考试不及格，我也绝不放弃。
• **Although** the problem is very complicated, **I will** solve it. 尽管问题很复杂，我也会解决。

重点单词

although [ɔ:l'ðəu] *conj.* 虽然，尽管
ballet ['bæleɪ] *n.* 芭蕾舞
avocation [ˌævəʊ'keɪʃn] *n.* 业余爱好
complicated ['kɒmplɪkeɪtɪd] *a.* 结构复杂的

7. Regardless of..., he... 不管……，他……

对话示例

— I want to buy some stock to make a quick buck.	— 我想炒股，赚点快钱。
— Which company are you going to buy into?	— 你打算买哪家公司的股票?
— I am going to put all my money in Baidu.	— 我打算把钱都放在百度上。
— Peter has sold his stock last week. This week the stock is through roof.	— 彼得上周把他的股票卖了。这周股价涨得很高。
— What a pity!	— 真遗憾!
— **Regardless of** how I tried to persuade Peter, **he** still sold his stock.	— 不管我怎么劝他，他仍然把股票卖了。

句型分析

Regardless of..., he... 该句型中，regardless of 其后可跟名词或者名词短语，regardless of 也可以引导让步状语从句。

句子示例

- **Regardless of** whether the manager is right or not, **he** has to abide by his plan. 不管经理正确与否，他不得不服从他的计划。
- **Regardless of** who caused it, **he** must be responsible for this. 不管是谁造成的，他必须对此负责任。
- **Regardless of** how often I correct him, **he** always makes the same mistake. 不管我怎样频繁地告诫他，他总是犯同样的错误。

重点单词

regardless [rɪ'gɑ:dləs] *ad.* 无论如何，不管怎样

stock [stɒk] *n.* 股票

through [θru:] *prep.* 通过，穿过

8. You could have... 你原本可以……

对话示例

— I have not finished the sales task of this month.	— 我没有完成这个月的销售任务。
— What happened to you?	— 发生了什么事?
— Some of my goods were seized by the customs.	— 我的一些货物被海关扣押了。
— In that regard, **you could have** finished the task.	— 这样看来，你原本可以完成销售任务的。

句型分析

You could have... 常用于表示过去本来有能力做到某事却没有做到，You could have 后跟动词的过去分词。

句子示例

- **You could have** done your homework. 你原本可以完成作业的。
- **You could have** prevented the accident. 你原本可以阻止这次的交通事故。
- **You could have** avoided saying anything to her. 你原本可以避免跟她说话。

重点单词

custom ['kʌstəm] *n.* 习惯，海关

prevent [prɪ'vent] *v.* 预防，阻碍

avoid [ə'vɔɪd] *v.* 避开，避免

9. I should have... 我本应该……

对话示例

— When is the meeting?	— 会议是什么时候?
— At 3:00 this afternoon.	— 下午三点整。
— How long do you expect the meeting to take?	— 会议开多长时间?
— About two hours.	— 大约两个小时。
— But there is another meeting at 4:30 in the meeting room.	— 但是在 4:30 会议室里还有一个会议。
— **I should have** told you to arrange it earlier.	— 我本应该提前让你安排的。

句型分析

I should have... 常用于表示过去应该做某事却没有做到。should have done 和 could have done 的区别在于，前者表示过去本应该做某事却没有做，后者表示过去有能力做某事却没有做。

句子示例

- **I should have** listened to the English report. 我本应该听英语新闻报道的。
- **I should have** told the truth to my parents. 我本应该告诉我父母实情的。
- **I should have** helped to build the relationship. 我本应该帮助建立关系的。

重点单词

expect [ɪk'spekt] *v.* 期望，预料

arrange [ə'reɪndʒ] *v.* 分类，整理

relationship [rɪ'leɪʃnʃɪp] *n.* 关系

10. You needn't have... 你原本不必……

对话示例

— When does the birthday party begin?	— 生日聚会什么时候开始?
— At eight o'clock tonight.	— 今晚 8 点整。
— But you told me to arrive here before seven o'clock.	— 但是你告诉我 7 点之前到这里。
— I am so sorry that I forgot to inform you to come at eight.	— 我很抱歉忘记通知你 8 点过来了。
— **You needn't have** told me to come earlier.	— 你原本不必让我早点过来的。

句型分析

You needn't have... 该句型通常用于表示“某事已经做了，但后来觉得没必要去做”，因此含有责备和遗憾之意。

句子示例

- **You needn't have** asked anybody to forgive you. 你原本不必乞求任何人的原谅。
- **You needn't have** added an item to the agenda. 你原本不必在议程里加一个议项。
- **You needn't have** decided a definite date. 你原本不必定出一个确切的日子。

重点单词

arrive [ə'raɪv] *v.* 到达

forgive [fə'gɪv] *v.* 原谅

agenda [ə'dʒendə] *n.* 议事日程

11. I ... only to... 我……，却……

对话示例

— Where have you been?	— 你去哪里了?
— I have been to the opera house to find Lisa.	— 我去戏剧院找丽萨了。
— Have you found her?	— 你找到她了吗?
— I arrived there **only to** find she has already got off work.	— 我到那里时却发现她已经下班了。
— Maybe you can find her in the gymnasium near her house.	— 或许你可以在她家附近的健身房里找到她。

句型分析

I ... only to... 该句型中的 only to do 常常容易与 only doing 混淆，only to 意为“不料（却）……，结果（却）……"，表示一个没有料到的结果；only doing 意为“结果就……"，表示一个意料之中的结果。

句子示例

- I hurried to the museum, **only to** find it was closed. 我匆忙赶到博物馆，它却已经关门了。
- I went to see my friend, **only to** learn that she had left the city last month. 我去看我的朋友，不料听说她已经在上个月离开了这个城市。
- I am there **only to** satisfy my curiosity. 我去那里，纯粹是为了满足我的好奇心。

重点单词

opera ['ɒprə] *n.* 歌剧

gymnasium [dʒɪm'neɪzɪəm] *n.* 健身房

curiosity [ˌkjʊərɪ'ɒsətɪ] *n.* 好奇心

12. She ..., on the contrary, he... 她……，相反，他……

对话示例

— Most modern people like to eat fried food.	— 大多数现代人喜欢吃油炸食品。
— My children like the fried food very much. What about your daughter and your son?	— 我的孩子们非常喜欢吃油炸食品。你的女儿和儿子呢?
— **She** likes to eat fried food, **on the contrary**, **he** likes to eat the light food.	— 她喜欢吃油炸食品，相反，他喜欢吃清淡的食物。
— Fired food is bad for our health.	— 油炸食品对我们的健康有害。

句型分析

She ..., on the contrary, he... 该句型中，on the contrary 表示“相反”之意，用于加强语气，在此句中作插入语，用以连接两个独立的句子。

句子示例

- **She** thinks the dress is beautiful, **on the contrary**, **he** thinks it is ugly. 她认为这条裙子很漂亮，相反，他认为很丑。
- **She** likes sweet food, **on the contrary**, **he** likes spicy food. 她喜欢吃甜食，相反，他喜欢辣的。
- **She** is good at skateboarding, **on the contrary**, **he** is useless at skateboarding. 她擅长玩滑板，相反，他不擅长玩滑板。

重点单词

contrary ['kɒntrərɪ] *a.* 相反的

fried [fraɪd] *a.* 油炸的

spicy ['spaɪsɪ] *a.* 辛辣的

skateboarding ['skeɪtbɔ:dɪŋ] *n.* 滑板运动

13. I would rather...than... 我宁愿……也不愿……

对话示例

— We are going to London next month.	— 我们打算下个月去伦敦。
— How do you go there, by train or by plane?	— 你们如何去那里，乘火车还是乘飞机?
— **I would rather** go there by train **than** by plane.	— 我宁愿乘火车也不愿乘飞机。

— Why? The plane can save you a lot of time.	— 为什么？飞机可以节省很多时间。
— But I am susceptible to airsickness.	— 但是我很容易晕机。

句型分析

I would rather...than... 句中的 would rather...than 意为“宁愿……也不愿……”，用以表达主语的意愿，强调经过选择后做其中一件事，而不愿做另一件事。

句子示例

- **I would rather** watch TV at home **than** go to the cinema. 我宁愿在家看电视也不愿去电影院。
- **I would rather** walk there **than** take a bus. 我宁愿步行去那里也不愿乘公共汽车。
- **I would rather** refuse you **than** borrow money from my friends. 我宁愿拒绝你也不愿向朋友借钱。

重点单词

rather ['rɑːðə] *ad.* 宁愿

susceptible [sə'septəbl] *a.* 易受影响的

airsickness ['eəsɪknəs] *n.* 晕机

14. John..., and yet ... 约翰……，可是……

对话示例

— I took John to a party by train last week.	— 上周我带约翰乘火车参加了一个聚会。
— It was a pleasant trip.	— 那一定是一段很开心的旅程。
— John is curious about everything. He told a woman she was ugly.	— 约翰对一切事情都很好奇。他还对一位女士说她很丑。
— It must be very interesting.	— 那一定很有趣。
— **John** was amused, **and yet** I was very embarrassed.	— 约翰很开心，可是我很尴尬。

句型分析

John..., and yet he... 在该句型中，yet 用作连词，与 but 一样主要用于转折，意为“但是，而”，可与并列连词 and 或 but 连用，构成习语 and yet 和 but yet，且两者大致同义，均相当于表转折的 but。

句子示例

- **John** has failed the match, **and yet** he will try again. 约翰比赛失败了，可是他还要尝试。
- **John** was stern, **and yet** completely fair. 约翰很严厉，可是他完全公正。
- **John** has made some progress, **and yet** he still has a long way to go. 约翰虽然取得了进步，可是还远远不够。

重点单词

embarrassed [ɪm'bærəst] *a.* 尴尬的

stern [stɜ:n] *a.* 严厉的，严峻的

completely [kəm'pli:tlɪ] *ad.* 完全地

15. He worked hard only to... 他这么努力，却……

对话示例

— Do you remember our last manager?	— 你记得我们上一个经理吗?
— Yes, he is an amiable manager.	— 记得，他是一位和蔼可亲的经理。
— He worked overtime before he left our company.	— 他在离开公司前经常加班。
— **He worked hard only to** fail to take the project.	— 他这么努力，却没有拿下那个项目。
— That hit him substantially.	— 那件事对他打击很大。

句型分析

He worked hard only to... 该句型中，主语是 he，谓语是 worked，only to 表示“不料竟会”，后必须跟动词原形。

句子示例

- **He worked hard only to** lose his job. 他这么努力，却丢了自己的工作。
- **He worked hard only to** go bankrupt. 他这么努力，却破产了。
- **He worked hard only to** owe a couple of million dollars. 他这么努力，却欠了几百万美元的债。

重点单词

amiable ['eɪmɪəbl] *a.* 和蔼可亲的

bankrupt ['bæŋkrʌpt] *a.* 破产的

substantially [səb'stænʃəlɪ] *ad.* 本质上，充分地

16. The boy..., whereas the others... 这个男孩……，而其他人……

对话示例

— Here is a photograph that was taken in Australia.	— 这是我们在澳大利亚拍的一张照片。
— **The boy** is running on the lawn, **whereas the others** are looking at him.	— 这个男孩正在草坪上跑，其他人正在看着他。
— Yes, the boy is my little son Robert.	— 是啊，这个男孩就是我的小儿子，罗伯特。
— Really? He was a fat boy at that time.	— 真的吗？他那个时候很胖。
— He is thinner than before.	— 他比之前瘦了。

句型分析

The boy..., whereas the others... 该句型中，whereas 是一个连词，可以引出表示对比、对立或直接相反的状语从句，比较正式，通常位于句中，也可置于句首。

句子示例

- **The boy** is playing football, **whereas the others** are playing cards. 这个男孩正在踢足球，而其他人正在打牌。
- **The boy** walks to school, **whereas the others** go to school on the school bus. 这个男孩步行去上学，而其他人坐校车去上学。
- **The boy** will go to Canada, **whereas the others** will go to America. 这个男孩将去加拿大，而其他人将去美国。

重点单词

whereas [ˌweər'æz] *conj.* 鉴于，然而

lawn [lɔːn] *n.* 草坪，草地

photograph ['fəʊtəgrɑːf] *n.* 照片

17. He is ... while his brother is ... 他正在……而他的哥哥正在……

对话示例

— Tell Tom and his brother to play basketball with us.	— 让汤姆和他哥哥跟我们一起去打篮球。
— I don't think they will go with us.	— 我认为他们不会跟我们一起去的。
— What is Tom doing?	— 汤姆正在干什么?
— **He is** playing the computer game, **while his brother is** playing chess with his father.	— 他正在玩电脑游戏，而他的哥哥正在和他爸爸下象棋。

句型分析

He is ... while his brother is ... 该句型中，while 作连词，在此句型中连接两个并列的句子，表示对比关系，while 也可以引导时间状语从句和让步状语从句。

句子示例

- **He is** listening to the music, **while his brother is** reading a book. 他正在听音乐，而他的哥哥正在看书。
- **He is** singing, **while his brother is** dancing. 他正在唱歌，而他的哥哥正在跳舞。
- **He is** doing his homework, **while his brother is** going for a walk. 他正在写作业，而他的哥哥正在散步。

重点单词

while [waɪl] *conj.* 在……期间，而

chess [tʃes] *n.* 棋，国际象棋

homework ['həʊmwɜːk] *n.* 家庭作业

18. In spite of... 尽管……

对话示例

— I'm under a lot of pressure.	— 我压力好大。
— The planning application will be ready to start operation next month.	— 这个项目的实施方案将于下个月投入运营。
— But there are still many problems to be	— 但是仍然还有很多问题需要解决。

solved.	
— Take it easy. **In spite of** many difficulties, we will stick to it.	— 放松点。尽管我们有很多困难，我们还会坚持到底。
— I really want to take a vacation.	— 我真想去度假。

句型分析

In spite of... 该句型中，in spite of 表示“尽管，虽然”，后可加单词或短语，在句中作状语，也可引导让步状语从句。

句子示例

- **In spite of** the rain, we will go to the cinema. 尽管下雨了，我们还会去看电影。
- **In spite of** many mistakes he has made, I will choose to believe him. 尽管他犯了很多错误，我还是选择相信他。
- **In spite of** her disappointment, she still encouraged him. 尽管她很失望，她还是鼓励他。

重点单词

pressure ['preʃə] *n.* 压力

operation [ˌɒpə'reɪʃn] *n.* 操作，经营

disappointment [ˌdɪsə'pɔɪntmənt] *n.* 失望

19. ... but... 虽然……但是……

对话示例

— What about the bonus in your company?	— 你们公司的奖金怎么样?
— I always get a quite handsome bonus every month.	— 我每个月都领一大笔奖金。
— Congratulations. I am not as lucky as you.	— 祝贺你。我就没有你那么幸运。
— Your company offers good benefits.	— 你们公司的福利很好。
— The welfare is really nice, **but** we can't get the bonus.	— 虽然福利确实很好，但是我们没有奖金。

句型分析

... but... 该句型中的 but 表示“但是”之意，可以连接词或短语，也可以连接句子。

句子示例

- It is snowing **but** not very cold today. 虽然正在下雪，但是今天一点也不冷。
- At first my daughter was a little shy, **but** now she acts more naturally. 虽然开始时我女儿有些腼腆，但现在她表现得很自然。
- There are lots of difficulties, **but** we can unite as a big family. 虽然有很多困难，但是我们可以像一个大家庭一样在团结在一起。

重点单词

bonus ['bəʊnəs] *n.* 奖金

naturally ['nætʃrəlɪ] *ad.* 自然地

unite [jʊ'naɪt] *v.* 团结，联合

Unit 4 强调

1. Don't let... 别让……

对话示例

— I would like to invite Max to join my birthday party.	— 我想邀请麦克斯参加我的生日聚会。
— You can inform him by telephone.	— 你可以打电话通知他。
— I telephoned him, but no one answered. Can you take a message for him?	— 我给他打过电话了，但是没有人接。你能给我带个口信吗？
— My pleasure.	— 我很乐意。
— Thank you. **Don't let** him forget to arrive on time.	— 谢谢。让他别忘记准时到达。

句型分析

Don't let... 该句型是祈使句的否定句，该句子是 let 引导的祈使句，这类祈使句是以第一人称和第三人称代词或者名词等作为祈使的对象。

句子示例

- **Don't let** him go to school by himself. 别让他一个人去上学。
- **Don't let** us waste our time arguing about it. 别让我们浪费时间争论这件事。
- **Don't let** Nina know the truth. 别让妮娜知道真相。

重点单词

invite [ɪn'vaɪt] *v.* 邀请

telephone ['telɪfəʊn] *n.* 电话 *v.* 打电话

argue ['ɑːgjuː] *v.* 争论，辩论

2. You'd better keep ... from... 你最好不要让……

对话示例

— What's wrong with you? You look very angry.	— 你怎么了？你看起来很生气。
— My son spends a lot of time playing computer games.	— 我的儿子花了太多时间玩电脑游戏。
— **You'd better keep** your son **from** playing computer games.	— 你最好不要让你儿子玩电脑游戏。
— Playing computer games too much is bad for children's studies and heart.	— 玩游戏太多的话不利于孩子的学习与内心。

句型分析

You'd better keep ... from... 该句型中，You'd 是 You had 的缩写， had better 的用法是 had better do sth，表示“最好做某事”； keep ... from... 用法是 keep sb from doing sth，表示“阻止某人做某事”。

句子示例

- **You'd better keep** your nephew **from** eating fried food. 你最好不要让你侄子吃油炸食物。
- **You'd better keep** Sunny **from** attending the meeting. 你最好不要让桑尼出席会议。
- **You'd better keep** consumers **from** buying the poor products. 你最好不要让消费者购买劣质产品。

重点单词

keep [ki:p] *v.* 保持，保留

angry ['æŋgrɪ] *a.* 生气的

product ['prɒdʌkt] *n.* 产品

3. Please... 请……

对话示例

— What can I do for you?	— 我能为你做些什么呢?
— **Please** erase my name from the list.	— 请把我的名字从名单上擦去。
— You must think it over seriously.	— 你必须认真考虑清楚。
— I have made up my mind.	— 我已经下定决心了。
— I will do that for you as soon as possible.	— 我会尽快给你办。

句型分析

Please... 在该句型中，please 是一个动词，表示“请”，please 后跟动词原形，句首加 please 表示客气的请求，通常在祈使句中使用。

句子示例

- **Please** lend me an English dictionary. 请借给我一本英语字典。
- **Please** check the balance in my account. 请核对一下我的账户余额。
- **Please** don't disturb me when I am working. 我工作的时候请不要打扰我。

重点单词

erase [ɪ'reɪz] *v.* 擦掉，抹去　　check [tʃek] *v.* 检查，核对

4. Never... 永远不要……

对话示例

— From what I understand, this item will be very popular this year.	— 据我了解，这款产品今年会很畅销。
— Our product sold remarkably fast during the trial sales period.	— 我们的这个产品在试销期间很抢手。
— What is your company mission?	— 你们公司的使命是什么？
— **Never** stop evolving the new product.	— 永不停止开发新产品。
— I hope we can cooperate happily.	— 我希望我们合作愉快。

句型分析

Never... 该句型中，never 是一个否定副词，表示“永远不要”之意，放在句首时，要部分倒装，即主语与谓语次序倒装。

句子示例

- **Never** have I seen a situation which made him so amazed. 我从来没有见过一个情况能使他这么吃惊。
- **Never** give up until you are successful. 永不言弃，直到成功。
- **Never** have I read such a book. 我从来没有读过这样的一本书。

重点单词

remarkably [rɪ'mɑ:kəblɪ] *ad.* 引人注目地

period ['pɪərɪəd] *n.* 时期

trial ['traɪəl] *n.* 试验

evolve [ɪ'vɒlv] *v.* 使发展，进化

5. No doubt... 毫无疑问……

对话示例

— This product combines many functions in one.	— 这种产品集多种功能于一身。
— It is handiness, elegance and beauty.	— 它轻巧、优雅又美观。
— **No doubt** this product will be popular with consumers.	— 毫无疑问这种产品非常受消费者的欢迎。
— We will find a good prospect in our products.	— 我们发现我们的产品前景非常好。

句型分析

No doubt... 该句型中，no doubt 可用作副词表示“毫无疑问”，通常位于句首，有时也可位于句中。

句子示例

- **No doubt** John will win the match. 毫无疑问约翰会赢得比赛。
- **No doubt** we will offer no charge for service. 毫无疑问我们会提供免费服务。
- **No doubt** he must guarantee he will never give up. 毫无疑问他必须保证决不放弃。

重点单词

combine [kəm'baɪn] *v.* 使结合

handiness ['hændɪnəs] *n.* 巧妙，轻便

function ['fʌŋkʃn] *n.* 功能，作用

guarantee [ˌgærən'ti:] *v. & n.* 保证，担保

6. Be... 要……

对话示例

— Who will be the host for tonight's program?	— 谁是今晚的节目主持人?
— Tina. **Be** quiet! It begins at once.	— 缇娜。请安静！节目马上就要开始了。
— We should turn off our phones now.	— 我们应该把手机关机。
— I hope we will enjoy the program.	— 希望我们能玩得开心。

句型分析

Be... 该句型中，be 放句首可以引导祈使句，这类祈使句的常用结构为“be+ 形容词 / 名词”，如：Be quiet! 请安静！

句子示例

- **Be** more careful next time! 下次要小心点！
- **Be** sure and come as soon as possible! 一定要尽快过来！
- **Be** patient and careful, and you will find the answer. 只要细心认真，你就能找到答案。

重点单词

host [həʊst] *v.* 当主人 *n.* 主人，主持人

soon [suːn] *ad.* 立刻，马上

7. Do... 务必……

对话示例

— I don't think I will put pure American English blurted out.	— 我觉得我不能把纯正的美语脱口而出了。
— I believe you can do it.	— 我相信你可以的。
— Can you give me some advice?	— 你能给我一些建议吗?
— The more you practice, the easier it gets.	— 你练习越多，就越简单。
— OK. Let me try.	— 我会试一试。
— **Do** listen to the English radio.	— 务必听英语广播。

句型分析

Do... 在该句型中，Do 可放在祈使句的句首，通常需要重读，用于说话人想特别强调他所说的话的场合。

句子示例

- **Do** come up with us quickly! 务必快点赶上我们！
- **Do** take the medicine three times a day! 务必一天吃三次药！
- **Do** agree to supply a complete set of equipment. 务必提供一整套设备。

重点单词

pure [pjʊə] *a.* 纯的，单纯的

blurt [blɜ:t] *v.* 脱口而出

equipment [ɪ'kwɪpmənt] *n.* 设备，装备

8. Let... 让……

对话示例

— Dad, I will take part in Linda's birthday party tonight.	— 爸爸，我今晚要参加琳达的生日聚会。
— You must arrive home before 10:00 p.m.	— 你必须在十点之前到家。
— **Let** me have the key to the front door.	— 让我带着前门的钥匙。
— No, you can't.	— 不可以。

句型分析

Let... 该句型中，let 引导的是祈使句，这类祈使句通常是以第一、第三人称作为祈使的对象，let 之后要加动词原形。

句子示例

- **Let** her translate the Japanese book. 让她翻译这本日语书。
- **Let** him supply his letter of resignation. 让他提供他的辞职信。
- **Let** us go to school together. 让我们一起去上学吧。

重点单词

translate [træns'leɪt] *v.* 翻译

supply [sə'plaɪ] *v.* 提供

resignation [ˌrezɪg'neɪʃn] *n.* 辞职，辞呈

9. ... made me... ……让我……

对话示例

— Why did you do this?	— 为什么要做这些?
— The director **made me** do the work.	— 主管让我做的。
— But you must inform the time of the meeting now.	— 但是你现在必须通知开会时间了。
— Thank you for your warning.	— 谢谢你的提醒。

句型分析

... made me... 该句型中，made 是 make 的过去式，“make +me+ 形容词”表示“让我……”，“make +me+ 动词原形”表示“让我……”。

句子示例

- It **made me** very unhappy. 它让我很不开心。
- That work **made me** exhausted. 那工作让我精疲力竭。
- You **made me** open the trunk. 你让我打开后备箱。

重点单词

warning ['wɔ:nɪŋ] *n.* 警告，告诫

exhausted [ɪg'zɔ:stɪd] *a.* 精疲力竭的

trunk [trʌŋk] *n.* 树干，后备箱

10. It is altogether fitting and proper that... ……是义不容辞的事

对话示例

— The basketball match will be held next week.	— 篮球比赛将在下周举行。
— Our team has been preparing for it for a long time.	— 我们队已经准备很久了。
— I hope you can get good grades this time.	— 我希望你们这次能取得好成绩。
— **It is altogether fitting and proper that** we should unite as one.	— 团结一致是我们义不容辞的事。

句型分析

It is altogether fitting and proper that... 该句型是一个强调句，强调句型的结构是：It+ be+ 被强调部分 + that + 句子其余部分。

句子示例

- **It is altogether fitting and proper that** we should do this for the children. 为孩子们做这些是我们义不容辞的事。
- **It is altogether fitting and proper that** she will be a volunteer teacher. 她成为一名志愿教师是义不容辞的事。
- **It is altogether fitting and proper that** we are always ready to help others. 乐于助人是义不容辞的事。

重点单词

altogether [ˌɔ:ltə'geðə] *ad.* 全部地，完全地　　proper ['prɒpə] *a.* 适当的

volunteer [ˌvɒlən'tɪə] *n.* 志愿者

11. Now it's the time to... 现在是……的时候了

对话示例

— Something is wrong with you today.	— 你今天有点不太对劲。
— Yeah, I was fired.	— 是啊，我被炒鱿鱼了。

— Don't let this get you down. You can go on a holiday to relax.	— 不要为此灰心丧气。你可以去度假放松一下。
— **Now it's the time to** take a vacation.	— 现在是去度假的时候了。

句型分析

Now it's the time to... 该句型中，It's the time to 后加动词原形表示“是时候……了”；而 It's the time for 也表示“是时候……了”，但其后加的是名词。

句子示例

- **Now it's the time to** have lunch at the school cafeteria. 现在是去学校食堂吃午餐的时候了。
- **Now it's the time to** tell the truth to our parents. 现在是告诉我们父母实情的时候了。
- **Now it's the time to** decide to reorganize the department. 现在是决定改组这个部门的时候了。

重点单词

relax [rɪ'læks] *v.* 放松

cafeteria [ˌkæfə'tɪərɪə] *n.* 自助餐厅

reorganize [rɪ'ɔːgənaɪz] *v.* 改组

12. It is evident that... 很显然……

对话示例

— How to get to the railway station?	— 我怎么去火车站？
— You can go there by bus.	— 你可以乘公交车。
— But there is often traffic jam in the rush hour.	— 但是在上下班高峰期经常出现交通堵塞。
— You are right. I suggest you go there by subway.	— 你说的对。我建议你乘地铁去。
— **It is evident that** I will accept your suggestion.	— 很显然我会接受你的建议。

句型分析

It is evident that... 该句型是一个强调句型，it 是形式主语，真正的主语是后面的 that 从句，“It is...that...”只是个固定的句型框架，表示强调意味，并不影响句意表达。

句子示例

- **It is evident that** the man won't take the ownership of our company. 很显然这位男士不会获得公司的所有权。
- **It is evident that** he won't accept my sympathies. 很显然他不会接受我的同情。
- **It is evident that** they are incredible. 很显然他们难以置信。

重点单词

evident ['evɪdənt] *a.* 明显的

traffic ['træfɪk] *n.* 交通

sympathy ['sɪmpəθɪ] *n.* 同情

13. It is only in this way that we can... 只有这样我们才能……

对话示例

— Have you read all the details in the contract?	— 你看过合同上的所有细节了吗?
— Yes. But I think we had better have another check.	— 看过了。但是我们最好再检查一下。
— OK. Let's check together.	— 好的。我们一起检查吧。
— **It is only in this way that we can** sign the contract.	— 只有这样我们才能签合同。

句型分析

It is only in this way that we can... 该句型是一个强调句型，强调句中的 be 动词，在强调结构中，无论被强调的是人还是物，是单数还是复数，be 动词都只能用单数 is / was。

句子示例

- **It is only in this way that we can** know your specific requirements. 只有这样我们才能知道你们的具体要求。
- **It is only in this way that we can** supply the materials on time. 只有这样我们才能准时提供原料。
- **It is only in this way that we can** complete the payment. 只有这样我们才能还清贷款。

重点单词

specific [spə'sɪfɪk] *a.* 具体的

complete [kəm'pli:t] *v.* 完成

payment ['peɪmənt] *n.* 付款，偿还

14. It is to be observed that... 值得一提的是……

对话示例

— I have something important to announce.

— What is it?

— **It is to be observed that** Nancy will be our finance director.

— Congratulations to Nancy.

— 我有重要的事情要宣布。

— 是什么？

— 值得一提的是南茜将会成为我们的财务总监。

— 祝贺南茜。

句型分析

It is to be observed that... 是一个强调句型，be observed 是被动形式，表示“被注意到……”；observe on 是固定搭配，表示“谈论，评论”。

句子示例

- **It is to be observed that** he has justified himself to us. 值得一提的是他向我们证明了他自己。
- **It is to be observed that** this plan's practicability is very strong. 值得一提的是这个计划的实用性很强。
- **It is to be observed that** he will be a big asset for our department. 值得一提的是他将会是我们部门的得力助手。

重点单词

observe [əb'zɜ:v] *v.* 观察，研究

finance ['faɪnæns] *n.* 财政

justify ['dʒʌstɪfaɪ] *v.* 证明

15. It need hardly be said that... 不用说……

对话示例

— Do you know who that is? She often gets much of the company's hospitality.	— 你知道那个人是谁吗？她经常受到很多公司的热情款待。
— **It need hardly be said that** Selena is an important client for every company in the region, even the entire city.	— 不用说，赛琳娜对于这个地区，甚至整个城市的所有公司来说，都是很重要的客户。
— Wow, she is really very rich and capable.	— 哇，她真的很有钱又很有能力。
— Certainly. I'm surprised you didn't know her. She is an honoured guest in our company.	— 是的，你竟然不知道她。她在我们公司是贵客。

句型分析

It need hardly be said that... 作为强调句，是为了强调后面存在的内容，用 hardly 表示后面的内容“几乎不用说”。

句子示例

- **It need hardly be said that** this man is an important client of our company. 不用说，这个人是我们公司的重要客户。
- **It need hardly be said that** this program is correct. 不用说，这个程序是正确的。
- **It need hardly be said that** he as an educator does not spread bad thoughts to children. 毋庸讳言，他作为一位教育者不会向孩子传播不好的思想。

重点单词

hospitality [ˌhɒspɪˈtæləti] *n.* 款待

surprised [səˈpraɪzd] *a.* 吃惊的，惊讶的

16. It is obvious that... 很显然……

对话示例

— **It is obvious that** the news brought us an unfavorable influence. What measures do you think we should take to contain it?	— 很显然这个消息给我们带来了不利的影响。你认为我们应该采取什么措施来遏制它?

— My suggestion is that our company should make a statement about the news first. This can show our attitude.	— 我的建议是我们公司应该先对这个消息作一个声明。这能表明我们的态度。
— Yes, then we can take practical measures according to the development of the situation.	— 是的。然后我们就可以根据事态的发展采取实际的措施。
— That's right.	— 没错。

句型分析

It is obvious that... 这是一个主语从句，it 在这里作形式主语，真正的主语是 that 引导的那部分，意为“（什么事情）是明显的”。

句子示例

- **It is obvious that** the new director is not qualified for the job. 很明显这个新来的主管不能胜任这个工作。
- **It is obvious that** this sales plan suits our company well. 很明显这个销售方案很适合我们公司。
- **It is obvious that** Mary makes a difference in the company. 很明显玛丽在这个公司发挥着她的影响力。

重点单词

qualified ['kwɒlɪfaɪd] *a.* 有资格的，能胜任的　　director [də'rektə] *n.* 主管

17. I feel sure that... 我确信……

对话示例

— Mike, do you think I can pass the interview?	— 麦克，你觉得我能通过面试吗?
— **I feel sure that** in terms of your ability, experience and qualifications, you will get the favor of the interviewer.	— 我确信就你的能力、经验和资格来说，你会获得面试官的青睐。
— Even so, I am still a little worried.	— 即便如此，我还是有一点担心。
— Don't worry.	— 不要担心。

句型分析

I feel sure that...that 引导我“确信”的内容，that 有时可以省略。I 是主语，feel 作系动词，sure 作表语。

句子示例

- **I feel sure that** you couldn't fulfill your promise. 我确信你没有能力履行自己的诺言。
- **I feel sure that** you're the only one who knows the truth. 我确信你是唯一知道这件事情真相的人。
- **I feel sure that** he lacks enough confidence in his work. 我确信他对自己的工作缺乏足够的信心。

重点单词

fulfill [fʊl'fɪl] *v.* 履行　　promise ['prɒmɪs] *n.* 诺言

18. It was the first time... 这是……第一次……

对话示例

— I heard that John was very nervous at the last speech.	— 我听说约翰在上次演讲时很紧张。
— Yes, **it was the first time** he'd spoken in public. But now he has become very confident.	— 是的，那是他第一次当众讲话。但是现在他已经变得很自信了。
— Did he attend any training course?	— 他参加过任何的培训课程吗？
— No. He just speaks up bravely in our company every time.	— 没有。他只是每一次在我们公司都勇敢地发言。

句型分析

It was the first time... 这个句型的关键是 was，因其是过去式，所以从句引导的动词需要是过去完成时；若 was 改为 is，那么从句动词就要用现在完成时。

句子示例

- **It was the first time** she had seen the star at the airport. 这是她第一次在机场见到明星。
- **It was the first time** professional players and amateurs had competed in the same competition. 这是专业选手和业余选手第一次在同一场比赛中竞争。

- **It was the first time** this natural landscape had been protected by legislation. 这是第一次这个自然景观通过立法保护。

重点单词

amateur ['æmətə] *n.* 业余爱好者

legislation [ˌledʒɪs'leɪʃn] *n.* 立法

19. Let it be understood once and for all that... 我要再一次地说清楚……

对话示例

— Here you are. This is a letter of apology wrote by Donald.	— 给你，这是唐纳德给你的道歉信。
— **Let it be understood once and for all that** I don't accept any form of apology from him.	— 我要再一次地说清楚我不接受他任何形式的道歉。
— Please, Mary. He really didn't mean to hurt you.	— 不要这样，玛丽。他真的是无心伤害你的。
— Enough.	— 够了。

句型分析

Let it be understood once and for all that... 这里的 it 作形式主语，that 后面引导的是我真正要说明的内容。

句子示例

- **Let it be understood once and for all that** I have no prejudice against any employee in the company. 我要再一次地说清楚，我对公司任何员工都没有偏见。
- **Let it be understood once and for all that** this report is not modified by me. 我要再一次地说清楚，这份报告不是我修改的。
- **Let it be understood once and for all that** this letter of accusation is definitely from our company. 我要再一次地说清楚，这封控告信绝对来自于我们公司。

重点单词

prejudice ['predʒʊdɪs] *n.* 偏见

accusation [ˌækjʊ'zeɪʃn] *n.* 控告，指责

20. He is the very person... 他就是……的人。

对话示例

— Look! **He is the very person** I always mentioned.	— 看！他就是我一直提到的人。
— Just as you say, he is indeed a shrewd man who knows how to recommend this technique to others in a clever way.	— 正如你说的，他确实是一个聪明又精明的人，懂得把这项技术以巧妙的方式推荐给他人。
— That's true. And all cases of our company are all about him.	— 是的。我们公司的所有案例都是在讲他。
— Wow! Can I meet him?	— 哇！我可以认识他吗？

句型分析

He is the very person... 这里的 very 是用来强调“他就是这样的一个人”，表示“正是、就是”，而关于是什么样的人要从 person 后的内容得知。这个句型后可跟从句，也可跟介词短语。

句子示例

- **He is the very person** our manager is looking for. 他正是我们经理要找的人。
- **He is the very person** that holds the key to the office. 只有他拿着办公室的钥匙。
- **He is the very person** for the job. 他是最适合这个工作的人。

重点单词

shrewd [ʃruːd] *a.* 精明的

recommend [ˌrekəˈmend] *v.* 推荐

21. I do... 我的确……

对话示例

— Linda, what's wrong with you? You've been absent-minded lately.	— 琳达，你怎么了？最近总是心不在焉的。
— I've been thinking about the mistake I made at work last time. Does it suggest that I am not fit for the job?	— 我一直在思考上次我在工作中所犯的错误。这是不是在暗示我不适合这个工作？

— Come on. That mistake did not cause any loss to the company. The manager scolded you is just to avoid similar mistakes made by others. I believe your ability.	— 得了吧。那个错误并没有给公司带来任何损失。经理骂你只是为了避免让别人犯类似的错误。我相信你的工作能力。
— Thank you. **I do** want you to comfort me.	— 谢谢。我的确想要你安慰我。

句型分析

I do... 这里的 do 在句子中起强调作用，放在谓语动词的前面，强调谓语动词。这里的主语是我，do 表示一般形式，如果是第三人称单数就要用 does，过去式要用 did。

句子示例

- **I do** hope you can forget the bad things. 我真的希望你能把那些不好的事情忘了。
- **I do** want you to read this email. 我的确想要你读一下这封电子邮件。
- **I do** lose my confidence because of that job. 我的确因为那份工作丢失了我的信心。

重点单词

comfort ['kʌmfət] *v.* 安慰　　scold [skəʊld] *v.* 责骂

22. I come close to... 我几乎……

对话示例

— Mary, **I come close to** passing the exam. But I read the time wrong, so I didn't finish my question.	— 玛丽，我这次考试差点就及格了。但是我看错了时间，所以我的题没有答完。
— That's all right. This indicates that you have the ability to pass the exam.	— 不要紧。这说明你有能力通过这个考试。
— Yes, I believe I can pass the exam next time.	— 是的，我相信我下次一定能通过考试。
— Yes, you can do it.	— 是的，你一定可以。

句型分析

I come close to... 这里的 close to 意为“几乎”， to 在这里作介词，后跟动名词，构成 come close to doing sth，意为“差一点做某事”，这里的 come 是系动词，相当于 be。

句子示例

- **I come close to** losing the ability to speak when the teacher asked me to answer the question. 当老师让我回答问题的时候我几乎丧失了说话的能力。
- **I come close to** losing my life in the accident. 我几乎在这次车祸中失去了生命。
- **I come close to** losing the manager's trust. 我几乎失去了经理的信任。

重点单词

accident ['æksɪdənt] *n.* 意外事故

indicate ['ɪndɪkeɪt] *v.* 显示

23. I'm the last person... 我是最不会……的

对话示例

— The relationship between my father and I is bad.	— 我和我父亲之间的关系很不好。
— You should always make time to communicate with your father.	— 你应该留点时间和你父亲沟通。
— **I'm the last person** that my father listens to.	— 我父亲最不愿听我说话。
— You may be able to write a letter to your father.	— 你或许可以给他写信。
— It might be a good idea.	— 那或许是个好主意。

句型分析

I'm the last person... 该句型属于主系表结构，主语是 I，系动词是 am，表语是 the last person，I'm the last person... 后可加从句。

句子示例

- **I'm the last person** my boss would think of. 我是我老板最不会考虑的人。

• **I'm the last person** to insist on your price. 我是最不会坚持你的价格的人。

• **I'm the last person** who would give up the transaction. 我是最不会放弃交易的人。

重点单词

insist [ɪn'sɪst] *v.* 坚持，强调　　transaction [træn'zækʃn] *n.* 交易，办理，业务

24. I'll... if I have to... 如果迫不得已……，我会……

对话示例

— Our factory will place some new products.	— 我们工厂打算订购一些新产品。
— **I'll** make a sample order first **if I have to** place the new varieties.	— 如果迫不得已订购新产品，我会先进行一次试订购。
— We want to make this a trial order, too.	— 我们也想用试订的方式。
— Oh, that's even better!	— 那就更好了！

句型分析

I'll... if I have to... 该句型中，含有一个 if 引导的虚拟条件句，I'll... 是主句，if I have to... 是从句，主句用一般将来时，从句用一般现在时。

句子示例

• **I'll** go bonkers **if I have to** wait any longer. 如果迫不得已继续等下去，我会发疯的。

• **I'll** finish the written contract **if I have to** finish it today. 如果迫不得已今天必须完成，我会完成书面合同。

• **I'll** choose a direct shipment **if I have to** transport by air. 如果迫不得已要空运，我会选择直运。

重点单词

variety [və'raɪətɪ] *n.* 多样，种类，多样化　　written ['rɪtn] *a.* 书面的，写成文字的

direct [də'rekt] *a.* 直接的，直的

Unit 5 重复省略

1. Did you see ... (that) ...? 你看见……的……了吗?

对话示例

— **Did you see** the model plane **that** I made?	— 你看见我制作的那个飞机模型了吗?
— Yes, I did. You put it in the container of the storage room.	— 我看见了，你把它放在储藏室的柜子里了。
— I am so careless.	— 我真是太粗心了。
— Remember to put things in order next time.	— 下次记得把东西按序放好。
— OK. I will.	— 好的，我会的。

句型分析

Did you see ... (that) ... 本句型中 that 是关系代词，在从句中作宾语，因此可以省略，如果在从句中作的是主语，千万不能省去。

句子示例

- **Did you see** the dictionary **that** I bought yesterday? 你看见我昨天买的那本字典了吗?
- **Did you see** the daffodils **that** John gave me last week? 你看见上星期约翰送给我的水仙花了吗?
- **Did you see** the map of the world **that** I borrowed from the library? 你看见我从图书馆借来的那张世界地图了吗?

重点单词

container [kən'teɪnə] *n.* 柜子，箱子

storage ['stɔ:rɪdʒ] *n.* 储藏，存储

daffodil ['dæfədɪl] *n.* 水仙花

map [mæp] *n.* 地图

2. This is the man (that) ... 这是……的人。

对话示例

— Do you know the man standing at the gate of our company?	— 你认识站在我们公司门口的那个人吗?
— **This is the man that** Maria loves very much.	— 这是玛利亚喜欢的那个人。
— I have never seen him before.	— 我以前从来没见过他。
— This is the third time that I've met him. We had dinner together before.	— 这是我第三次见他。我们之前一起吃过饭。
— Are you familiar with him?	— 你对他很熟悉吗?
— No. Maria just introduced him to me.	— 不。玛利亚只是把他介绍给我认识而已。

句型分析

This is the man that... 本句型中 that 为关系代词，在句子中作宾语，可以省略。

句子示例

- **This is the man that** Alice hates very much. 这是爱丽丝很讨厌的那个人。
- **This is the man that** we are proud of. 这是我们都引以为豪的那个人。
- **This is the man that** Bill wants to beat. 这是比尔想打败的那个人。

重点单词

familiar [fə'mɪlɪə] *a.* 熟悉的，知晓的

introduce [ˌɪntrə'dju:s] *v.* 提出，介绍

3. Here is ... (that) you are asking for. 这是你需要的……

对话示例

— **Here is** the document **that you are asking for**.	— 这是你要的那份文件。
— You have finished it so fast.	— 你这么快就整理好了。
— Yes. I used my lunch time to finish it.	— 是的，我利用午饭时间完成的。
— Great. Thank you very much.	— 太棒了。谢谢你。
— You are welcome.	— 不客气。

句型分析

Here is ... (that) you are asking for. 本句型中 that 是关系代词，在句子中作宾语，可以省略，ask for 是固定搭配，意为“需要，请求”。

句子示例

- **Here is** the black pen **that you are asking for**. 这是你需要的黑色钢笔。
- **Here is** the cassette **that you are asking for**. 这是你需要的盒式磁带。
- **Here is** the flashlight **that you are asking for**. 这是你需要的手电筒。
- **Here is** the hammer **that you are asking for**. 这是你需要的锤子。

重点单词

cassette [kə'set] *n.* 盒式磁带，录音带　　hammer ['hæmə] *n.* 锤子 *v.* 击打

4. ... (which)...is my favorite. ……的……是我的最爱。

对话示例

— It seems that you have been wearing this sweater for many years.	— 你这件毛衣似乎已经穿了很多年了。
— The sweater **which** my mother made for me **is my favorite**.	— 我妈妈为我织的这件毛衣是我的最爱。
— Your mother is so clever. I really envy you!	— 你的妈妈这么聪明，真羡慕你！
— In fact, your mother is very great. You don't always quarrel with her.	— 其实你的妈妈也很伟大，你不要总是和她吵架。
— All right. I will try to avoid quarrelling with her later.	— 好的，我以后尽量避免和她吵架。

句型分析

... (which)...is my favorite. 本句型中 which 在从句中作宾语，因此可以省去。

句子示例

- The skirt **which** my father bought me **is my favorite**. 我爸爸给我买的这条裙子是我的最爱。
- The cabbage soup **which** my grandmother cook for me **is my favorite**. 奶奶给我做的白菜汤是

我的最爱。

• The uniform **which** my uncle gave me **is my favorite**. 我的叔叔给我的那件制服是我的最爱。

重点单词

cabbage ['kæbɪdʒ] *n.* 白菜，卷心菜   uniform ['ju:nɪfɔ:m] *n.* 制服，军装

5. I will...if I have to. 如果有必要……，我会……

对话示例

— There is an academic exchange activity in Japan next week. Do you want to go?	— 下周在日本有一个学术交流活动。你要去吗?
— **I will** take part in this activity **if I have to**.	— 如果有必要参加学术交流活动，我会参加。
— Of course. Because a famous professor will tell us some of his own experiences.	— 当然有必要。因为会有一个著名的教授讲一些他自己的心得体会。
— I must go there.	— 那我一定去。
— OK. See you then.	— 好的，到时候见。

句型分析

I will...if I have to 本句型中省略了 have to 后面的动词。在包含动词不定式的句子中，如果不定式后面的动词与前面所出现的动词一样，就可以省去。

句子示例

• **I will** go on business trip **if I have to**. 如果有必要出差，我会出差。

• **I will** write dissertations **if I have to**. 如果有必要写论文，我会写论文。

• **I will** revise some terms of the contract **if I have to**. 如果有必要修改合同中的一些条款，我会修改。

重点单词

dissertation [ˌdɪsə'teɪʃn] *n.* 论文，学术演讲   revise [rɪ'vaɪz] *v.* 修改，校正

term [tɜ:m] *n.* 条款，学期

6. She was dancing with... 她一边跳舞，一边……

对话示例

— What was Mary doing at 8 o'clock last night?	— 玛丽昨天晚上 8 点在干什么？
— **She was dancing with** listening to the music.	— 她一边跳舞，一边听音乐。
— So what about her dance?	— 那她的舞蹈练得怎么样了？
— I think it is so graceful.	— 我觉得特别优美。
— Let's dance with her at this Christmas party.	— 那今年的圣诞晚会我们和她一起跳舞吧。

句型分析

She was dancing with... 本句型中省略了关系副词 when，with 表示一种伴随状态，强调的是前后两个动作同时发生。

句子示例

- **She was dancing with** her eyes full of tears. 她一边跳舞，一边眼眶泛泪。
- **She was dancing with** her face full of confidence. 她一边跳舞，一边脸上充满了信心。
- **She was dancing with** her face turning red. 她一边跳舞，一边脸红了。

重点单词

graceful ['greɪsfl] *a.* 优美的，得体的　　confidence ['kɒnfɪdəns] *n.* 信心

7. ... be speaking with... 某人……地说着话。

对话示例

— What do you think of our new department manager?	— 你觉得我们新来的部门经理怎么样？
— I don't like him.	— 我不喜欢他。
— Why?	— 为什么？
— Because he **is speaking with** guns blazing.	— 因为他说话的态度很强势。
— Maybe it's his habit.	— 可能这是他的习惯。

句型分析

... be speaking with... 本句型中，with 表示一种伴随状态，表示前后的动作是同时发生的，后面要用现在分词或者过去分词。

句子示例

- John **is speaking with** his head down. 约翰说话的时候低着头。
- The old man **is speaking with** his legs crossed. 这个老人两腿交叉说着话。
- They **are speaking with** their arms held. 他们双臂交叉说着话。

重点单词

gun [gʌn] *n.* 枪 *v.* 射击　　　　habit ['hæbɪt] *n.* 习惯

8. ... can ... if...want to. ……可以……，如果……想。

对话示例

— Do you have any plans for the holiday?	— 这个假期你有什么打算?
— I haven't thought about it yet.	— 我还没有考虑好。
— You **can** travel to Europe **if** you **want to**.	— 如果你想的话，你可以去欧洲旅行。
— It must take me a lot of money. I have been poor lately.	— 这一定会花费我很多钱。我最近比较穷。
— If you really want to go, I can lend you money.	— 如果你真的想去，我可以借钱给你。

句型分析

... can ... if...want to. 本句型中省略了 want to 后面的动词，因为在包含不定式的句子当中，前后的动词如果相同，不定式后的动词就可以省略。

句子示例

- You **can** go to the party **if** you **want to**. 你今天晚上可以去参加派对，如果你想去的话。
- Eric **can** go to see the magic show **if** he **wants to**. 埃里克可以去看魔术表演，如果他想去的话。
- He **can** go to court to sue me **if** he **wants to**. 如果他想的话他可以去法院控告我。

重点单词

magic ['mædʒɪk] *n.* 魔术，戏法

sue [su:] *v.* 控诉，控告

9. This is ...(whom) I have thought highly of. 这就是……，我对……评价很高。

对话示例

— I have never seen this man. Who is he?	— 我从来没见过这个人。他是谁？
— **This is** our new biology teacher **whom I have thought highly of**.	— 这就是我们新来的生物学老师，我对他评价很高。
— Why do you say that?	— 为什么这样说？
— Because I heard that he had published a lot of articles about biology before.	— 因为我听说他之前发表过很多关于生物学的文章。

句型分析

This is ...(whom) I have thought highly of. 本句型中关系代词 whom 在从句中充当宾语，因此可以省去。如果在从句中充当主语，千万不可省略。

句子示例

- **This is** the prestigious headmaster **whom I have thought highly of**. 这就是那位有声望的校长，我对这位校长的评价很高。
- **This is** the brilliant girl **whom I have thought highly of**. 这就是那个才华横溢的女孩，我对这个女孩的评价很高。
- **This is** the lettered man **whom I have thought highly of**. 这就是那个有学问的男人，我对这个男人的评价很高。

重点单词

biology [baɪ'ɒlədʒɪ] *n.* 生物，生物学

publish ['pʌblɪʃ] *v.* 发表，出版

prestigious [pre'stɪdʒəs] *a.* 有声望的

lettered ['letəd] *a.* 有学问的，有文化的

10. ... , which... gave me, is made of... ……送我的……，是……制成的。

对话示例

— Yesterday was your birthday. What did Paul give you for your birthday?	— 昨天是你的生日，保罗送你什么生日礼物了?
— He gave me a beautiful cheongsam	— 他送了我一件漂亮的旗袍。
— Can you tell me what your cheongsam is made of?	— 你能告诉我你的旗袍是什么材质的吗?
— The cheongsam, **which** he **gave me, is made of** silk.	— 他送给我的这件旗袍，是由丝绸制成的。
— It must be very expensive.	— 那一定特别贵。

句型分析

... , which... gave me, is made of... 本句型中 which 引导定语从句，指代的是前面的主语。be made of 是固定搭配，意为“由……制成”。

句子示例

- The bangle, **which** my father **gave me, is made of** gold. 我爸爸送我的这只手镯，是由黄金制成的。
- The briefcase, **which** my girlfriend **gave me, is made of** leather. 我女朋友送我的这个公文包，是由皮革制成的。
- The table, **which** my boss **gave me, is made of** wood. 我老板给我的这张桌子，是由木头制成的。

重点单词

cheongsam [tʃɒŋ'sæm] *n.* 旗袍

bangle ['bæŋgl] *n.* 手镯，手链

briefcase ['bri:fkeɪs] *n.* 公文包

leather ['leðə] *n.* 皮革

11. Those who ... won't be successful. 那些……的人是不会成功的。

对话示例

— The old employees of our company always feel that life is out of hope.	— 公司的老员工总觉得生活没有希望。
— **Those who** are very passive **won't be**	— 那些消极的人是不会成功的。

successful.	
— As a psychologist, you can enlighten them properly.	— 作为一名心理医生，你可以适当地开导一下他们。
— OK, I'll make an appointment with them.	— 好的，我和他们约个时间。
— Thank you very much.	— 真是太感谢你了。
— Not at all.	— 不客气。

句型分析

Those who ... won't be successful. 本句型中 those 指代的是其后的定语从句中所指的所有人，关系代词 who 不可以省略。

句子示例

- **Those who** are very lazy **won't be successful**. 那些非常懒惰的人是不会成功的。
- **Those who** don't want to work hard **won't be successful**. 那些不愿意付出努力的人是不会成功的。
- **Those who** are opportunistic **won't be successful**. 那些投机取巧的人是不会成功的。

重点单词

passive ['pæsɪv] *a.* 消极的，被动的

enlighten [ɪn'laɪtn] *v.* 开导，启发

psychologist [saɪ'kɒlədʒɪst] *n.* 心理医生，心理学家

opportunistic [ˌɒpətju:'nɪstɪk] *a.* 投机取巧的，机会主义的

12. Those who... will make mistakes easily. 那些……的人很容易犯错。

对话示例

— Several students in our class didn't come home until daybreak.	— 我们班的好几个学生竟然到天亮才回家。
— Do you know where they went?	— 你知道他们去哪里了吗?
— I guess they seem to have gone to the Internet bar.	— 我猜他们去了网吧。
— **Those who** are addicted to the Internet **will make mistakes easily**.	— 那些沉迷于网络的人很容易犯错。
— I need to talk to their parents.	— 我需要和他们的父母好好谈谈。

句型分析

Those who... will make mistakes easily. 本句型中 those 指代的是其后的定语从句中所指的所有人，关系代词 who 不可以省略。make mistakes 为固定搭配，意为“犯错，出错”。

句子示例

- **Those who** are very careless **will make mistakes easily**. 那些特别粗心的人很容易犯错。
- **Those who** are conceited **will make mistakes easily**. 那些骄傲自大的人很容易犯错。
- **Those who** are crossed in love **will make mistakes easily**. 那些情场失意的人很容易犯错。

重点单词

daybreak ['deɪbreɪk] *n.* 天亮，黎明

conceited [kən'si:tɪd] *a.* 骄傲自大的

13. ... belong to those who... ……是属于那些……的人。

对话示例

— What are they talking about?	— 他们在说什么?
— They are complaining that they have no bonus this year.	— 他们在抱怨今年没有奖金。
— Bonuses **belong to those who** often work overtime.	— 奖金是属于那些经常加班的人。
— That's all right. It's impossible for them to have bonuses because they are late for the work all day.	— 没错。像他们这样整天迟到的人是不可能有奖金的。

句型分析

... belong to those who... 本句型中 those 指代的是定语从句中所指的所有人，关系代词 who 不可以省略。belong to 为固定搭配，意为“属于”。

句子示例

- The future **belongs to those who** are willing to work hard for their dreams. 未来是属于那些愿意为他们自己的梦想付出努力的人。
- The happiness **belongs to those who** are easy to be satisfied. 幸福是属于那些容易满足的人。

• The pain of defeat **belongs to those who** are indecisive. 失败的痛苦属于那些优柔寡断的人。

重点单词

satisfy ['sætɪsfaɪ] *v.* 满足，满意

indecisive [ˌɪndɪ'saɪsɪv] *a.* 优柔寡断的，犹豫的

14. ... be looking for a man whose name is ... ……在找一个名叫……的人。

对话示例

— Excuse me, what can I do for you?	— 打扰一下，有什么可以帮你的吗?
— **I am looking for a man whose name is** Aaron. Do you know where he lives?	— 我在找一个名叫艾伦的人。你知道他住在哪里吗?
— Sorry, he has moved to another city.	— 不好意思，他已经搬到另一个城市了。
— Why did he move?	— 他为什么要搬家?
— Because he is a drummer of a popular rock band, he is always going to perform in different cities.	— 因为他是一个很受欢迎的摇滚乐队的鼓手，所以经常要去不同的城市演出。

句型分析

... be looking for a man whose name is... 本句型中 name 和先行词 man 是所属关系，意为“那个人的名字”。whose 是 who 和 which 的所有格，它可以指人，也可以指物。

句子示例

• I **am looking for a man whose name is** Richard. 我在找一个名叫理查德的人。
• They **are looking for a man whose name is** George. 他们在找一个名叫乔治的人。
• Tina **was looking for a man whose name is** Jack. 蒂娜在找一个名叫杰克的人。

重点单词

drummer ['drʌmə] *n.* 鼓手

band [bænd] *n.* 乐队 *v.* 连接

15. We knew the girl whose... 我们认识那个……的女孩。

对话示例

— **We knew the girl whose** car is red.	— 我们认识那个拥有红色汽车的女孩。
— How do you know her?	— 你们是怎么认识她的？
— We met at a coffee shop before, and she picked up my wallet.	— 我们之前在一家咖啡馆遇见过，她捡到了我的钱包。
— She is an honest girl.	— 她是一个诚实的女孩。
— Yeah, so we became good friends.	— 是啊，所以我们成了好朋友。

句型分析

We knew the girl whose... 本句型中 whose 后面的名词和先行词 the girl 是所属关系，whose 意为“谁的”，在句中不能省略，knew 是 know 的过去式。

句子示例

- **We knew the girl whose** eyes are big and bright. 我们认识那个眼睛又大又亮的女孩。
- **We knew the girl whose** parents are pharmacists. 我们认识那个父母都是药剂师的女孩。
- **We knew the girl whose** voice is sweet. 我们认识那个嗓音很甜美的女孩。

重点单词

wallet ['wɒlɪt] *n.* 钱包，皮夹　　pharmacist ['fɑːməsɪst] *n.* 药剂师

16. ... will meet in a store whose name is... ……在一家名叫……的商店见面。

对话示例

— I introduced Robin to Kate.	— 我把罗宾介绍给凯特了。
— Did you tell them where they date?	— 你告诉他们在哪里约会了吗？
— Yes, I did. They **will meet in a store whose name is** Emma's Bakery.	— 告诉他们了。他们将在一家名叫“艾玛的蛋糕”的店见面。
— Do you think they are going to be lovers?	— 你觉得他们会成为恋人吗？
— Yes. Because Robin told me that he had carried a torch for her for one year.	— 是的。因为罗宾之前和我说他单恋凯特一年了。

句型分析

... will meet in a store whose name is... 本句型中 name 和先行词 a store 是所属关系，意为“一家商店的名字”。whose 是 who 和 which 的所有格，它可以指人，也可以指物，在本句型中 whose 指的是物。

句子示例

- We **will meet in a store whose name is** Dora's Cabin. 我们将在一家名叫“朵拉的小屋”的店见面。
- Jack and Rose **will meet in a store whose name is** Sunny's Cafe. 杰克和露丝将在一家名叫“桑妮的咖啡馆”的店见面。
- They **will meet in a store whose name is** Green Bar. 他们将在一家名叫“绿色的酒吧”的店见面。

重点单词

torch [tɔːtʃ] *n.* 手电筒，火把　　　cabin ['kæbɪn] *n.* 隔间，木屋

17. Do you know the woman who...? 你认识那个……的女人吗？

对话示例

— **Do you know the woman who** is wearing the purple coat?	— 你认识那个穿紫色大衣的女人吗？
— Yes, she is Mike's stepmother.	— 认识。她是麦克的继母。
— How did you know her?	— 你怎么会认识她？
— I went to Mike's house for dinner before, so I met her.	— 我之前去麦克的家里吃饭，所以见过她。
— Is she friendly to Mike?	— 那她对麦克友善吗？
— Yes. She treats Mike as if she treated her own son.	— 非常好，她对待麦克就像对待自己的亲生儿子一样。

句型分析

Do you know the woman who... 本句型属于定语从句，who 是先行词，也是关系代词，指代前面的人，可以和 that 相互替换。

句子示例

- **Do you know the woman who** works at a bank? 你认识那个在银行工作的女人吗?
- **Do you know the woman who** lives in your neighborhood? 你认识那个住在你隔壁的女人吗?
- **Do you know the woman who** is ragged? 你认识那个衣衫褴褛的女人吗?

重点单词

stepmother ['stepmʌðə] *n.* 继母

neighborhood ['neɪbəhʊd] *n.* 附近；街坊

ragged ['ræɡɪd] *a.* 衣衫褴褛的，衣冠不整的

18. The movie which...was great. ……的电影很棒。

对话示例

— Long time no see! What did you do on your vacation?	— 好久不见！你假期都干什么了?
— I often went to the cinema to see the movies alone.	— 我经常一个人去电影院看电影。
— Are you interested in the film?	— 你对电影很感兴趣吗?
— Yes. **The movie which** is named *The Lord of the Rings* **was great**. I have seen it three times.	— 是的，那个名叫《指环王》的电影很棒。我都看了三遍了。
— OK. If I have time, I will go and see it.	— 好吧。如果我有时间，我也去看看。

句型分析

The movie which... was great. 本句型中关系代词 which 指代的是先行词 movie。当先行词是物时，可以用 which 来指代。

句子示例

- **The movie which** was shown yesterday **was great**. 昨天上映的电影很棒。
- **The movie which** Tom invited me to see last week **was great**. 汤姆上周邀请我去看的那场电影很棒。
- **The movie which** Bill saw **was great**. 比尔看的那部电影很棒。

重点单词

lord [lɔ:d] *n.* 上帝，王

ring [rɪŋ] *n.* 铃声，指环，戒指 *v.* 打电话

19. What we have to do is... 我们唯一要做的就是……

对话示例

— We are going to graduate soon. What are you going to do after graduation?	— 我们快要毕业了，你毕业以后打算做什么？
— I haven't considered it yet. **What we have to do is** finish our final paper before November 5.	— 我还没有考虑过这些事。我们唯一要做的就是在 11 月 5 日之前完成最终论文。
— However, I have been in a bad mood recently and have no intention to write my paper.	— 可是，我最近心情不好，没有心思去写论文。
— Well. Let's go shopping this weekend. It can relieve your pressure.	— 那我们这周末去购物吧。这样可以缓解一下你的压力。
— OK. Thank you.	— 好的，谢谢你。

句型分析

What we have to do is... 本句型中 is 后面要跟动词原形，have to 是固定搭配，意为“必须，需要”。记住，本句型 is 后面千万不能跟动名词。

句子示例

- **What we have to do is** believe him absolutely. 我们必须要做的就是完全相信他。
- **What we have to do is** tell her the truth. 我们唯一要做的就是告诉她真相。
- **What we have to do is** mend this machine. 我们唯一要做的就是修理这台机器。
- **What we have to do is** mop the floor before Mom comes back. 我们唯一要做的就是在妈妈回来之前把地拖干净。

重点单词

November [nəʊ'vembə] *n.* 十一月

absolutely ['æbsəlu:tlɪ] *ad.* 完全地，绝对地

mop [mɒp] *v.* 拖地，擦地 *n.* 拖把

intention [ɪn'tenʃn] *n.* 目的，意图

mend [mend] *v.* 修理，修补

20. He hired the boy whom... 他雇佣了一个……的男孩。

对话示例

— Have you found a new job?	— 你找到新工作了吗?
— Not yet. Last week I went to an interview, but **he hired a boy whom** he quarreled with before.	— 还没有。上周我参加了一个面试，但是他雇佣了一个之前和他吵架的男孩。
— That boss is so strange!	— 那个老板真奇怪!
— I also think it is incredible. Am I useless?	— 我也觉得不可思议。我是不是很没用?
— Don't lose heart. You are the best.	— 别灰心。你是最棒的。

句型分析

He hired the boy whom... 本句型是定语从句。whom 作为先行词指代的是前面的 the boy，whom 在从句中充当的是谓语动词的宾语。此句型中 whom 可以和 that 相互替换，也可以省去。

句子示例

- **He hired the boy whom** he is very fond of. 他雇佣了一个他非常喜欢的男孩。
- **He hired the boy whom** he talked with before. 他雇佣了那个之前和他说话的男孩。
- **He hired the boy whom** he met in the street. 他雇佣了他在街上遇见的那个男孩。

重点单词

quarrel ['kwɒrəl] *v.* 争吵，吵架

incredible [ɪn'kredəbl] *a.* 不可思议的，不可相信的

fond [fɒnd] *a.* 喜欢的

Unit 6 否定

1. We have no option but to... 我们只能……没有其他选择。

对话示例

— I have missed John since he went to Japan.	— 自从约翰去日本之后，我就一直很想念他。
— I miss him, too. But **we have no option but to** stay here.	— 我也很想念他，但是我们别无选择，只能待在这里。
— We can go to apply for a passport, so we can go to Japan to visit him.	— 我们可以一起去办个护照，这样就可以去日本看望他了。
— Well, we can go there this Friday.	— 好啊，那我们就约在这个星期五去吧。
— OK. See you then.	— 好的，到时候见。

句型分析

We have no option but to... 本句型中 to 后面要跟动词原形。本句型可用于表达“我们只能做某事，没有其他选择”。

句子示例

- **We have no option but to** select such an obscure place for camping. 我们别无选择，只能选择这么隐蔽的地方野营。
- **We have no option but to** pass over the subject. 我们别无选择，只能回避这个话题。
- **We have no option but to** tie the dog with a rope. 我们别无选择，只能用绳子绑住这只狗。

重点单词

option [ˈɒpʃn] *n.* 选项，选择

obscure [əbˈskjʊə] *a.* 隐蔽的，昏暗的

apply [əˈplaɪ] *v.* 申请，运用

2. Promise not to... 答应我不要……

对话示例

— It's time to leave now.	— 我现在要走了。
— Take care of yourself.	— 照顾好你自己。
— OK. **Promise not to** contact with your ex-husband.	— 好的。答应我不要和你前夫联系了。
— I will try.	— 我尽量。
— You must do it. Otherwise, he will keep pestering you.	— 你必须做到。否则他会一直缠着你的。

句型分析

Promise not to... 本句型中to后面必须跟动词原形。promise sb to do sth，意为"答应某人做某事"，promise sb not to do sth，意为"答应某人不要做某事"。本句型可用于表达请求对方不要做某事。

句子示例

Promise not to forget to walk the dog. 答应我不要忘记去遛狗。

Promise not to ruffle the manager's feather. 答应我不要激怒经理。

Promise not to talk to the strangers. 答应我不要和陌生人说话。

Promise not to unbuckle the seat belt. 答应我不要解开安全带。

重点单词

pester ['pestə] *v.* 纠缠，为难

ruffle ['rʌfl] *v.* 激怒，打扰

feather ['feðə] *n.* 羽毛，状态

unbuckle [ˌʌn'bʌkl] *v.* 解开

3. Nobody would... 没有人会……

对话示例

— Tina says she plays the guitar at home every day.	— 蒂娜说她每天都会在家弹吉他。
— **Nobody would** believe her words.	— 没有人会相信她的话。
— I don't believe it, either. She is not good at	— 我也不相信。她一点儿也不擅长弹吉他。

playing the guitar.	
— I think she can go to the training class to study. After all, she is interested in the guitar.	— 我认为她可以去培训班学习一下。毕竟，她对吉他很感兴趣。

句型分析

Nobody would... 本句型中 would 是情态动词，是 will 的过去式，后面要跟动词原形。本句型可用于表示“没有人会做某事”。

句子示例

- **Nobody would** believe the rogue. 没有人会相信那个无赖。
- **Nobody would** go jogging every day. 没有人会每天都去慢跑。
- **Nobody would** paint the walls. 没有人会刷墙壁。
- **Nobody would** accompany you for a lifetime. 没有人会陪伴你一辈子。

重点单词

guitar [gɪ'tɑː] *n.* 吉他

rogue [rəʊg] *n.* 无赖，流氓

jogging ['dʒɒgɪŋ] *n.* 慢跑

4. I dare not... 我不敢……

对话示例

— Someone came to see you just now when you went out.	— 刚才你出去的时候有人来找你。
— Who's looking for me?	— 谁来找我了?
— I don't know him. So **I dare not** tell him your telephone number.	— 我不认识他。所以我不敢把你的电话号码给他。
— Didn't he wait here for me for a moment?	— 他没有在这里等我一会儿吗?
— No, maybe he doesn't have anything urgent.	— 没有。可能他没有什么紧急的事情吧。

句型分析

I dare not... 本句型中 not 后面必须跟动词原形。本句型可用于表示自己不敢做某事。它可以和 I don't dare... 相互替换。

句子示例

- **I dare not** go to play by the brook. 我不敢去小溪边玩耍。
- **I dare not** get close to the woman, because she is a fraud. 我不敢靠近这个女人,因为她是个骗子。
- **I dare not** buy high-class furniture. 我不敢买高档家具。
- **I dare not** offer you a quotation based on the internal price. 我不敢按内部的价格给你报价。

重点单词

dare [deə] *v.* 敢，敢于

brook [brʊk] *n.* 小溪 *v.* 忍受

fraud [frɔ:d] *n.* 骗子，冒牌货

furniture ['fɜ:nɪtʃə] *n.* 家具

5. I can't make out why... 我不明白为什么……

对话示例

— What did you do after graduation?	— 你毕业以后做了什么?
— I have been looking for a job, but I haven't found a suitable job yet.	— 我一直在找工作，但是还没有找到一个合适的岗位。
— My job was arranged by one of my relatives.	— 我的工作是我的一个亲戚安排的。
— **I can't make out why** the employment rate is so low now.	— 我不明白为什么现在的就业率这么低。
— Because the current economic crisis is serious.	— 因为现在的经济危机很严重。

句型分析

I can't make out why... 本句型中 make out 为固定搭配，意为“明白，理解”，why 后面要跟一个完整的句子，句子要用陈述句的语序。本句型可用于表达自己不明白某事的原因。

句子示例

- **I can't make out why** he can get a job in kindergarten. 我不明白为什么他可以在幼儿园找到一份工作。
- **I can't make out why** the party was delayed. 我不明白为什么这个派对被推迟了。
- **I can't make out why** you want to ask for a full refund. 我不明白你为什么想要全额退款。
- **I can't make out why** he wanted to look over the draft of the contract. 我不明白为什么他想看合同的草稿。

重点单词

rate [reɪt] *n.* 比例，比率

kindergarten ['kɪndəgɑ:tn] *n.* 幼儿园

current ['kʌrənt] *a.* 当前的，现在的

delay [dɪ'leɪ] *v.* 延迟，推后

6. It is no use... ……没有用

对话示例

— Why do you always go shopping?	— 你为什么总是去购物?
— I just bought a dressing mirror.	— 我只是买了一个穿衣镜而已。
— **It is no use** buying such a big dressing mirror.	— 买这么大的穿衣镜是没有用的。
— Why? I don't understand.	— 为什么？我不明白。
— Because our house doesn't have enough space at all.	— 因为我们家根本没有足够的空间。

句型分析

It is no use... 本句型中 use 后面要跟动名词结构，本句型可用于表达做某事是没有用的。

句子示例

- **It is no use** handing in the homework now. 现在上交作业是没有用的。
- **It is no use** explaining to her about the case. 向她解释这件事是没有用的。
- **It is no use** reporting it to the senior. 向上级报告这件事是没有用的。
- **It is no use** sympathizing with him. 同情他是没有用的。

重点单词

mirror ['mɪrə] *n.* 镜子

sympathize ['sɪmpəθaɪz] *v.* 同情，可怜

senior ['si:nɪə] *n.* 上级 *a.* 年长的，级别高的

7. It is not enough to... ……是不够的

对话示例

— The final exam is coming. Do you have confidence in the exam?	— 期末考试就要到了。你对这次考试有信心吗?
— Of course. I have been doing a lot of exercises.	— 当然，我已经做了大量的习题。
— **It is not enough to** do these exercises.	— 只做习题是远远不够的。
— So do you have any good suggestions?	— 那你有什么好的建议吗?
— I think you can sum up the key knowledge while doing exercises.	— 我认为你可以在做习题的同时总结出重点知识。

句型分析

It is not enough to... 本句型中 to 后面必须跟动词原形。本句型可用于表达只做某件事是远远不够的。

句子示例

- **It is not enough to** write answers on the paper. 只在纸上写出答案是远远不够的。
- **It is not enough to** draw up a draft of the contract. 只拟出合同的草稿是远远不够的。
- **It is not enough to** investigate and research. 只做调查和研究是远远不够的。
- **It is not enough to** meet these needs. 只满足这些要求是远远不够的。

重点单词

sum [sʌm] *v.* 概括，总结　　draft [drɑ:ft] *n.* 草稿，草图

investigate [ɪn'vestɪgeɪt] *v.* 调查

8. There is not time for us to... 我们没有时间……

对话示例

— Have you made a plan for the trip?	— 你制定好旅行的计划了吗?
— Yes. But **there is not time for us to** travel.	— 是的，但是我们没时间去了。
— Why do you say that?	— 为什么这样说?

— Because the boss told us to work overtime for a week.	— 因为老板临时通知我们加班一星期。
— I'm sorry to hear that, but if you work overtime in the holiday, you will have a double salary.	— 虽然很遗憾，但是如果你在假期加班，就会有双倍的工资。

句型分析

There is not time for us to... 本句型中 to 后面要跟动词原形，本句型可用于表达我们没有时间去做某事。

句子示例

- **There is not time for us to** realize our dreams. 我们没有时间去实现梦想了。
- **There is not time for us to** attend Maria's wedding. 我们没有时间去参加玛利亚的婚礼了。
- **There is not time for us to** prepare the dinner. 我们没有时间去准备晚饭了。
- **There is not time for us to** visit the photo exhibition. 我们没有时间去看摄影展了。

重点单词

double ['dʌbl] *a.* 双倍的，两人的　　wedding ['wedɪŋ] *n.* 婚礼，结婚

dinner ['dɪnə] *n.* 晚餐，正餐

9. It is impossible to... ……是不可能的

对话示例

— Do you know who got the first place in the final exam?	— 你知道谁期末考试得了第一名吗?
— It is Jenny.	— 是珍妮。
— **It is impossible to** get the first place for her.	— 她不可能得第一名的。
— I can't believe it,either, because she never hands in the homework on time.	— 我也不敢相信，因为她从来都不会按时交作业。
— Maybe she is a lucky dog.	— 可能她是个幸运儿吧。

句型分析

It is impossible to... 本句型中 to 后面要跟动词原形，it 是形式主语，真正的主语是 to 后面的不定式。本句型可用于表示“做某事是不可能的”。

句子示例

- **It is impossible to** finish the project in September. 在九月份完成这个项目是不可能的。
- **It is impossible to** build a new school. 建立一个新学校是不可能的。
- **It is impossible to** reach an agreement with these officials. 和这些行政官员达成共识是不可能的。

重点单词

impossible [ɪm'pɒsəbl] *a.* 不可能的，难以做到的　　official [ə'fɪʃl] *a.* 官方的 *n.* 行政官员

10. It's not for ...to... ……没有责任去……

对话示例

— Tony, can you give me a cup of coffee?	— 托尼，你能给我一杯咖啡吗?
— Sorry, **it's not for** me **to** do that because I am not your secretary.	— 对不起，我没有责任那样做。因为我不是你的秘书。
— I know. But my secretary has asked for leave. I'm very busy now.	— 我知道，但是我的秘书请假了，我现在特别忙。
— OK. But I don't know where the coffee beans are.	— 好的，但是我不知道咖啡豆放在哪里。

句型分析

It's not for ...to... 本句型中 to 后面必须跟动词原形，it 是形式主语，真正的主语是 to 后面的不定式。本句型可用于表达某人没有责任或者义务去做某事。本句型可与 ... have no responsibility to... 相互替换。

句子示例

- **It's not for** me **to** take charge of his work. 我没有责任去接管他的工作。
- **It's not for** John **to** buy the coffee for the guest. 约翰没有责任去为那个客人买咖啡。
- **It's not for** our parents **to** raise us all the time. 我们的父母没有一直养育我们的责任。

重点单词

charge [tʃɑːdʒ] *v.* 充电，控告 *n.* 接管，负责

guest [gest] *n.* 客人

raise [reɪz] *v.* 抚养，筹集

11. He had no idea of... 他不知道……

对话示例

— Frank looks very frustrated. What happened to him?	— 弗兰克看起来很失落。发生了什么?
— He lost Peter's bike. **He had no idea of** how to deal with it.	— 他弄丢了彼得的自行车，不知道该怎么办。
— It doesn't matter. Peter is very kind; he won't complain about Frank.	— 没关系。彼得很善良，他不会抱怨弗兰克的。
— I hope so.	— 希望如此。

句型分析

He had no idea of... 本句型中 of 为介词，后面跟名词、动名词、代词等。本句型可用于表达某人不知道某事。

句子示例

- **He had no idea of** where the laundry is. 他不知道洗衣房在哪里。
- **He had no idea of** how to get to the metro station. 他不知道如何到达地铁站。
- **He had no idea of** how to catch the mouse. 他不知道如何捉到那只老鼠。

重点单词

laundry ['lɔːndrɪ] *n.* 洗衣房

metro ['metrəʊ] *n.* 地铁

mouse [maʊs] *n.* 老鼠，鼠标

12. It was not often that... 不经常……

对话示例

— I went to Kate's wedding yesterday.	— 我昨天去参加凯特的婚礼了。
— What do you think of her wedding?	— 你认为她的婚礼怎么样?
— Very wonderful. But there are few classmates in her wedding.	— 很完美，但是她的同学好像很少。
— Because **it was not often that** she kept in touch with her classmates.	— 因为她不经常和她的同学联系。

句型分析

It was not often that... 本句型中 that 后面要跟主语从句，从句要用陈述句的语序。因为前面用的是 was，所以从句也要用过去时。本句型可用于表达某人不经常做某事。

句子示例

- **It was not often that** the youngsters washed clothes at home. 年轻人在家不经常洗衣服。
- **It was not often that** the boy worked overtime. 这个男孩不经常加班。
- **It was not often that** I had western food. 我不经常吃西餐。

重点单词

youngster ['jʌŋstə] *n.* 年轻人，青少年　　western ['westən] *a.* 西方的，西部的

13. ... couldn't remember... ……想不起来……

对话示例

— My grandmother is so old that she often forgets something.	— 我奶奶年纪太大了，以至于她经常会忘记一些事。
— You should spend more time with her, and take her out for a walk.	— 你们应该多陪陪她，带她出去逛逛。
— Tomorrow is her birthday, but she **couldn't remember** it.	— 明天是她的生日，但是她想不起来。
— How are you going to celebrate her birthday?	— 那你们打算怎么庆祝她的生日?

— We are going to have a special party for her.	— 我们准备为她举办一个特别的生日派对。

句型分析

... couldn't remember... 本句型中 remember 后面可以跟名词、动名词、代词和从句。因为前面用的是 couldn't，所以从句也要用过去时态。本句型可用于表示“某人想不起来某事”。

句子示例

- The little girl **couldn't remember** when she turned off the light. 这个小女孩想不起来她什么时候把灯关了。
- I **couldn't remember** where the shampoo is. 我想不起来洗发水在哪里。
- The old man **couldn't remember** how to use the mobile phone. 这个老人想不起来如何使用手机。

重点单词

shampoo [ʃæm'puː] *n.* 洗发水

mobile ['məʊbaɪl] *a.* 可以移动的 *n.* 手机，电话

14. I'm not sure that... 我不确定……

对话示例

— Will you see Kathy tomorrow?	— 你明天会见到凯西吗?
— **I'm not sure that** she will come to the company, because her child is ill.	— 我不确定她明天会不会来公司，因为她的孩子生病了。
— If you see her, please give her a message for me.	— 如果你见到她了，请帮我给她捎个口信。
— OK, but if you have urgent things, I can give you her address.	— 好的，但是如果你有特别紧急的事，我可以把她家的地址给你。
— That's great!	— 那真是太好了!

句型分析

I'm not sure that... 本句型中 that 引导的是宾语从句，从句要用陈述句的语序。本句型可用于表达“某人不确定某事”。

句子示例

- **I'm not sure that** he will come back home at 6 o'clock. 我不确定他会 6 点钟回家。
- **I'm not sure that** John will answer your questions. 我不确定约翰会回答你的问题。
- **I'm not sure that** she will pay a deposit for the hotel. 我不确定她会为这个酒店付押金。

重点单词

address [ə'dres] *n.* 地址　　deposit [dɪ'pɒzɪt] *n.* 押金，保证金

15. We could do nothing to... 我们无法……

对话示例

— **We could do nothing to** go hiking this weekend.	— 我们这周末无法去远足了。
— Why?	— 为什么?
— Because the manager rejected my proposal, so I have to work overtime on weekends.	— 因为经理否决了我的提案，所以我周末得加班。
— It is not fair to take your rest time.	— 经理占用你们的休息时间是不公平的。

句型分析

We could do nothing to... 本句型中 to 后面要用动词原形。本句型可用于表示“某人无法去做某事”。

句子示例

- **We could do nothing to** call off this activity. 我们无法取消这次活动。
- **We could do nothing to** bear the little boy's bad temper. 我们无法忍受这个小男孩的坏脾气。
- **We could do nothing to** accept the fact. 我们无法接受这个事实。

重点单词

reject [rɪ'dʒekt] *v.* 否定，拒绝　　bear [beə] *v.* 忍受 *n.* 熊

temper ['tempə] *n.* 脾气

16. I don't care... 我不在乎 / 关心……

对话示例

— Kelly is going to study in England next week.	— 凯丽下周要去英国留学了。
— **I don't care** where she is going.	— 我才不关心她去哪里。
— What's wrong with you? Did you have a fight?	— 怎么了？你们吵架了？
— She actually said I was a liar yesterday.	— 她昨天居然说我是个骗子。
— Maybe she misunderstood you.	— 她可能误会你了。

句型分析

I don't care... 本句型中 care 后面可以跟名词、动名词、代词、疑问不定式和完整的句子。本句型可用于表达“自己不关心或者不在乎某事”。

句子示例

- **I don't care** whether he would believe me. 我不在乎他是否会相信我。
- **I don't care** the registrar's attitude. 我不在乎教务主任的态度。
- **I don't care** whether my wife likes to eat strawberries. 我不关心我的妻子是否喜欢吃草莓。

重点单词

liar ['laɪə] *n.* 骗子，说谎的人　　registrar [ˌredʒɪ'strɑ:] *n.* 教导主任，登记员

strawberry ['strɔ:bərɪ] *n.* 草莓

17. I'm not likely to... 我不可能……

对话示例

— Do you like English class?	— 你喜欢上英语课吗？
— No, **I'm not likely to** be interested in English.	— 不，我不可能对英语感兴趣。
— Why? Is your English teacher very strict?	— 为什么？你的英语老师很严厉吗？
— No, because I'm not good at grammar.	— 不，因为我在语法方面不是很擅长。
— You can ask your teacher for help.	— 你可以向老师请求帮助。

句型分析

I'm not likely to... 本句型中 to 后面跟动词原形。本句型可用于表示“自己不可能做某事”。它可与 It is impossible for me to... 相互替换。

句子示例

- **I'm not likely to** earn money by selling cucumbers. 我不可能靠卖黄瓜挣钱。
- **I'm not likely to** betray my friends. 我不可能出卖我的朋友。
- **I'm not likely to** allow you to bother my husband. 我不可能允许你去打扰我的丈夫。

重点单词

earn [ɜ:n] *v.* 得到，赚到 cucumber ['kju:kʌmbə] *n.* 黄瓜

18. There is no occasion to... 还不是……的时机。

对话示例

— Jenny was injured in a car accident yesterday.	— 珍妮昨天在一场车祸中受伤了。
— We should tell her parents about it.	— 我们应该把这件事告诉她的父母。
— **There is no occasion to** tell them. Her parents are on business abroad now.	— 还不是告诉她父母的时机。她父母现在在国外出差。
— We can take turns to go to the hospital to take care of her.	— 那我们可以轮流去医院照顾她。
— OK.	— 好的。

句型分析

There is no occasion to... 本句型中 to 后面要跟动词原形。本句型可用于表示“还不是做某事的时机”。

句子示例

- **There is no occasion to** sign the contract with him. 还不是和他签订合同的时机。
- **There is no occasion to** sell the stock. 还不是出售股票的时机。
- **There is no occasion to** plant poplars. 还不是种植杨树的时机。

重点单词

occasion [ə'keɪʒn] *n.* 时机，机会

poplar ['pɒplə] *n.* 杨树

19. I know of no way of... 我不知道怎么……

对话示例

— Why do you eat in a restaurant?	— 你为什么在餐馆吃饭?
— There is something wrong with my induction cooker, so I can't cook at home.	— 因为我家的电磁炉坏了，所以不能在家做饭了。
— You should repair it. It's a waste of money to eat out.	— 你应该修一下，在外面吃饭太浪费钱了。
— But **I know of no way of** repairing it.	— 但是我不知道怎么去修理它。
— You'd better buy a new one.	— 那你最好买一个新的。

句型分析

I know of no way of... 本句型中 of 为介词，因此后面要跟动名词结构。本句型可用于表示“自己不知道如何去做某事”。

句子示例

- **I know of no way of** checking in. 我不知道怎么办理登机手续。
- **I know of no way of** braking the car lightly. 我不知道怎么轻踩刹车。
- **I know of no way of** communicating with people on such occasions. 我不知道怎么在这种场合和人交流。

重点单词

induction [ɪn'dʌkʃn] *n.* 电磁感应

brake [breɪk] *v.* 刹车 *n.* 刹车，制动器

lightly ['laɪtlɪ] *ad.* 轻轻地，容易地

20. It's not my habit to... ……不是我的一贯作风。

对话示例

— Kate is really a sharp-tongued girl. What do you think of her?	— 凯特真是个说话尖酸刻薄的女孩。你认为她是一个什么样的人?
— **It's not my habit to** comment others privately.	— 私下评论别人不是我的一贯作风。
— I just want to know your opinions of her.	— 我只是想知道你对她的看法。
— Sorry. I don't want to say this.	— 对不起，我不想说这个。

句型分析

It's not my habit to... 本句型中 to 后面要跟动词原形。本句型可用于表达做某事不是自己的一贯作风或者习惯。

句子示例

- **It's not my habit to** censure the students. 批评学生不是我的一贯作风。
- **It's not my habit to** work overtime at the weekend. 周末加班不是我的一贯作风。
- **It's not my habit to** drive on the left side of the road. 在路的左侧开车不是我的一贯作风。

重点单词

privately ['praɪvətlɪ] *a.* 私下地　　opinion [ə'pɪnjən] *n.* 看法，主张

censure ['senʃə] *v.* 批评，责备 *n.* 指责，批评

21. You have no right to... 你没有权力……

对话示例

— Nancy, what are you doing now?	— 南希，你在干什么?
— I am looking at Emma's diary.	— 我在看艾玛的日记。
— **You have no right to** read her diary. You are invading her privacy.	— 你没有权力去翻看她的日记。你这样是在侵犯她的隐私。
— I am curious about her.	— 我就是对她比较好奇。
— It's not right for you to do it.	— 你这样做是不对的。

句型分析

You have no right to... 本句型中 to 后面跟动词原形，right 在此为名词，意为“权力”。本句型可用于表示对方没有权力做某事。

句子示例

- **You have no right to** use his computer. 你没有权力使用他的电脑。
- **You have no right to** forbid me to drive the car. 你没有权力阻止我开车。
- **You have no right to** swear at me. 你没有权力咒骂我。

重点单词

curious ['kjʊərɪəs] *a.* 好奇的

forbid [fə'bɪd] *v.* 阻止，禁止

swear [sweə] *v.* 咒骂，发誓

22. ...would by no means... ……坚决不……

对话示例

— The weather forecast said there will be a typhoon recently.	— 天气预报说最近会有台风。
— I **would by no means** believe that the typhoon is coming.	— 我坚决不会相信台风就要来了。
— Why don't you believe it?	— 你为什么不相信呢?
— Because our city belongs to the monsoon climate of medium latitudes, it doesn't have the conditions for the formation of the typhoon.	— 因为我们城市属于温带季风气候，不具备台风形成的条件。
— You are so clever!	— 你真是太聪明了!

句型分析

...would by no means... 本句型中 means 后面需要跟动词原形。本句型可用于表达某人坚决不会去做某事，表明了一种坚决的态度。

句子示例

- I **would by no means** be full of hostility with him. 我坚决不会对他充满敌意。
- He **would by no means** try to apologize to me. 他坚决不会试着向我道歉。
- Maria **would by no means** make friends with those who are unprincipled. 玛利亚坚决不会和那些毫无原则的人交朋友。

重点单词

forecast ['fɔ:kɑ:st] *n.* 预言，预报

hostility [hɒ'stɪlətɪ] *n.* 敌意

latitude ['lætɪtju:d] *n.* 范围，纬度

unprincipled [ʌn'prɪnsəpld] *a.* 毫无原则的，没有道德的

23. ...had no intention of... ……无意……

对话示例

— Mike and Paul have been good friends since they were very young.	— 麦克和保罗在他们很小的时候就是好朋友了。
— But Mike **had no intention of** inviting Paul to take part in his birthday party.	— 但麦克无意邀请保罗去参加他的生日派对。
— You are wrong, because he know Paul has no time.	— 不是这样的，因为他知道保罗没有时间。
— What is he doing now?	— 那保罗在忙什么?
— He is busy conferring with the customer on the contract.	— 他在忙着和客户协商合同。

句型分析

...had no intention of... 本句型中 of 为介词，因此其后要跟动名词形式。本句型可用于表达某人无意做某事。

句子示例

- I **had no intention of** hearing their conversation. 我无意听他们的谈话。
- Alice **had no intention of** revealing her identity. 爱丽丝无意暴露她的身份。
- They **had no intention of** standing up to greet me. 他们无意起身向我打招呼。

重点单词

confer [kən'fɜː] *v.* 协商，授予

identity [aɪ'dentətɪ] *n.* 身份

greet [griːt] *v.* 打招呼，致意

24. It wasn't long before... 没过多久……

对话示例

— Are Bill and Tom still in a cold war?	— 比尔和汤姆还在冷战吗?
— No, **it wasn't long before** they reconciled.	— 不是的，没过多久他们就和好如初了。
— After all, there was nothing serious that happened.	— 毕竟也没有发生什么严重的事情。
— Because they are manly people.	— 因为他们都是有男子汉气概的人。
— Of course.	— 当然。

句型分析

It wasn't long before... 本句型中 before 后面必须跟完整的句子，句子要用陈述句的语序。本句型可用于表达“某人没过多久就做某事了”。

句子示例

- **It wasn't long before** he was married with the pretty girl. 没过多久他就和那个漂亮的女孩结婚了。
- **It wasn't long before** I finished the formidable task. 没过多久我就完成了那项艰巨的任务。
- **It wasn't long before** the young woman received a bundle of lilies. 没过多久这个年轻的女人就收到了一束百合花。

重点单词

reconcile ['rekənsaɪl] *v.* 和解，和好

formidable ['fɔːmɪdəbl] *a.* 艰巨的，可怕的

lily ['lɪlɪ] *n.* 百合花

manly ['mænlɪ] *a.* 有男子汉气概的

bundle ['bʌndl] *n.* 束，捆

25. No wonder that... 难怪……

对话示例

— The professor said Kate obtained the doctor's degree.	— 刚才教授说凯特获得了博士学位。
— **No wonder that** she is so happy.	— 难怪她这么开心。
— Do you know how hard she worked?	— 你知道她付出了多少努力吗?
— Of course. Every time when we went out to play, she was reviewing her lessons.	— 当然，每次我们出去玩的时候她都在复习功课。

句型分析

No wonder that... 本句型中 that 后面必须跟完整的句子，句子要用陈述句的语序。本句型可用于表示对某事感到特别惊讶或者恍然大悟。

句子示例

- **No wonder that** he bullied the alcoholic. 难怪他欺负那个酗酒者。
- **No wonder that** she was tired of this boring life. 难怪她厌倦了这种枯燥的生活。
- **No wonder that** the woman said it is a happy thing to have a dream. 难怪这个女人说拥有梦想是一件幸福的事情。

重点单词

wonder ['wʌndə] *v.* 怀疑，好奇 *n.* 奇迹 *a.* 奇妙的

obtain [əb'teɪn] *v.* 得到，获得

alcoholic [ˌælkə'hɒlɪk] *n.* 酗酒者 *a.* 有酒精的

26. I could no longer... 我不再……

对话示例

— **I could no longer** be interested in painting.	— 我不再对绘画感兴趣了。
— Why? You are good at drawing, aren't you?	— 为什么？你最擅长绘画了，不是吗?
— Since I went to a concert last week, I have been crazy about classical music.	— 自从上周我听完音乐会之后，我就迷上了古典音乐。
— You are really a changeable person.	— 你真是一个多变的人。

句型分析

I could no longer... 本句型中 could 是情态动词，no longer 是插入语，所以后面必须跟动词原形。本句型可用于表达自己不再做某事了，可以和 I could not... any longer 相互替换。

句子示例

- **I could no longer** destroy the environment. 我不再破坏环境了。
- **I could no longer** sit up since I became nearsighted. 自从我眼睛近视之后，我就不再熬夜了。
- **I could no longer** play baseball. 我不再打棒球了。

重点单词

changeable [ˈtʃeɪndʒəbl] *a.* 多变的，易变的

destroy [dɪˈstrɔɪ] *v.* 破坏，毁坏

nearsighted [ˌnɪəˈsaɪtɪd] *a.* 眼睛近视的

27. You're not supposed to... 你不应该……

对话示例

— There are a lot of books in the bookstore.	— 书店里有很多书。
— I like reading books.	— 我喜欢阅读。
— Me too. I want to take some books away.	— 我也是。我想带走一些书。
— **You're not supposed to** take the books out of the rooms.	— 你不应该把这些书带出去。
— Of course. I will pay the money first.	— 当然。我会先付钱的。

句型分析

You're not supposed to... 该句型常常在否定别人的观点的场合中使用，其中 suppose 是一个动词，表示"假定，猜想，让"。

句子示例

- **You're not supposed to** smoke in the church. 你不应该在教堂里吸烟。
- **You're not supposed to** wear the suit on such an occasion. 你不应该在这种场合穿西装。
- **You're not supposed to** use that photocopier. 你不应该用那台复印机。

重点单词

church [tʃɜ:tʃ] *n.* 教堂　　photocopier ['fəʊtəʊkɒpɪə] *n.* 复印机

28. Don't even think about... 连想都不要再想……

对话示例

— I really want to take a vacation.	— 我真想去度假。
— **Don't even think about** it.	— 连想都不要再想它。
— What happened?	— 怎么了?
— We will have a lot of work to do.	— 我们将有很多工作要做。
— Well, I should say that work is exhausting.	— 好吧，我得说那工作真叫人精疲力竭。

句型分析

Don't even think about... 该句型中，Don't 用于祈使句的句首表示否定，even 是一个副词表示“甚至”，其中 think about 表示“考虑，回想”，后可加名词、名词短语、动名词以及从句。

句子示例

- **Don't even think about** why that procedure would be like that. 连想都不要再想为什么那个程序会是那样。
- **Don't even think about** the practicability of this plan. 连想都不要再想这个方案的可行性。
- **Don't even think about** doing something else. 连想都不要再想做些其他的事。

重点单词

procedure [prə'si:dʒə] *n.* 程序，手续　　practicability [ˌpræktɪkə'bɪlətɪ] *n.* 可行性

Chapter 5
疑问用语句型

Unit 1 一般疑问句

1. Are you aware that...? 你知道……吗?

对话示例

— **Are you aware that** the acountant has been dismissed?	— 那个会计师被解雇了，你知道吗?
— How come?	— 怎么会这样呢?
— It is said that he abused the financial power of our company.	— 据说他滥用我们公司的财政权。
— Such a bad man should be fired.	— 像这种坏人就应该被解雇。
— Our boss should employ some honest people.	— 我们的老板应该雇佣一些诚实的人。

句型分析

Are you aware that... 句型中，系动词are放在句首构成一般疑问句，be aware that / of是固定搭配，意为“察觉到，意识到”，that 后面的从句要用陈述句的语序。

句子示例

- **Are you aware that** the young man is a lawyer? 那个年轻人是一位律师，你知道吗?
- **Are you aware that** the voice of the speaker is very familiar? 你知道吗? 那位演讲者的声音特别熟悉。
- **Are you aware that** the company will lay off some staff members? 公司将要裁减一些员工，你知道吗?

重点单词

aware [ə'weə] *a.* 意识到的，知道的，察觉到的

dismiss [dɪs'mɪs] *v.* 解雇，遣散，搁置

familiar [fə'mɪlɪə] *a.* 熟悉的，通晓的 *n.* 常客，密友

abuse [ə'bju:s] *v.* 滥用，虐待，辱骂

staff [stɑ:f] *n.* 参谋，全体职工 *a.* 职员的，行政工作的 *v.* 任职于

2. Is there any way...? 有办法……吗?

对话示例

— Alice looks very sad. What happened?	— 爱丽丝看起来很难过，发生什么了?
— Because her father died of cancer last week.	— 因为上周她的父亲由于癌症去世了。
— **Is there any way** to get her out of sorrow?	— 有什么办法可以让她走出悲伤吗?
— I think she should adjust her mind, and then she can travel.	— 我认为她应该调整一下心态，然后可以去旅行。
— That's a good idea!	— 真是个好主意!

句型分析

Is there any way... 本句型后面必须跟动词不定式，充当目的状语。

句子示例

- **Is there any way** to reduce the environmental pollution? 有什么办法能减少环境污染吗?
- **Is there any way** to prevent them from playing computer games? 有什么办法阻止他们玩电脑游戏吗?
- **Is there any way** to make him become a responsible boy? 有什么办法能让他成为一个有责任心的男孩吗?

重点单词

sorrow [ˈsɒrəʊ] *n.* 悲伤，悔恨 *v.* 伤感，遗憾
reduce [rɪˈdju:s] *v.* 减少，缩小，减弱
responsible [rɪˈspɒnsəbl] *a.* 有责任心的，尽职尽责的
adjust [əˈdʒʌst] *v.* 适应，调整
pollution [pəˈlu:ʃn] *n.* 污染，腐败
prevent [prɪˈvent] *v.* 防止，阻止

3. Is there nobody to...? 没有人……吗?

对话示例

— Tomorrow is Michael's birthday.	— 明天是迈克尔的生日。
— **Is there nobody to** attend his birthday party?	— 没有人去参加他的生日派对吗?
— You know he likes simple life, so he doesn't	— 你知道他喜欢简单的生活，所以他不打算

intend to hold a party.	举办派对。
— But we should prepare birthday presents for him.	— 但是我们应该为他准备生日礼物。
— OK. Let's go to the mall.	— 好的。那我们去购物中心吧。

句型分析

Is there nobody to... 句型中 to 后面的动词充当的是不定代词 nobody 的定语，起限定作用。

句子示例

- **Is there nobody to** be angry at this traffic accident? 没有人对这场车祸感到愤怒吗?
- **Is there nobody to** take care of the old man? 没有人来照顾这个老人吗?
- **Is there nobody to** want to know about her past? 没有人想要知道她的过去吗?

重点单词

attend [ə'tend] *v.* 参加，出席

mall [mɔ:l] *n.* 购物中心，林荫小路

accident ['æksɪdənt] *n.* 事故，偶然

past [pɑ:st] *a.* 过去的 *n.* 过往，过去的事 *prep.* 超过，大于

4. Is it true that...? ……是真的吗?

对话示例

— I heard that Betty is going to Australia next month.	— 我听说贝蒂下个月要去澳大利亚。
— **Is it true that** she will be married to a 40-year-old foreigner?	— 她要嫁给一个 40 岁的外国人，这是真的吗?
— Yes. It's incredible.	— 是的，太不可思议了。
— But I still hope that she can live a happy life.	— 但我还是希望她能过着幸福的生活。
— Of course.	— 那当然。

句型分析

Is it true that... 句型中 it 充当形式主语，真正的主语是 that 引导的从句。

句子示例

- **Is it true that** we will have a bonus this month? 这个月我们会有奖金，是真的吗?
- **Is it true that** the tall boy is his son? 那个个子高高的男孩是他的儿子，是真的吗?
- **Is it true that** the timid woman is a lawyer? 那个胆怯的女人是一名律师，是真的吗?
- **Is it true that** our boss divorced last week? 我们的老板上星期离婚了，是真的吗?

重点单词

bonus ['bəʊnəs] *n.* 奖金，利润，退休金

timid ['tɪmɪd] *a.* 胆小的，胆怯的

lawyer ['lɔ:jə] *n.* 律师，法学家

5. Do you know who...? 你认识 / 知道……吗?

对话示例

— Yesterday you were absent for school, we had a calligraphy competition.	— 昨天你没来学校，我们举行了书法比赛。
— Unfortunately, I didn't take part in it.	— 很遗憾我没有参加。
— **Do you know who** won the first?	— 你知道是谁赢得了第一名吗?
— It must be Nancy. I know her writing is so beautiful.	— 当然是南希了。我知道她的字写的特别漂亮。
— You are wrong. It's our new classmate.	— 你错了。是我们班新来的同学。

句型分析

Do you know who... 本句型中 do 放在句首构成一般疑问句，who 引导的是一个宾语从句，要用陈述句的语序。

句子示例

- **Do you know who** donated clothes and books for those poor children? 你知道是谁为那些贫困的孩子们捐赠衣服和书籍的吗?
- **Do you know who** is strict with us? 你知道是谁对我们这么严厉吗?

• **Do you know who** forgot the report? 你知道是谁忘记了那份报告吗?

重点单词

calligraphy [kə'lɪgrəfɪ] *n.* 书法

competition [ˌkɒmpə'tɪʃn] *n.* 竞争，比赛

6. Does it mean that...? 这是否意味着……?

对话示例

— Environmental pollution has always been a concern for us.	— 环境污染一直是我们担心的问题。
— We have complained to the related staff members, but there is still no one to solve it.	— 我们已经向相关的工作人员投诉了，但还是没有人解决。
— **Does it mean that** we must put up with the pollution? And we can do nothing about it.	— 这是否意味着我们要忍受污染呢? 而且我们还不能做任何事。
— I think we should explain to the government leaders.	— 我认为我们可以向政府领导解释。

句型分析

Does it mean that... 句型中 it 是形式主语，真正的主语是 that 引导的从句，从句的时态要根据句意而定。

句子示例

• **Does it mean that** the summer vacation is coming? 这是否意味着暑假即将到来?
• **Does it mean that** he is a rude man? 这是否意味着他是一个粗鲁的人?
• **Does it mean that** we will have a wonderful future? 这是否意味着我们将会有一个美好的未来?

重点单词

concern [kən'sɜːn] *v.* 涉及，关心 *n.* 关心，关系，考虑

explain [ɪk'spleɪn] *v.* 解释，说明

government ['gʌvənmənt] *n.* 政府，政体

rude [ruːd] *a.* 粗鲁的，简单的

wonderful ['wʌndəfl] *a.* 壮观的，精彩的，美妙的

7. Have you ever...? 你有没有……?

对话示例

— How could we win the speech contest?	— 我们怎样才能赢得演讲比赛呢?
— I have no idea now.	— 我现在也没主意。
— **Have you ever** thought we could ask returned students for help?	— 你有没有想过我们可以向留学生求助?
— But their ideas are so different from us.	— 但是他们的想法和我们区别太大了。
— We can take their advice properly.	— 我们可以适当地采纳他们的建议。

句型分析

Have you ever... 本句型用现在完成时，ever 后面要跟动词的过去分词形式。

句子示例

- **Have you ever** bought cakes at this bakery? 你有没有在这家面包店买过蛋糕?
- **Have you ever** noticed a mole on his neck? 你有没有注意到他的脖子上有一颗痣?
- **Have you ever** thought why she was so angry? 你有没有想过她为什么如此生气?
- **Have you ever** been to South Africa? 你有没有去过南非?

重点单词

contest ['kɒntest] *v.* 竞争，辩论 *n.* 比赛，竞赛

bakery ['beɪkərɪ] *n.* 面包店，烘焙坊

neck [nek] *n.* 脖子，颈部，衣领

properly ['prɒpəlɪ] *a.* 适当地，正确地

mole [məʊl] *n.* 痣，鼹鼠

8. May I venture to...? 我可否冒昧地……?

对话示例

— Why are you always busy with your business?	— 你为什么总是忙着事业?
— Because I want to create a good living condition for my family.	— 因为我想为我的家庭创造一个良好的生活条件。
— **May I venture to** remind you that you haven't been home for many days.	— 我可否冒昧地提醒你一下，你已经好多天没回家了。

— Do you think I'm a competent father?	— 你认为我是一个称职的父亲吗？
— Of course, everything you do is for your family.	— 当然，你做的一切都是为了你的家庭。

句型分析

May I venture to... 句型中 may 是情态动词，表示一种委婉的语气，venture to do sth 意为“敢于做某事”，to 后面必须跟动词原形。

句子示例

- **May I venture to** ask whether anyone was injured in the accident? 我可否冒昧地问一下这场事故中有没有人受伤？
- **May I venture to** say something about his behaviour? 我可否冒昧地对于他的行为说几句？
- **May I venture to** ask whether you agree with the idea of manager? 我可否冒昧地问一下你是否同意经理的想法？

重点单词

venture ['ventʃə] *v.* 冒险 *n.* 冒险

injure ['ɪndʒə] *v.* 损坏，受伤，伤害

competent ['kɒmpɪtənt] *a.* 称职的，可以胜任的，能干的

behaviour [bɪ'heɪvjə] *n.* 行为，举止，态度

9. Can you imagine that...? 你能想象……吗？

对话示例

— Paul has been reviewing the lessons recently.	— 保罗最近一直在复习功课。
— Yes, he is preparing for the final exam.	— 是的，他正在为期末考试做准备。
— **Can you imagine that** he is reciting the English text carefully?	— 你能想象他正在认真背诵英语课文吗？
— I guess he must have done the ideological struggle for a long time.	— 我猜他一定做了很长时间的思想斗争。
— Maybe.	— 也许。

句型分析

Can you imagine that... 句型中 that 引导的从句要用陈述句的语序，时态要根据句意来定。

句子示例

- **Can you imagine that** the prices are rising all the time? 你能想象物价一直上涨吗?
- **Can you imagine that** he is wearing glasses? 你能想象他戴眼镜的样子吗?
- **Can you imagine that** there is a robot in the living room? 你能想象，在客厅里有一个机器人吗?

重点单词

imagine [ɪ'mædʒɪn] *v.* 想象，猜测，以为

recite [rɪ'saɪt] *v.* 背诵，叙述

ideological [ˌaɪdɪə'lɒdʒɪkl] *a.* 思想上的，意识上的

struggle ['strʌgl] *v.* 斗争，战斗，努力 *n.* 斗争，奋斗

10. Did you refuse to...? 你拒绝……?

对话示例

— I want to give up this project.	— 我想放弃这个项目了。
— What's up? **Did you refuse to** accept Mike's help?	— 怎么了? 你拒绝接受麦克的帮助了吗?
— Yes. I want to finish it on my own.	— 是的，我想自己独立完成。
— Come on. I believe you can do it.	— 加油，我相信你可以的。
— Thank you.	— 谢谢你。

句型分析

Did you refuse to... 本句型中 do 放在句首构成一般疑问句，to 后面跟动词原形，refuse to do sth 意为“拒绝做某事”。本句型可用于询问对方“拒绝做某事吗”。

句子示例

- **Did you refuse to** pay the bill in advance? 你拒绝预先付款了吗?
- **Did you refuse to** go camping? 你拒绝去露营了吗?
- **Did you refuse to** quit smoking? 你拒绝戒烟了吗?
- **Did you refuse to** play badminton with her? 你拒绝和她一起打羽毛球了吗?

重点单词

camp [kæmp] *v.* 露营，宿营

badminton ['bædmɪntən] *n.* 羽毛球

11. Is it not a fact that...? ……难道这不是事实吗?

对话示例

— Sometimes the manager's attitude is really unacceptable.	— 有时候经理的态度真的让人无法接受。
— They were just arguing because of disagreement.	— 他们只是因为意见不合才导致激烈争吵。
— **Is it not a fact that** he is really autocratic?	— 他真的是太专制了，难道这不是事实吗?
— We should give him more advice.	— 我们应该多给他一点建议。
— But he did not listen to our ideas.	— 但是他根本不听我们的想法。

句型分析

Is it not a fact that... 句型中 it 指代 that 引导的从句，从句要用陈述句的语序，否定词 not 也可以放在 it 之前。

句子示例

- **Is it not a fact that** he often tells lies to us? 他经常对我们撒谎，这难道不是事实吗?
- **Is it not a fact that** his father used to be a spy? 他的父亲以前是一名间谍，难道这不是事实吗?
- **Is it not a fact that** the senior staff member leaked the quotation of the company? 那位资深的员工泄露了公司的报价单，难道这不是事实吗?

重点单词

fact [fækt] *n.* 事实，真相，实际

autocratic [ˌɔ:tə'krætɪk] *a.* 专制的，垄断的，独裁的

leak [li:k] *v.* 透漏，泄露 *n.* 漏洞，透漏

argument ['ɑ:gjʊmənt] *n.* 争吵，辩论

spy [spaɪ] *n.* 间谍，侦探

quotation [kwəʊ'teɪʃn] *n.* 报价单，引用

12. Shall we put an end to...? 我们是不是应该终止……？

对话示例

— The Japanese student seems not very active. He looks like a girl.	— 那个日本学生好像不是很活跃。他像一个女孩子一样。
— **Shall we put an end to** this topic?	— 我们是不是应该终止这个话题?
— Oh, sorry. I shouldn't talk about others at random.	— 对不起。我不应该随便议论别人。
— Don't do this again.	— 下次别这样做了。
— OK, I'll remember what you said.	— 好的，我记住你说的话了。

句型分析

Shall we put an end to... 本句型中 shall 为情态动词，表示一种委婉的请求。put an end to 是固定搭配，意为“终止，结束”，后面一般跟名词和代词，但有时也可跟动词。

句子示例

- **Shall we put an end to** the heated discussion? 我们是不是应该终止这次热烈的讨论?
- **Shall we put an end to** this unpleasant conversation for our friendship? 为了我们的友谊，我们是不是应该终止这次不愉快的谈话?
- **Shall we put an end to** the contract because of our company's interests? 为了我们公司的利益，我们是不是应该终止这份合同?
- **Shall we put an end to** this trip because he stumbled and fell? 他摔倒了，我们是不是应该终止这次旅行?

重点单词

active ['æktɪv] *a.* 活跃的，积极主动的

conversation [ˌkɒnvə'seɪʃn] *n.* 谈话，交流

random ['rændəm] *a.* 随意的，任意的

stumble ['stʌmbl] *v.* 摔倒，蹒跚 *n.* 绊倒，差错

13. Are...capable of...? ……能……吗?

对话示例

— The show is about to begin right away. Are all the preparations ready?	— 演出马上就要开始了。一切准备工作都做好了吗?
— Jacke hasn't arrived yet. What should we do?	— 只有杰克还没有到。我们应该怎么办?
— **Are you capable of** performing instead of him?	— 你能代替他去表演吗?
— OK. But I'm not sure I can do it well.	— 好的，但是我不确定我可以表演好。
— It doesn't matter.	— 没关系。

句型分析

Are...capable of... 句型中 of 为介词，后面必须跟名词或者动名词。be capable of 意为“具备……的能力”。

句子示例

- **Are you capable of** adjusting the life abroad? 你能适应国外的生活吗?
- **Are you capable of** finishing the task with him before the weekend? 你能在周末之前和他一起完成任务吗?
- **Are you capable of** using this new machine? 你能使用这台新机器吗?
- **Are you capable of** getting a discount on these goods? 你能得到这些商品的折扣吗?

重点单词

perform [pə'fɔ:m] *v.* 表演，演出

machine [mə'ʃi:n] *n.* 机器，机械

discount ['dɪskaʊnt] *n.* 折扣 *v.* 打折，减价

goods [gʊdz] *n.* 商品，产品

14. Do you intend to...? 你打算……?

对话示例

— I heard that we'll have a week's holiday.	— 我听说我们将有一星期的假期。
— **Do you intend to** go traveling with your	— 你打算和你的家人一起去旅行吗?

family?	
— Of course. What about you?	— 当然。你呢?
— I am going to the countryside to visit my grandparents.	— 我要去乡下看望我的爷爷奶奶。
— Haven't you seen them for a long time?	— 你已经很久没见他们了吗?
— Yes. I've been working on my graduation thesis these days.	— 是的，最近我在忙着写毕业论文。

句型分析

Do you intend to... 本句型中 do 为助动词，放在句首，构成一般疑问句。to 后面跟动词原形。intend to do sth 意为“打算做某事”。本句型用于表示询问对方“打算做某事吗? ”。

句子示例

- **Do you intend to** go boating on rainy days? 你打算在下雨天去划船吗?
- **Do you intend to** tell your parents the truth? 你打算对你父母说实话吗?
- **Do you intend to** meet all his requirements? 你打算满足他所有的要求吗?

重点单词

intend [ɪn'tend] *v.* 计划，打算

thesis ['θi:sɪs] *n.* 论文，命题

meet [mi:t] *v.* 遇见，满足 *n.* 会议

requirement [rɪ'kwaɪəmənt] *n.* 要求，必需品

15. Do you really think that...? 你真的认为……吗?

对话示例

— I went to visit Maria's villa yesterday. There is also a small garden in it.	— 我昨天去参观了玛利亚的别墅。里面还有一个小花园。
— You envy her again.	— 你又在羡慕她了。
— I also want to buy a villa.	— 我也想买一栋别墅。
— **Do you really think that** we have enough money to buy it?	— 你真的认为我们有足够的钱去买别墅吗?
— From now on, let's save money.	— 那从现在开始，让我们攒钱吧。

句型分析

Do you really think that... 本句型中 really 是一个程度副词，修饰动词 think，that 引导的从句的时态要根据句意而定。

句子示例

- **Do you really think that** they will elect you as a director? 你真的认为他们会选你当主管吗?
- **Do you really think that** he is an optimistic boy? 你真的认为他是一个乐观的男孩吗?
- **Do you really think that** he will remind us of danger? 你真的认为他会提醒我们注意危险吗?
- **Do you really think that** he was suspicious of our teammates? 你真的认为他怀疑我们的队友吗?

重点单词

villa ['vɪlə] *n.* 别墅

elect [ɪ'lekt] *v.* 选举，选择

optimistic [ˌɒptɪ'mɪstɪk] *a.* 乐观的，积极的

envy ['envɪ] *n.* 羡慕，嫉妒 *v.* 羡慕，嫉妒

director [də'rektə] *n.* 主管，导演

suspicious [sə'spɪʃəs] *a.* 怀疑的，可疑的

16. Have you any objection to...? 你会反对……吗?

对话示例

— I really don't know how to deal with this matter.	— 我真的不知道该怎么解决这件事。
— **Have you any objection to** asking those European tourists for help?	— 你会反对向那些欧洲游客求助吗?
— Of course not. But my spoken English is very poor.	— 当然不会。但是我的英语口语特别差。
— Don't worry. I can help you.	— 别担心。我会帮助你的。
— OK. I would appreciate it if you can help me.	— 好的，如果你可以帮助我，我将不胜感激。

句型分析

Have you any objection to...? 本句型中 have 为实义动词，意为“有”，它可以直接放在句首，构成一般疑问句。have objection to doing sth，意为“反对做某事”。

句子示例

- **Have you any objection to** booking the hotel in advance? 你会反对提前预订酒店吗?
- **Have you any objection to** cancelling our lunch break? 你会反对把我们的午休取消吗?
- **Have you any objection to** buying goods that are about to expire? 你会反对买快要过期的商品吗?

重点单词

objection [əb'dʒekʃn] *n.* 反对
advance [əd'vɑ:ns] *n.* 预先，提前
expire [ɪk'spaɪə] *v.* 到期
European [ˌjʊərə'pi:ən] *a.* 欧洲的 *n.* 欧洲人
cancel ['kænsl] *v.* 取消，注销

17. Is there any particular and special reason for...? ……有什么特殊原因吗?

对话示例

— I guess this studio was created by his father.	— 我猜这个工作室是他的父亲为他创立的。
— **Is there any particular and special reason for** your saying?	— 你这么说是有什么特殊原因吗?
— I heard that his father is a boss of the securities company.	— 我听说他的父亲是一家证券公司的老板。
— Oh, dear! He was born in such a rich family!	— 哦，天哪！他竟然出生在一个如此富裕的家庭里。
— He is so lucky!	— 他真是太幸运了！

句型分析

Is there any particular and special reason for...? 本句型是 There be 句型的一般疑问句形式。particular and special 作定语修饰 reason。for 为介词，后面跟名词、动名词、代词。

句子示例

- **Is there any particular and special reason for** your being interested in classical dance? 你对古典舞这么感兴趣，是有什么特殊原因吗?
- **Is there any particular and special reason for** your saying her ideas are not practical? 你说她的想法不切实际，是有什么特殊原因吗?

• **Is there any particular and special reason for** your believing he will win the first place in the competition? 你认为他将在比赛中赢得第一名，是有什么特殊原因吗？

重点单词

particular [pəˈtɪkjələ] *a.* 特殊的，独特的

practical [ˈpræktɪkl] *a.* 实际的

securities [sɪˈkjʊərɪtɪs] *n.* 证券

18. Do you wish me to...? 你希望我……吗？

对话示例

— He was determined to fight against Thomas.	— 他下定决心要与托马斯为敌。
— Anyway, it's his own business.	— 不管怎么说，这是他自己的事情。
— **Do you wish me to** persuade him?	— 你希望我去说服他吗？
— He is very stubborn, maybe he will not follow your advice.	— 他特别固执，或许他不会听从你的建议。
— Let me have a try.	— 我试一下。

句型分析

Do you wish me to...? 本句型中 wish sb to do sth，意为“希望某人做某事”，本句型可用于询问对方希望自己做某事。

句子示例

• **Do you wish me to** invite the professor who is very wacky. 你希望我邀请那位性格古怪的教授吗？

• **Do you wish me to** catch the bus at my peril? 你希望我冒险去追那辆公交车吗？

• **Do you wish me to** protest this comment? 你希望我抗议这个评论吗？

重点单词

persuade [pəˈsweɪd] *v.* 劝说，说服

wacky [ˈwækɪ] *a.* 古怪的，怪癖的

protest [ˈprəʊtest] *v.* 反对，抗议 *n.* 抗议

stubborn [ˈstʌbən] *a.* 固执的，顽强的

peril [ˈperəl] *n.* 冒险，危险

comment [ˈkɒment] *n.* 评论

19. Are you sure that...? 你确定……吗?

对话示例

— I have never been to Japan.	— 我从来没去过日本。
— **Are you sure that** you want to go to Japan? Earthquakes occur frequently in Japan.	— 你确定你想要去日本吗? 日本经常会发生地震。
— You think too much, it does not matter.	— 你想得太多了，没关系的。
— But 50 people died in the last earthquake.	— 但是最近的一次地震有 50 人死亡。
— How terrible! I won't go there recently.	— 真是太恐怖了! 最近我不会去那里了。

句型分析

Are you sure that...? 本句型中 that 引导的是一个从句，从句的时态要根据句意而定。本句型可用于询问对方“确定做某事吗? ”。

句子示例

- **Are you sure that** there is a story book on the desk? 你确定课桌上有一本故事书吗?
- **Are you sure that** he can't speak French? 你确定他不会说法语吗?
- **Are you sure that** you want to sign this agreement? 你确定你想要签订这份协议吗?

重点单词

earthquake ['ɜːθkweɪk] *n.* 地震　　terrible ['terəbl] *a.* 恐怖的，吓人的

French [frentʃ] *n.* 法语，法国人 *a.* 法国的，法国人的

20. Can it be possible...? ……可能……吗?

对话示例

— I heard that Emma left without saying goodbye.	— 我听说艾玛没打一声招呼就离开了。
— She must have reasons for that.	— 她一定有她自己的理由。
— **Can it be possible that** she had pressing matters to deal with?	— 她有没有可能有紧急的事情要处理?

— Maybe. As her friends, we should understand her. — 有可能。作为她的朋友，我们应该理解她。

— I hope she can call me back afterwards. — 我希望她日后可以给我回个电话。

句型分析

Can it be possible...? 本句型中 possible 后面可以跟 that 引导的从句或动词不定式。

句子示例

- **Can it be possible** to make the design more distinctive? 有没有可能让这个设计更加与众不同?
- **Can it be possible** to avoid talking with strangers? 有没有可能避免和陌生人说话?
- **Can it be possible** that he drove to find his son? 他有没有可能开车去找他儿子了?
- **Can it be possible** that the old man lives in a quiet village? 这个老人有没有可能住在一个安静的村子里?

重点单词

pressing [ˈpresɪŋ] *a.* 紧急的，急迫的

distinctive [dɪˈstɪŋktɪv] *a.* 特别的，与众不同的

avoid [əˈvɔɪd] *v.* 避免

Unit 2 特殊疑问句

1. What does it mean to...? ……是什么意思?

对话示例

— The waiter apologized to me reluctantly.	— 那个服务生不情愿地向我道了歉。
— **What does it mean to** say that?	— 你这样说是什么意思?
— He broke my glass, and his service attitude is very poor.	— 他打碎了我的酒杯，而且他的服务态度特别差。
— Don't be so stingy. He didn't mean to break the glass.	— 不要这么吝啬。他也不是故意要打碎酒杯的。

句型分析

What does it mean to... 本句型中 to 后面必须跟动词原形。本句型可用于询问“某人做某事是什么意思或者意味着什么”。

句子示例

- **What does it mean to** be a successful leader? 成为一个成功的领导意味着什么?
- **What does it mean to** say that? 这样说意味着什么?
- **What does it mean to** offer such a proposal? 提出这样的提议意味着什么?

重点单词

reluctantly [rɪ'lʌktəntlɪ] *ad.* 勉强地，不情愿地

attitude ['ætɪtju:d] *n.* 看法，态度

stingy ['stɪndʒɪ] *a.* 吝啬的，小气的

2. When will you...? 你什么时候……？

对话示例

— Long time no see! What do you do now?	— 好久不见！你现在做什么工作？
— I'm a student. I haven't graduated yet.	— 我是一名学生，还没毕业。
— **When will you** get a master's degree?	— 那你什么时候才能拿到硕士学位？
— Next year. What's your job?	— 明年。那你的工作是什么呢？
— I work in a bank.	— 我在一家银行工作。

句型分析

When will you... 本句型中 will 是情态动词，后面跟动词原形，will do sth 意为“将要做某事”。

句子示例

- **When will you** hand in your homework? 你什么时候上交你的家庭作业？
- **When will you** graduate from the college? 你什么时候大学毕业？
- **When will you** go to Africa to see the migrations of animals? 你什么时候去非洲看动物迁徙？

重点单词

graduate [ˈɡrædʒuət] *v.* 毕业　　migration [maɪˈɡreɪʃn] *n.* 移居，迁徙

3. What's the use of...? ……有什么用？

对话示例

— You'd better describe the details again.	— 你最好再描述一下细节。
— **What's the use of** doing that?	— 这样做有什么用？
— The manager may reconsider your plan.	— 经理可能会重新考虑你的方案。
— He's not going to agree to my plan.	— 他不会同意我的方案。
— You can try to convince him.	— 你可以试着去说服他。

句型分析

What's the use of... 本句型中 what 是引导词，放在句首构成特殊疑问句。use 是不可数名词，意为“作用，价值”，of 是介词，后面必须跟名词、动名词或代词。

句子示例

- **What's the use of** inviting this unknown actor? 邀请那位不知名的演员有什么用?
- **What's the use of** buying some unhealthy snacks? 买一些不健康的零食有什么用?
- **What's the use of** playing those silly jokes? 开那些无趣的玩笑有什么用?

重点单词

describe [dɪ'skraɪb] *v.* 描述，描写

convince [kən'vɪns] *v.* 说服，使相信

unknown [ˌʌn'nəʊn] *a.* 未知的，不知名的 *n.* 未知的事物，不知名的人

4. However have you managed to...? 你究竟是怎么设法……的?

对话示例

— My little sister always cries when she eats dinner.	— 我妹妹吃晚饭的时候总是哭。
— You should make friends with her. My sister and I are good friends.	— 你应该和她交朋友。我和我妹妹就是好朋友。
— **However have you managed to** make friends with your sister?	— 你究竟是怎么设法和她交朋友的?
— I often play with her in my spare time.	— 我经常会在闲暇时间陪她一起玩。
— But I was so busy that I didn't have time to play with her.	— 但是我总是太忙了，没有时间陪她玩。

句型分析

However have you managed to... 本句型中 to 后面要跟动词原形，manage to do sth 意为“设法做某事”。本句型可用于询问对方是“怎么设法做某事的”。

句子示例

- **However have you managed to** cheer him up? 你究竟是怎么设法使他振作起来的?

· **However have you managed to** catch the escaped prisoner? 你究竟是怎么设法抓到那个逃犯的?
· **However have you managed to** ruin their appointment? 你究竟是怎么设法破坏他们的约会的?

重点单词

prisoner ['prɪznə] *n.* 犯人，囚犯

ruin ['ru:ɪn] *v.* 破坏，损失，破产 *n.* 灭亡，损失

5. How would you know...? 你怎么知道……?

对话示例

— His mistake caused the loss of our whole department.	— 他的失误造成了我们整个部门的损失。
— It doesn't matter. Maybe he will compensate us for the loss.	— 没关系。或许他会赔偿我们的损失。
— **How would you know** that he will compensate?	— 你怎么知道他会赔偿?
— We had dinner together last night, and he told me that.	— 昨天晚上我们一起吃晚饭，他告诉我的。
— But it would cost him several months' wages.	— 但是这样会花费他好几个月的工资。

句型分析

How would you know... 本句型中疑问词 how 放在句首构成特殊疑问句，would 是情态动词，所以后跟动词原形 know。know 后面可以跟名词、代词、that 引导的宾语从句。

句子示例

· **How would you know** that the Smiths migrated to America? 你怎么知道史密斯一家人移居到了美国?
· **How would you know** the frightening secret? 你怎么知道这个惊人的秘密?
· **How would you know** that he could understand the importance of this issue? 你怎么知道他会理解这件事的重要性?

重点单词

frightening ['fraɪtnɪŋ] *a.* 惊人的，令人害怕的

issue ['ɪʃu:] *n.* 事情，问题

wage [weɪdʒ] *n.* 工资

6. Why did not you...? 你为什么不……?

对话示例

— Yesterday was Paul's birthday. **Why didn't you** go to his birthday party?	— 昨天是保罗的生日。你为什么没去参加他的生日派对?
— Because we had a fight last week, and it was obvious that he was wrong, but he didn't apologize to me.	— 因为我们上周吵架了。很明显是他错了，他还不向我道歉。
— You should forgive him. After all, he is our classmate.	— 你应该原谅他。毕竟，他是我们的同学。
— OK, I will invite him to see a film tomorrow.	— 好的，那我明天邀请他去看电影。
— It's very kind of you.	— 你真是太好了。

句型分析

Why did not you... 本句型中 why 放在句首构成特殊疑问句，did 为助动词，所以 you 后面要跟动词原形。本句型可用于询问“对方为什么不做某事”。

句子示例

Why did not you go hiking with us? 你为什么不和我们一起去远足?

Why did not you think about it again? 你为什么不再考虑一下?

Why did not you cancel the flight? 你为什么不取消航班?

重点单词

forgive [fə'gɪv] *v.* 原谅，宽恕

hiking ['haɪkɪŋ] *v.* 远足 *n.* 徒步

7. How can we...? 我们怎么做才能……?

对话示例

— Professor Paul will come to our school to give a speech tomorrow.	— 保罗教授明天会来我们学校做一个演讲。
— We can learn some methods and techniques of studying from him.	— 我们可以向他学习一些学习方法和技巧。
— But **how can we** make full use of this opportunity?	— 但是我们怎么做才能充分利用这次机会呢?
— We can write a letter to him.	— 我们可以给他写一封信。
— That's a good idea!	— 好主意!

句型分析

How can we... 本句型中 how 为特殊疑问词，放在句首构成特殊疑问句。can 为情态动词，所以 we 后面要跟动词原形。本句型可以用于询问对方“自己要怎么做”。

句子示例

- **How can we** prevent him from taking drugs? 我们怎么做才能阻止他吸毒?
- **How can we** get him out of trouble? 我们怎么做才能让他摆脱困境?
- **How can we** make this book become a best seller? 我们怎么做才能使这本书成为畅销书?

重点单词

method ['meθəd] *n.* 方法

technique [tek'ni:k] *n.* 技术，技巧

drug [drʌg] *n.* 毒品，药物

8. Why did you choose to...? 你为什么选择……?

对话示例

— What did you buy yesterday?	— 你昨天都买了些什么?
— I bought a microwave and a refrigerator.	— 我买了一个微波炉和一个电冰箱。
— **Why did you choose to** buy this brand?	— 你为什么会选择买这个品牌?
— Because everyone says that the quality of	— 因为大家都说这个品牌的质量特别好。

this brand is so good.	
— Okay, I will also choose this brand next time.	— 好的，那我下次也选择这个品牌。

句型分析

Why did you choose to... 本句型中 to 后面要跟动词原形，choose to do sth 意为“选择做某事”。本句型可用于询问对方“为何要选择做某事”。

句子示例

- **Why did you choose to** conceal the fact that he resigned? 你为什么选择隐瞒他辞职的事实?
- **Why did you choose to** refuse her invitation? 你为什么选择拒绝她的邀请?
- **Why did you choose to** believe in magic? 你为什么选择相信巫术?

重点单词

microwave ['maɪkrəweɪv] *n.* 微波炉

refrigerator [rɪ'frɪdʒəreɪtə] *n.* 冰箱

brand [brænd] *n.* 商标，品牌

9. How dare you...? 你怎么敢……?

对话示例

— What are you talking about?	— 你们在讨论什么?
— We are saying that the teacher is very eccentric to Mary.	— 我们在说老师对玛丽很偏心。
— **How dare you** say that?	— 你怎么敢这样说?
— That is the truth.	— 这本来就是事实。
— I believe that our teacher is fair to every student.	— 我相信我们老师对每个学生都是公平的。

句型分析

How dare you... 本句型中 dare 为情态动词，意为“敢，敢于”，后面跟动词原形。本句型可用于询问对方“怎么敢做某事”。

句子示例

- **How dare you** quarrel with the boss? 你怎么敢和老板吵架?
- **How dare you** violate his privacy? 你怎么敢侵犯他的隐私?
- **How dare you** drink so much carbonated drinks? 你怎么敢喝这么多碳酸饮料?

重点单词

eccentric [ɪk'sentrɪk] *a.* 偏心的，不同寻常的

violate ['vaɪəleɪt] *v.* 违反，侵犯

carbonated ['kɑːbəneɪtɪd] *a.* 含有二氧化碳的

10. What about...? ……怎么样?

对话示例

— Tomorrow is Christmas Eve. How are you going to celebrate?	— 明天就是平安夜了。你打算怎么庆祝?
— **What about** seeing the fireworks show?	— 去看烟花表演怎么样?
— I think it is too dangerous.	— 我认为这太危险了。
— So what do you want to do?	— 那你想干什么?
— We can hold a party at home.	— 我们可以在我家举办一个派对。

句型分析

What about... 本句型后面可以跟名词、动名词、代词。本句型可用于表达委婉的请求或者建议，或者询问某事怎么样。本句型可以和 How about... 替换。

句子示例

- **What about** climbing the mountain tomorrow? 明天去爬山怎么样?
- **What about** the talkative man? 那个健谈的人怎么样?
- **What about** buying this stock? 买这支股票怎么样?

重点单词

firework ['faɪəwɜːk] *n.* 烟花，烟火

talkative ['tɔːkətɪv] *a.* 健谈的，爱说话的

stock [stɒk] *n.* 股票，库存

11. How come you...? 你怎么会……?

对话示例

— Do you know our new PE teacher?	— 你知道我们新来的体育老师吗?
— Yes. He used to be an athlete of our country, but he's retired now.	— 他曾经是国家运动员，不过现在退役了。
— **How come you** know this?	— 你怎么会知道这些?
— I listened to the teachers saying when I went to the teacher's office yesterday.	— 昨天我去老师办公室的时候，听老师们说的。

句型分析

How come you... 本句型中 how come 是固定搭配，意为“怎么会”，本句型后面要跟完整的句子，句子的时态要根据句意而定。

句子示例

- **How come you** are sent to the United States on business? 你怎么会被派到美国出差?
- **How come you** say that it's permissible to smoke here? 你怎么会说这里允许抽烟?
- **How come you** know that he was a murderer? 你怎么会知道他曾经是一个杀人犯?

重点单词

retire [rɪ'taɪə] *v.* 退休，退役

permissible [pə'mɪsəbl] *a.* 许可的，允许的

murderer ['mɜ:dərə] *n.* 杀人犯，谋杀犯

12. Who is to...? 谁将会……?

对话示例

— There will be a job fair next week.	— 下周会有一次工作招聘会。
— **Who is to** be responsible for this activity?	— 谁将会负责这次活动?
— I think it should be Paul. Because he was responsible for all previous activities, and he was familiar with the details.	— 我认为应该是保罗。因为以前的活动都是他负责的，而且他对这些细节都比较熟悉。
— Considering these factors, our boss will choose him.	— 考虑到这些因素，老板肯定会选择他的。

句型分析

Who is to... 本句型中 to 后面跟动词原形，be to do sth 是固定搭配，意为“将要，打算做某事”。不定式结构在本句型中充当表语。

句子示例

- **Who is to** indulge in computer games during the vacation? 谁将会在假期沉迷于电脑游戏?
- **Who is to** preside over the meeting? 谁将会主持这次会议?
- **Who is to** know what the theme of the debate is? 谁将会知道这次辩论的主题是什么?

重点单词

previous ['pri:vəs] *a.* 以前的，之前的

indulge [ɪn'dʌldʒ] *v.* 沉迷于

factor ['fæktə] *n.* 因素

preside [prɪ'zaɪd] *v.* 主持，指挥

13. Why would you want to...? 你为什么会想要……?

对话示例

— You feel like a million dollars. What happened to you?	— 你看起来很开心。发生了什么?
— I got a new job today, and I signed a contract for five years.	— 我今天找到了新工作，而且我签订了一份五年的合同。
— **Why would you want to** sign such a contract?	— 你为什么会想要签订这样一份合同?
— I don't think there is anything wrong with the contract.	— 我不觉得这份合同有什么不对。
— You are so foolish.	— 你真是太傻了。

句型分析

Why would you want to... 本句型中 to 后面要跟动词原形，want to do sth 是固定搭配，意为“想要做某事”。本句型可用于询问对方“想做某事的原因”。

句子示例

- **Why would you want to** take steps to protect the wildlife? 你为什么会想要采取措施去保护野生

动物？

- **Why would you want to** take the external examination? 你为什么会想要参加校外的考试？
- **Why would you want to** execute the woman's command? 你为什么会想要执行这个女人的命令？

重点单词

million ['mɪljən] *n.* 百万

external [ɪk'stɜːnl] *a.* 外面的，外用的

14. What steps can be taken to...? 可以采取什么措施来……？

对话示例

— Yesterday I read the newspaper and it said that a criminal ran away.	— 昨天我看报纸说一个罪犯逃跑了。
— Where did the criminal escape?	— 那个罪犯逃到哪里了？
— He is said to have escaped to the border.	— 据说他逃到边境了。
— **What steps can be taken to** arrest him at the border crossing?	— 可以采取什么措施在边境地带抓到他？
— Sorry. It's not mentioned in the newspaper.	— 不好意思。报纸上没有提到。

句型分析

What steps can be taken to... 本句型中 to 后面要跟动词原形，不定式结构在句中作目的状语，本句型属于被动语态。本句型可以用于询问对方“可以采取什么措施来做某事”。

句子示例

- **What steps can be taken to** cure the cancer? 可以采取什么措施来治愈这种癌症？
- **What steps can be taken to** help him when the crunch comes? 可以采取什么措施在紧急情况时帮助他？
- **What steps can be taken to** accomplish our purpose? 可以采取什么措施来达到我们的目的？

重点单词

border ['bɔːdə] *n.* 边境，边界

cure [kjʊə] *v.* 治疗，治愈

crunch [krʌntʃ] *n.* 紧急情况

accomplish [ə'kʌmplɪʃ] *v.* 达到，完成，实现

15. What do you think of...? 你怎么看待……？

对话示例

— We have a new neighbor who is Spanish.	— 我们有一个新邻居是西班牙人。
— **What do you think of** the Spanish?	— 你怎么看待这个西班牙人？
— She seems to be very rich. Because I often see her go shopping.	— 她好像特别有钱，因为我经常看见她去购物。
— I don't know much about her.	— 我对她不是很了解。

句型分析

What do you think of... 本句型中 of 为介词，后面跟名词、动名词、代词。think of 为固定搭配，意为“考虑，认为，看待”。本句型可用于询问对方如何看待某事。

句子示例

- **What do you think of** our chief financial officer? 你怎么看待我们的财务总监？
- **What do you think of** taking advantage of the good opportunity? 你认为利用这个好机会怎么样？
- **What do you think of** these people who have nothing to do? 你怎么看待这些无所事事的人？

重点单词

Spanish ['spænɪʃ] *n.* 西班牙人，西班牙语 *a.* 西班牙的，西班牙人的

chief [tʃi:f] *n.* 主管 *a.* 最主要的

advantage [əd'vɑ:ntɪdʒ] *n.* 优点，有利条件

16. What could be more...than...? 还有什么比……更……？

对话示例

— Shall we go to the stadium to watch the football match tomorrow?	— 明天我们一起去体育场看球赛吧？
— Sorry, I am going to the amusement park with my son.	— 对不起，我要和我儿子去游乐场玩。
— You can go with him next time.	— 你可以下次陪他去。
— **What can be more** important **than** my son?	— 还有什么比我儿子更重要的吗？
— I can't understand you. Probably because I have no children.	— 我不能理解你，可能是因为我没有孩子。

句型分析

What could be more...than... 本句型中 could 为情态动词，后跟动词原形 be，more...than...，意为“比……更……”，more 后面要跟多音节的形容词。

句子示例

- **What could be more** terrible **than** the fact that he divorced? 还有什么比他离婚更糟糕的吗?
- **What could be more** exciting **than** winning the prize? 还有什么比得奖更令人激动的吗?
- **What could be more** important **than** taking the final exam? 还有什么比参加期末考试更重要的吗?

重点单词

stadium ['steɪdɪəm] *n.* 体育场，运动场

amusement [ə'mju:zmənt] *n.* 娱乐活动

probably ['prɒbəblɪ] *ad.* 可能，也许

17. For what purpose do you...? 你……有什么目的?

对话示例

— Do you know the boss's new assistant?	— 你知道老板新来的助理吗?
— Yes. What's up?	— 知道。怎么了?
— I want to know what her character is like?	— 我想知道她的性格怎么样?
— **For what purpose do you** know that?	— 你想知道这些有什么目的?
— Nothing. I just want to know a little about our colleague.	— 并没有。我只是想简单了解一下我们的同事而已。

句型分析

For what purpose do you... 本句型是由 for what purpose 引导的特殊疑问句，do 是助动词，所以其后要跟动词原形。本句型可用于询问对方“做某事是出于什么目的”。

句子示例

- **For what purpose do you** make trouble for the salesman? 你故意给那个售货员制造麻烦有什么目的?
- **For what purpose do you** unfold your plan to him? 你向他透露你的计划是有什么目的?
- **For what purpose do you** stay at home alone? 你独自一人留在家里有什么目的?

• **For what purpose do you** prop up the industry? 你资助这个产业有什么目的?

重点单词

salesman ['seɪlzmən] *n.* 售货员

industry ['ɪndəstrɪ] *n.* 产业，工业

unfold [ʌn'fəʊld] *v.* 展开，透露，显示

18. What else could it be that made me...? 还有什么可以让我……?

对话示例

— I've never been as happy as I am now.	— 我从来没有像现在这样高兴。
— Are you happy for the success of our team this time?	— 你是在为我们小组这次的成功而感到高兴吗?
— Of course. **What else could it be that made me** feel so happy?	— 当然。还有什么能让我感到如此高兴的?
— Let's have a party to celebrate the success tonight.	— 我们今晚开个派对来庆祝一下这次胜利吧。
— Great.	— 太棒了。

句型分析

What else could it be that made me... 本句型中 what else 放在句首构成特殊疑问句，could 为情态动词，后跟动词原形 be，it 在句中是形式主语，真正的主语是 that 引导的从句。

句子示例

• **What else could it be that made me** feel so depressed? 还有什么可以让我感到这么沮丧的?

• **What else could it be that made me** become a great scientist? 还有什么可以让我成为一位伟大的科学家?

• **What else could it be that made me** enthusiastic about my job? 还有什么可以让我热衷于我的工作?

重点单词

depressed [dɪ'prest] *a.* 沮丧的，低落的，萧条的

enthusiastic [ɪnˌθju:zɪ'æstɪk] *a.* 热情的，狂热的

19. What could I...? 我能……什么？

对话示例

— Our company is going to go bankrupt.	— 我们的公司即将破产。
— **What could I** do when I am faced with this situation?	— 面对这样的局面，我能怎么做？
— Maybe we can rebuild a company.	— 也许我们可以重建一个公司。
— It's impossible. Let's get ready for finding a new job.	— 这是不可能的事。我们还是做好准备去找新工作吧。
— What a pity!	— 真是太遗憾了！

句型分析

What could I... 本句型是由 what 引导的特殊疑问句，could 为情态动词，因此 I 后面要跟动词原形。

句子示例

- **What could I** do if those orphans are bullied? 如果那些孤儿被人欺负，我能怎么做？
- **What could I** do to protect our environment? 我能做些什么去保护我们的环境？
- **What could I** do with the sales decreasing this month? 这个月的销售额下降，我能做些什么？

重点单词

orphan ['ɔːfn] *n.* 孤儿

bully ['bʊlɪ] *v.* 欺负

20. What do we mean when we say that...? 我们说……意义何在？

对话示例

— Paul seems to have some difficulties in learning English.	— 保罗好像在学习英语上有些困难。
— We should try our best to help him.	— 我们应该尽最大的努力去帮助他。
— **What do we mean when we say that** we should help him?	— 当我们说到我们应该帮助他的时候，意义何在？
— Because we are good friends. Good friends should help each other, don't they?	— 因为我们是好朋友。好朋友之间就应该相互帮助，难道不是吗？
— You are so right!	— 你说的太对了！

句型分析

What do we mean when we say that... 本句型中 what 放在句首引导特殊疑问句，包括 when 引导的时间状语从句和 that 引导的宾语从句。

句子示例

- **What do we mean when we say that** we have a lot of work every day? 我们所说的我们每天都有大量的工作，指的是什么?
- **What do we mean when we say that** people's living standards are improving gradually? 我们说的人们的生活水平不断提高，意思是什么?
- **What do we mean when we say that** the nurse was absent without any reasons? 我们说那名护士无故缺席，意思是什么?

重点单词

gradually ['grædʒʊəlɪ] *a.* 逐渐地　　standard ['stændəd] *n.* 标准

21. What is the best way to...? ……的最好办法是什么?

对话示例

— Jane lost her love last week. She is in a bad mood every day.	— 简上周失恋了。她现在每天都萎靡不振。
— **What is the best way to** comfort her?	— 安慰她的最好办法是什么?
— We can often go shopping, go traveling and watch movies with her.	— 我们可以经常和她去购物、旅行、看电影。
— That's a good idea! Let's watch movies with her on weekend.	— 好主意！那我们周末一起去陪她看电影吧。
— OK.	— 好的。

句型分析

What is the best way to... 本句型中 what 放在句首构成特殊疑问句，to 后面要跟动词原形。the best way 在句中作表语，不定式在句中作 the best way 的定语。